Fellow Travelers

UNIVERSITY PRESS OF FLORIDA

Florida A&M University, Tallahassee
Florida Atlantic University, Boca Raton
Florida Gulf Coast University, Ft. Myers
Florida International University, Miami
Florida State University, Tallahassee
University of Central Florida, Orlando
University of Florida, Gainesville
University of North Florida, Jacksonville
University of South Florida, Tampa
University of West Florida, Pensacola

Fellow Travelers

Indians and Europeans Contesting the Early American Trail

Philip Levy

University Press of Florida
Gainesville/Tallahassee/Tampa/Boca Raton
Pensacola/Orlando/Miami/Jacksonville/Ft. Myers

Copyright 2007 by Philip Levy
Printed in the United States of America on acid-free, recycled paper
All rights reserved

12 11 10 09 08 07 6 5 4 3 2 1

Library of Congress Cataloging-in-Publication Data:
Levy, Philip, 1963–
Fellow travelers: Indians and Europeans contesting the early American trail / Philip Levy.
p. cm.
Includes bibliographical references and index.
ISBN-13: 978-0-8130-3058-6 (alk. paper)
1. Indian trails—United States—History. 2. Indian roads—United States—History. 3. Indians of North America—First contact with Europeans. 4. Indians of North America—History—Colonial period, ca. 1600–1775. 5. United States—History—Colonial period, ca. 1600–1775. 6. United States—Discovery and exploration. I. Title.
E98.T7L48   2007
973.2—dc22   2006030877

The University Press of Florida is the scholarly publishing agency for the State University System of Florida, comprising Florida A&M University, Florida Atlantic University, Florida Gulf Coast University, Florida International University, Florida State University, University of Central Florida, University of Florida, University of North Florida, University of South Florida, and University of West Florida.

University Press of Florida
15 Northwest 15th Street
Gainesville, FL 32611-2079
http://www.upf.com

For Ward Stavig

Contents

Preface ix

Introduction: Setting Off on the Trail 1

1. The Paradox of the Conquistadors' Trail 11

2. "Upon Proper Terms": The Rewards of Guidance 37

3. "Quite Contrary to the Custom" 63

4. None but the Rattlesnakes! 81

5. Sex, Difference, and the Ideal Traveler 105

6. Going Out 134

Notes 147

Bibliography 173

Index 189

Preface

This book began in North Carolina's Smoky Mountains on the Appalachian Trail. Some years ago, my wife and I took off from our flatland home and drove up to the garishly down-at-the-mouth town of Cherokee. We ditched the car, kitted up, and set off into the American woods, having arranged with a friend to pick us up in about ten days. As short-term "Section Hikers," we were second-class citizens compared with the real stars, the "Through Hikers," who set out in the spring to walk from Georgia to Maine. Our walk was early enough in the season to overlap with the first few weeks of many northbound Through Hikers still fired up at the prospect of making the full hike; the broken ankles, intestinal parasitosis, and the myriad other problems which sideline many hikers were then still in the future. Each night we all slept in the open-fronted log shelters, which were built and maintained by hiker volunteers and which the Park Service required all Smokey Mountain hikers to make their nightly home. Some evenings these were packed full of people; other nights we were part of a much smaller company. Since all hikers had to share the shelters, each evening we saw many of the same people, the fastest ones being well settled in before we arrived (and having taken the driest sleeping spots), the slowest arriving long after we were tucked in.

These repeated meetings made for many chances to get to know one another. And it was only a matter of time before conversation turned to who each of us was when not nursing blisters, pump-filtering the water, and sharing a small hole near a tree as a toilet. When it came my turn, I revealed that in civilian life I was a graduate student studying Indian-colonial relations.[1] My confession resulted in a flurry of questions about Indians generally and local lore specifically. My cabin mates were eager to know whatever I had to share about Indian dining and hunting practices, how Indians traveled, what kinds of shelters they built, and so on. Many of these questions had a sort of practical edge—they dealt with how Natives survived in conditions in many ways similar to the ones we then shared. It was as if my reading might have revealed some trick for finding the best water or doing better than our open-air latrines. But some hikers were also interested in less tangible and practical Native habits and knowledge. They wondered how Indian peoples understood the landscape we now walked through; might a particularly large rock or narrow passage have been some special place once upon a time? Some hikers imagined the trail as something Indigenous in and of itself and their experience of it something akin to "going Native."[2]

What I knew then, but did not want to let out, was that the Appalachian Trail (A.T.) itself has no Native past per se, at least in its current form. The trail was the brainchild and creation of twentieth-century Americans steeped in the logic of Frederick Jackson Turner and who held a fear that the American woods were vanishing. The land through which the trail ran had indeed once been Native, but in those days most Indian trails ran not along the crests of ridges but instead took the gentlest paths, where possible following river lines or traversing the best mountain passes. By the time the Appalachian Trail's founders laid out its course, the once extensive network of Native trails had long since been appropriated by European colonists and their descendants and turned into (in sequence) wagon roads, dirt roads, toll roads, and state roads. It was not until the 1950s that American road planners, aided by heavy machinery and high explosives, abandoned the long-standing, albeit reshaped, Native trail network and blasted vast six-lane ribbons of tar and rest stops through mountains and across plains. The A.T. runs where it does, not because it replicates something Native, but because the Appalachian ridge was just about the only stretch of unbroken woods running along the eastern states when the trail was first blazed.[3]

Nevertheless, for many modern Americans, walking in the woods conjures up something Indian in their minds, even if it is only a sort of ecological woodsman stereotype informed principally by the tearful image of Iron Eyes Cody in his famous antipollution television-ad appearances.[4] During my Smoky Mountains hike I also was thinking about Indians, but not so much to frame my experiences. Instead, I was thinking about what my doctoral dissertation would be—I knew it would deal with Indians during the colonial era, yet I did not know was what it would focus on. But with each hiker's question, I gradually realized that there was a Native story here, even if it was not focused specifically on the A.T. I also became more aware of how place and experience can merge, and why it is that A.T. hikers conflate the two in the single term "the trail," a term I use throughout this book toward the same end. I continued to think about all of this when I got home, and as the topic came into focus I discussed it with James Axtell, my dissertation director at the College of William and Mary, and other senior scholars who liked the project. My fellow hikers' questions began to make me think about how Native and European travelers related to each other while traveling in each others' company. What did they talk about when they sat near campfires? How did they treat each other? Did they share their burdens as fellow travelers might, or did they work against each other along the way? Did the larger dynamics of colonization shape these relationships, or was there something in the specific conditions of travel which marked it as distinctive—a realm apart from greater colonial processes? These were some of the questions and ideas I brought from the trail back to Williamsburg.

What followed was reading, lots of it, mostly in the College of William and Mary's Earl Gregg Swem Library, but also at the University of Arizona Library and at Harvard University's Widner Library. Later I spent considerable time in the University of South Florida's Tampa Campus Library and the University of Mary Washington's Simpson Library. During this time I read hundreds of colonial-era travel narratives, searching for the presence of Indians in this grand old literature. Some of these stories were published in their day; others have been collected into wonderful multivolume collections like *Jesuit Relations, Original Narratives of Early American History*, and the *Coronado Cuarto Centennial Publications*. Still others are hidden away in the older editions of historical journals or in state and colonial papers. Most of my reading was in published material, as so much of this literature has been published. No doubt there is much more of it stashed away in archives, but the vast body of published material, my desire to keep as large a temporal and regional focus as possible, and the fact that these texts have become standards in the scholarly literature on Indian-colonial relations all meant that there was enough here to keep me busy for some considerable time. As often happens, not all of the texts I read made it into this book nor does very single example of what I found. And I apologize to readers who do not find herein a treatment of their favorite travel moment or a special focus on any specific region or people. I came to see all early modern travelers as constituting a sort of community of their own, as well as inhabiting (at least for the time of their travels) their own space—the trail—and this book's shape and selections reflect that vision.

There are many people whom I wish to thank for helping me create this book. First and foremost is James L. Axtell, whose advice and encouragement have been invaluable aids in this and many other projects. So much of what I have become I owe to his direction, mentorship, and friendship. Daniel H. Usner Jr. set me off on my own early American trail so many years ago, and his help and advice have been indispensable. James P. Whittenburg and Kris E. Lane both offered input on the dissertation phase, and I thank them once again for their time and insightful comments. Paul Hoffman read and commented on "The Paradox of the Conquistadors' Trail" and answered some vital questions. Bernard Bailyn, Peter Wood, and my fellow participants in the 2004 International Seminar on the History of the Atlantic World, 1500–1825, read and commented on "None but the Rattlesnakes" in an engaging session at Harvard University. William Cummings took the time to carefully read an early draft and offered just the right advice at just the right time. William O'Reilly also read the manuscript and provided encouragement as well. Richard White let me bend his ear on this topic and graciously offered to read and comment on the manuscript. I thank him warmly for his time, interest, and advice. Colin Calloway took time to help shape this book at a crucial juncture and his warmth and professionalism mean a great deal.

The staff at the University Press of Florida have been the best partners an author could wish for. I especially thank Derek Krissoff, whose hard work and confidence in the project have seemed boundless. Thanks also to Eli Bortz and Jacqueline Kinghorn Brown for all of their efforts and patience. John Coombs, one of my closest and dearest friends, also read the book through, and what is more, test-drove an early draft of it in his Early American History Seminar at Florida International University. I thank him for his endless patience, indulgence, and endurance at every stage of this project. Likewise David Muraca has been both a mentor and best friend and, it seems as though he has walked every step of this journey with me. He has always offered nothing but his unflinching confidence and support. My beloved wife, my *bashaer*t, Sarah Carleton has lived with this project and all its permutations, serving as sounding board, copy editor, and muse. Our son Felix has been a great source of joy and amusement when these were needed.

Don Welsh and Sheila Brown of Swem Library looked under endless rocks and cleared innumerable obstacles during my research there. My friends and colleagues at the University of South Florida—most notably William Murray, Fraser Ottanelli, Giovanna Benadusi, Robert Ingalls, Golfo Alexopolous, John Behlolavek, Lu Ann Jones, Paul Dosal, Barbara Berglund, David K. Johnson, Kathleen Paul, and John McKiernan Gonzales—provided advice, support, and clarity of purpose. Daniel Ingram, Elizabeth Kelly Gray, Anthony DeStefanis, James Spady, and Amy Kowalski Muraca have also weighed in with a needed good word, a fresh take on material, or a strong editorial hand. My family, be they Levys or Carletons, has been the backbone I have so often needed. I also wish to thank the staff at the George Washington Fredericksburg Foundation and Marley R. Brown III, Kennan Ferguson, Carolyn Eichner, Judy Drawdy, Sylvia Wood, Michael Decker, Graydon "Jack" Tunstall, Tamara Zwick, Julie Langford-Johnson, Daniel Belgrad, Elizabeth Fraser, Friedemann Buschbeck, Jeffery Oppenhiem, Daniel Zogott, Jerry Colonna, Uriel Rivkin, Lazer Rivkin, Menachem M. Schneerson, Daniel Peck, John Heins, and Margaret Gonglewski.

As I prepared this manuscript for publication, my academic home, the Department of History at the University of South Florida, suffered a devastating loss. Professor Ward Stavig passed away in the company of friends and family. Ward was a first-rate scholar, fabulous teacher, devoted and loving father and husband, and, as all who knew him can attest, a truly wonderful human being. Ward helped me begin to understand how to balance being an academic and a father and how to keep focused on the things that matter most. His loss can never be repaired. It is to him that I dedicate this book.

Introduction

Setting Off on the Trail

> *Oh. What a reckless blunder! What greater crime can a leader commit than to lead people into a land that neither he nor another of his group had ever been in before?*
>
> Gonzalo Fernández de Oviedo

When Europeans first edged up to North American shores they came to a continent crisscrossed by a well-trodden network of trails. Tracks through woodlands, passes between mountains, fords over rivers, and portages between waterways all connected innumerable Indian communities with one another. Sometimes these paths served as the avenues of trade, visitation, or hunting. Other times they were the routes for warriors or raiding parties. Some trails were equipped with such amenities as well-maintained huts, fire pits, and grinding stones ready for travelers' corn. Others were less well appointed, or ran through forbidding tundra lands or harsh deserts. But trails were vital arteries all over Native North America. For the many people living along this network, knowing the varied twists and turns of a given path or the eddies and pools of a local river was often essential for survival.

On arriving in the Americas, European colonizers quickly learned that access to the Native trail network would become essential to the success of their varied endeavors. From its earliest days, European North American colonization frequently depended on knowing the shape of the coast, what lay at a river's headwaters, or where paths led. Who and what was to be found up a trail or river were crucial questions for colonizers, and for that reason virtually all early settlements made great effort to learn their surrounding geography. This need did not end once European forts and towns became well established. Far from it. As the various colonial powers expanded their activities, the scale of their territorial interest and reach grew as well. The expansion of European colonial trade and diplomacy relied on knowledge of and access to distant territory. Native trails quickly became the avenues along which traders, missionaries, diplomatists, and naturalists traveled as they reached ever deeper into the continent. And so the colonial era saw a steady flow of European travelers tramping North American trails and visiting the many destinations to which they led.[1] But throughout those centuries, European travel beyond the bounds of settlements and their immediate hinterlands invariably required some amount of Native aid, in the form of either guidance, hunting, carrying baggage, or a variety of other travel-related tasks. In short, travel, that most fundamental of colonial activities, depended in no small measure on the skills, knowledge, and goodwill of the very Native people most often squarely in colonization's crosshairs.

The continuing intersection of European need and Native ability enabled the creation of one of the most enduring types of colonial relationships, that of European travelers and the Native guides, porters, hunters, and other assistants on whom they depended. This book is a study of these relationships in North America from the sixteenth to the nineteenth centuries, based on the writings of European travelers who took to trails and rivers ranging from the Rio Grande to the very edges of the Arctic.[2] The following chapters focus on what my research led me to see as the defining element of those relationships, an ongoing and often highly personalized competition between Native and European travel companions, or "fellow travelers" as I call them.[3] The stories which follow explore the many forms this competition took, its many consequences, and how in some cases these often small and seemingly inconsequential contests contributed to the larger shape and course of colonial travel. This is no small matter. Choosing one path over another, accepting or rejecting proffered advice, and conflict over whose travel habits to respect on the trail all influenced the small footsteps which in their thousands made up every colonial trek. These social dimensions of travel frequently shaped where Europeans went, whom they met, and what they saw along the way, and this in turn shaped the contours of the alliances and trade networks which ultimately were the tendrils of European North American empires. Simple conflicts and disagreements between Native and European travel companions had implications well beyond the immediate issue and the development of something far larger, making shared travel an important and distinctive arena of colonial encounter.[4]

Recent writing has reawakened for many an overly heroic image of European travelers and explorers and downplayed the contingent and dependent nature of these endeavors.[5] This book recasts colonial-era travel as its own contentious arena of colonization as opposed to being an advance of European power and knowledge. Natives were vital to the success (however defined) of European travel. Native advice and knowledge shaped European courses on countless trips, small and large. Native skills cleared newcomers' paths, worked to fill their bellies, and met other hungers too. Native abilities and knowledge got Europeans safely past innumerable obstacles and helped them survive many ailments and dangerous situations. Native backs often bore the loads and lashes of European travelers. In some cases, Europeans worked hard to control the shape and pace of travel; other times, Europeans were effectively guests on Native trips, and acted like it. But in either case, the well-known heroes of colonial expansion, from the Age of Exploration to natural science tourism, were only one part of the expeditions which often bear their names.[6]

Although Europeans could be cumbersome baggage for Native travelers, they were not always burdens. Europeans could also be valuable additions and play special roles on Native trips. In some cases, having a European in a travel party could add social prestige to a journey. A European travel companion could be a vehicle for building an alliance, settling a score, or bringing greater rewards in trade. European travel plans could be the basis for new and interesting travels which, without European initiation, might not have occurred, and in some situations a European's travel plans might provide the safety and permission to travel for people with otherwise limited or restricted travel horizons. Many Indian travelers also came to rely on an array of European manufactured goods, which changed long-standing travel habits. In one way or another, colonial-era North American Indian and European travelers quickly became tightly enmeshed in many aspects of each other's wanderings.

In sharing the rigors and burdens of the trail, and relying on one another in a variety of ways, Indians and Europeans entwined their fates as travelers. When it rained on one, it rained on all, and when it froze, all froze. When the food ran low, all went hungry, and churning river rapids made no distinction between Native and European paddlers of canoes. Time on the trail also put travelers together in a uniquely close setting removed from the comforts of home and the usual trappings of social stature and security. This meant that the comfortable, socially situating amenities of kin, friends, and daily routine, and sometimes possessions and the trappings of identity and social prestige as well, were often removed, or at least not readily on hand to assure and soothe. This was certainly true for many Europeans, but it was also the case for many Native travelers as well. Early modern travel could be a form of social alienation, throwing individuals back on the bare transportable essentials of how they constructed their identities on the move.[7]

On this level, the realities of the trail potentially blurred distinctions between people eating the same food, treading the same path, and often wearing similar clothes.[8] Or so it would be if colonial-era travelers of many types had not worked so hard to locate, describe, and fuss over the differences between themselves and the people with whom they traveled. Just as shared travel threatened to melt identities, it also provided innumerable opportunities to explore the implications of cultural differences between Natives and Europeans, and they appear to have worked hard to maintain distinctions.

Intercultural travelers spent considerable time in the company of people quite different from themselves—for many it was the most time they would ever spend in such company. Common travel therefore provided numerous opportunities for observation and inquiry while the trail itself provided a shared body of experiences against which to judge the merits and value of their fellows. Travelers' different ways of getting along on the trail were brought into crisp outline as travel companions confronted new and alien ways of moving, eating, camping, and conceptualizing the meanings and goals of travel. The result was that the trail, and how best to survive on it, was the setting and focus of a long-term discussion of the differences between Native and European travel companions conducted on the trail itself and in stories told afterwards by the travelers. Furthermore, the numerous dangers of early modern travel meant that issues of different practice were more than merely curiosities: making the "right" choice at a turn in the trail or bend in the river could be a matter of life and death. Fellow travelers came face-to-face with just how different their varying understandings of the world could be, and were confronted with the limitations of their culturally informed travel habits.[9] The trail brought out in its denizens a need to differentiate. The dangers of travel suffused habits, practices, and solutions with an urgent immediacy, with competition being one of the by-products.[10]

Observing, questioning, emulating, ridiculing, and challenging were all ways that fellow travelers tested and evaluated one another and the merits of each other's habits. These contests took many forms, as we shall see. Travel partners collided over the rules and pace of travel, disagreed over the course, intent, and meaning of shared travel, and argued about how best to avoid the trail's many dangers. They squabbled over whose cosmology should rule, and they demeaned each other as travelers. As so many of the travelers were men, frequently their own manliness became an object of contention. Rather than building a consensus about how best to get along on the trail born of shared conditions and the many cultural borrowings between partners, these Native and European travelers instead engaged in an ongoing tug-of-war to see whose rules, practices, and interpretations should govern their common travel, even as they appropriated what they saw as most useful in each other's habits. In this way, travelers battled not only the elements on the trail, but also each other over how best to cope with those elements. The specifics of this competition tacked and turned somewhat over the colonial era, as did elements of the language and context of cultural contest. But compete they did, with remarkable fortitude and in ways which set patterns that lasted the whole of the colonial era, if not longer.

What it took to get along on the trail in 1500 was not all that different from the conditions and travails one would have encountered in 1799. The realities of travel remained largely constant over the time this book covers—and while the trail was not a single transhistorical place, it was typified more by continuity than by change. Therefore, the following stories do not reveal a world in constant flux or even one gradually changing in some of its most crucial defining attributes. Instead, since the trail changed little over the three centuries covered herein, a similar constancy played out in travel relationships. Certainly local conditions, both social and environmental, varied, and larger events effected the tone of Indian colonial relations, but in so many important ways the trail was on its own clock and was almost always a world more or less unto itself.

In order for a travel relationship to appear in this study, two separate things must have occurred. The first is that an Indian and a European had to have traveled in each other's company. The second is that someone (almost always European, as it happens) had to record the events of their shared travel. These two conditions were met most often at the edges of European settlements—in those areas of interest to Europeans, but still well in the hands of Indians, those places where Europeans wanted to travel throughout the colonial era but could only do so with Indian aid and cooperation.[11] Therefore this study is not a comprehensive review of all travel literature, nor is it an attempt to describe every aspect or implication of common travel, nor is it an attempt to take apart the beliefs of any single group of people or travel writer. Instead, what follows is an attempt to insert questions of European-Native cultural conflict into the literature of travel and exploration and make a sustained argument for the centrality of spaces in forming these relationships.[12] All of the relationships portrayed in this book could only have taken shape within the spaces of travel, which in this study I have collectively called "the trail." The trail includes all the North American tracks, portages, rivers, and coasts fellow travelers shared. The trail was both the setting for these relationships and their context and was often the object under critique. Therefore, the trail is more than a neutral setting or a backdrop—in its way, it is a principal actor as well.[13]

Humankind has a long history of seeing travel and travelers as engaging in some sort of epic, heroic, self-defining venture, even if long-distance trips have become something more mundane and commonplace in our own era.[14] Travelers from many societies and many epochs saw their varied wanderings as being significant, defining, and even transcendent experiences. Scholars of many disciplines have explored the ways that travel made people anew and brought them social prestige and influence back in their hometowns.[15]

Native North Americans had numerous ways of marking the trail and of signifying travelers as special and having undergone a special experience. In many Native societies, great travelers and the blazers of new trails were heroes whose deeds marked them as possessing great power. On the trail, specific rocks, waterfalls, pools, and other features required special offerings and rituals of each Native traveler who passed them. Rituals like the offering of tobacco, stones, or other goods kept travelers safe and maintained balance in the world at large—travelers' good acts or misdeeds had great significance. Travelers themselves also required special handling at the beginning and ending of their trips.[16] Some Native peoples sang, leaped, or fired off guns in welcome. Others rubbed or washed new arrivals' bodies, and still others carried travelers bodily into towns as both a sign of respect and in recognition of the arduousness of traveling. Some peoples offered their new guests food, drink, tobacco, and respectful silence while they recovered from their travels and composed their thoughts, while others immediately convened for great celebrations of eating, dancing, and singing. All of these acknowledged the rigors, both physical and existential, which travelers endured.

Europeans also had an array of habits through which they marked travel as distinctive. Masses and benedictions called upon God to bless and protect those who faced travel's dangers. Along their way European travelers took measurements, recorded distances, and described what they saw—all of which helped control and contain their experiences.

But for historians, the most significant ritual of European travel was without a doubt the widespread desire to record a trip's events in some form of report or narrative. Travelers and stay-at-homes alike understood that these journeys were something rare and special, something worthy of recording, and something they wished to share with audiences present and future. For some travelers, reporting was a duty born of bureaucratic demands or the need to publicize activity to help fund the next venture. For others, penning their stories was the single greatest literary act of their lives, an act which suggests that their travels were also of deep personal significance. In either case, the people and institutions involved in European colonial-era North America understood that what happened on the trail mattered and needed to be reviewed, encapsulated, and remembered. The writings of travelers served many purposes for authors and their readers alike. They provided edification and entertainment for readers while allowing armchair travelers to passively partake in colonial activity. They brought the places and peoples of the New World into European homes in a very real way. They helped describe and codify these "new" places. They highlighted areas of differences and similarities between Natives and newcomers, and became part of a prolonged, multivoice discussion of the nature, location, and maintenance of cultural differences. In these ways, travel stories were important components of larger colonial enterprises, in that they brought the places and peoples of the New World into European homes and minds in ways which fascinated readers and validated colonization itself by helping to create both the logic of colonization and showing America and her peoples as being fit to be colonized.[17]

Some of these travel writers were highly skilled travelers. Men like Pierre Espirit Radisson, Alexander Henry, and David Thompson were well-seasoned in the ways of North American travel. Others were dabblers, men who made only one or two trips before committing their experiences to writing. A few types of European travelers proved to be the most prolific writers, and consequently much of what we know about colonial-era intercultural travel we see through their imperfect eyes. Territorial explorers, be they ambitious mariners like Jacques Cartier, restless soldiers like John Smith, or fur traders like Samuel Hearne, often wrote detailed accounts of their travels as reports for backers at home, or simply to garner for themselves as much praise and reward as they could. Missionaries of many European churches and nations described the events of their wanderings as a testament to their own faith and missionary zeal, as admonitions to the less faithful, and as recorded witness to the faith of new converts. Eighteenth-century naturalists, and others adopting a scientific stance, created detailed accounts of their findings in order to share their knowledge and experience with kindred spirits. And on occasion the odd diarist, like the ever-candid planter William Byrd II, simply wrote out of a love of the exercise. Because these explorers, fur traders, missionaries, scientists, and colonial administrators recorded so much colonial travel, they are by necessity the types of European travelers most commonly appearing in this study.

But Europeans were not the only travelers to walk along, and talk about, the trail. Native peoples also had their own histories as travelers and likewise were also tellers of travel tales. Like Europeans, Native travelers came in many types, although we know much less about who they were than we do of Europeans. Nevertheless we can see many types of Native travelers in European documents. Native traders brought goods between peoples. Mystics, visionaries, and healers brought their words and skills to distant villages. Individuals seeking guidance and solace from nonhuman forces might set off on vision quests, many of which involved travel. Warriors ranged the land in parties small and large looking to wreak vengeance, score blows, and bring home captives. Hunters tracked beasts great and small in every habitat. As in European societies, travelers could be great heroes. The blazers of new trails often took on legendary status, and the ability to control trade goods, geographic access, and information from great distance brought great prestige.[18] In North American travel stories though, we see most clearly and most often those types of Native travelers Europeans found most useful to their own ends. Guides, porters, hunters, and warriors are the most common Native travelers in European writing, but we have to assume that this is only a small selection of the many types of travelers once walking North America's vast trail network.

The book's chapters are organized thematically to highlight the various competitive aspects of travel relationships. The first chapter, "The Paradox of the Conquistadors' Trail," looks at the marches of three North American Spanish conquistadors—Pánfilo de Narváez, Hernando de Soto, and Vázquez de Coronado—and reveals how a flawed strategy of coercing guides and aids from the people they met on the march ultimately worked against the marches' goals and in time made the model itself untenable. The heavy hand of the earliest European arrivals was somewhat short lived and soon yielded to less overt forms of coercion.

The growth of European colonial settlements changed the basis for European and Indian travel partnerships by ending the Age of Exploration's heaviest hand. Travel companions now found themselves compelled to travel together by demands of alliances, economic ties, and a host of other personal motivations. This pattern had a long life, beginning early in the seventeenth century and lasting throughout the rest of the colonial era. Chapters dealing with the socio-economic rewards of common travel, the conflicts brought out by different travel habits, and the formation of what I call "ideal travelers," all explore the terrain on which fellow travelers enacted their differences. In some cases, the consequences of differences were dramatic—the differences undermined the viability of expeditions and erupted in sustained conflicts. In other cases, the consequences were small-scale and focused on simple acts, such as when to start a travel day or how best to ride a horse.

The second chapter, "'Upon Proper Terms,'" examines the economic logic which came to hold sway on the trail. By dividing relationships into those stemming from an Indian's offering assistance and those forming when Europeans begged aid, the chapter outlines how Natives turned European need and ignorance to their own ends. Chapter 3, "'Quite Contrary to the Custom,'" focuses on how intercultural travel partners' travel habits differed and how questions of the best ways to travel became a bone of contention on the trail.

Chapter 4, "None but the Rattlesnakes!" takes this idea a bit further by focusing in some detail on one particular highly charged source of conflict—the right way to comprehend and cope with a rattlesnake in the trail. The fifth chapter, "Sex, Difference, and the Ideal Traveler," explores how travelers used ridicule and contest to test each other and thereby reveal in outline the traits they most prized in themselves. Competing ideals of manhood played a special role on the trail as European and Native men challenged each others' masculinity and European travelers in particular worked to restrict the roles Native women played in their travels.

By the end of the eighteenth century things had changed somewhat for Indian-European travel. While Indians and Europeans continued to travel together well after the colonial era ended, there was some change in the circumstances surrounding these relationships. The book's last chapter, "Going Out," looks at how an increasing presence of Europeans on the trail both facilitated more and more intimate travel relationships, while also pushing Indians to the margin of some larger European trips. As more and more Europeans became skilled North American travelers over the seventeenth and into the end of the eighteenth centuries, it became increasingly possible for European travelers to rely on colonial woodsmen, and less exclusively on Indians, for some kinds of travel assistance. The cross-continental treks of Sir Alexander Mackenzie and Lewis and Clark, for example, relied first and foremost on the strength, skill, and endurance of European woodsmen, whereas earlier endeavors of this scale looked far more centrally to Native aids. What resulted was a distancing of Natives from the core of some high-profile travels. This did not end intercultural relationships, but it did introduce a new dimension, and meant that in some cases Indians were forced more to the edges of Europeans' travel, their skills and knowledge more easily marginalized and overlooked.

This book is first and foremost about the experiences of travel and how people interact within a distinct setting. As such, it is a broadly comparative history and an essay on the nature and implications of cultural difference examined within an arena that provides us with a unique setting for and lens on the location, creation, and maintenance of these differences. The literature on which the study is based is a fascinating and engaging body of stories which are illustrative and edifying in their own right in hundreds of different ways. These travel stories reveal to us how much the travels of colonial-era explorers, missionaries, traders, diplomatists, naturalists, and even tourists were hardly their own. Native peoples shaped and used European travel in myriad creative ways—so much so that the travels which usually bear the name of a European chronicler were really mobile microcosms of the larger world of Indian-

European contact and mutual exploration. The tales these travels produced can be heartrending, terrifying, infuriating, and amusing—they teach us about how people confronted dangers and hardships almost unimaginable to modern travelers. They show us how travelers formed their identities out of conflict and compromise, and how they made and understood the worlds through which they passed.

1

The Paradox of the Conquistadors' Trail

In the fall of 1539, the Spanish invasion of North America came to the central Florida village of Aguacaleyquen. A small number of men riding out in advance of Hernando de Soto's main column would have been the first into the town, but soon after, the rest of expedition's over-six-hundred-strong company would have come tramping through the village's center. Spanish spirits were still high that fall, and the crew of petty nobles, experienced conquistadors, and common folk were flushed with high hopes for the expedition they had eagerly signed on to. Their leader was a man with considerable New World experience under his sword belt. He had marched through Peru and received four full shares of the booty for his troubles. Now he held papers from Charles V appointing him governor—*adelantado*—of Cuba and this new land of La Florida, with the right to claim nearly six hundred coastal miles as his own new colony, and royal permission to distribute Native land and labor rights to his followers.[1] Soto was the third of Charles's subjects in the past twenty years to become adelantado of La Florida, and must have seemed to be the type of man who succeeded best in these endeavors.[2] When the small fleet of support ships disgorged its cargo of men, horses, supplies, weapons, chains, and a mobile forge at Tampa Bay's eastern shore the previous spring, there was every reason to believe that the name of La Florida would soon join those of Mexico and Peru in the annals of Iberian colonial legend.[3]

When the line of march came to Aguacaleyquen, the Spaniards were in search of the two things these *entradas*, or entries, most needed: food and information. Indeed, such pursuits would be an almost daily concern on the trail for the next four years, as the party marched a winding course from Florida into Texas and then back to the Mississippi. A few days earlier, scouts had found a "pretty town," where they raided the local supply of "very delicious small chestnuts" and other eatables.[4] But the glowing description of town and dainty food contrasted with the ugly means of acquisition. Before their feast of chestnuts they had set loose "a noble greyhound from Ireland," which bolted after a Timucuan man fleeing his would-be captors. The beast's jaw seized the man and "held him by the fleshy part of the arm in such a manner that the Indian was thrown down and apprehended."[5] It would seem that all of Soto's company, both man and beast, ate at the expense of La Florida's Native population.

As the Spaniards rode on through the palmettos and live oaks, they must have reflected on the events of the last few days and the possibilities awaiting them in the next village. But the clipped, perfunctory style of the Soto expedition's few chroniclers did not extend to long asides about the travelers' states of mind.[6] The march's documentary evidence leaves even less from which to reconstruct the experiences of people like those of Aguacaleyquen, who found themselves suddenly front and center in the most important drama of the age.

The towns of central Florida were in fairly close contact—roads on which the conquistadors traveled were the arteries of Indigenous trade, diplomacy, and warfare. Goods and people traveled these roads, and so did news between the towns.[7] Most likely, word of the strangers, their herds of strange animals, and their long line of Native porters—many of whom were chained hand and foot—had reached Aguacaleyquen's Timucuans along this extensive network well before the advancing column's dust was first visible. There must have been time for the villagers to take a few hurried precautions and protect who and what mattered most. Some people moved the freshly harvested corn from its usual raised cribs to hidden caches. Others took their children and elders and fled to the nearby fields and hummocks, seeking what shelter they could find. But soon the strangers were there, filling the town clearing, brandishing glinting steel weapons, poking in and out of homes, making demands in unintelligible tongues, and freely taking what they wanted wherever they found it.

The sounds of clanking armor and horses' hooves trampling the dying corn told a man and woman hiding in a field that their race was run. The sight of two hungry sweaty strangers now in front of them must have been as overwhelming as the din of the riders' barked-out, incomprehensible questions and threats and the stomping of their horses. Whether through gestures or the menacing waving of a corn stalk, the Indian woman somehow understood the solders' demands, despite a language gulf as wide as the Atlantic. Food. She led them to the cached bounty they had carefully tended all summer. The loss of this food supply could mean that her people would have to go hungry and many might even starve. They would be weak and vulnerable to their enemies. There may not even be enough seed to plant a new crop for the next season, endangering the future survival of the town. At Aguacaleyquen, as at countless other Native towns, corn was life, and its loss or destruction a disaster. But corn was also life to Soto and his men, who had been living on dwindling supplies for days. The entrada marched with its own herd of pigs, and always carried some food from its last provisioning stop, but this mobile larder was never quite enough to keep the hidalgo-led horde fully fed on the march. The plan, therefore, was to take the food they needed from the villages along their route. But the land did not produce food by itself—the food resulted from Native hard work and sweat; if anyone thanked the Aguacaleyquen woman for the village's labor and sacrifice, Rodrigo Rangel, the woman's captor and the event's chronicler, did not record it.

Meanwhile, the Indian man faced his own crisis. The words of demand and coercion are lost to history, as are the reasoning of the unnamed man. But the result is not, having been recorded in the perfunctory style of the expedition's few accounts. The Indian man showed Captain Balthasar de Gallegos where seventeen of his fellow villagers had hidden themselves from the sudden invasion that was undoing their world. Soto's secretary described the result of the seizure, which was in most ways unremarkable from the Spanish point of view, noting with satisfaction that the seventeen included the daughter of the cacique of Aguacaleyquen. Her capture was fortunate for the Spaniards because "it seemed reasonable that this would make her father come in peace."[8] The cooperation of a local chief—what the Spanish invariably called by the Lucayo word *cacique*—was often essential for the success of an expedition. The most famous of the conquistadors—men like Hernán Cortés and the Pizarro brothers, whose legendary achievements whetted the appetite of each new expedition—relied heavily on the aid and knowledge of Indigenous rulers. Soto and other would-be legends knew that carrying a ruler through his own territory greatly enhanced the chances that the Spaniards and their retinue would get through the land expeditiously, safely, and well fed. When possible, the soldiers brought local chiefs with them as guides and tickets for safe passage. To get this valuable aid, the armies employed threats and deception or tried to win over the chief with a promise to march against his enemies. But when no chief was around, conquistadors like Soto were happy to rely on the frequently problematic testimony of the first Native captive to tell the intruders a good and useful story of what the trail ahead led to.

After a few days' rest, and the construction of a pine log bridge over a nearby river, Soto's men resumed their march northward. They left loaded down with Aguacaleyquen's harvest. They also took with them the town's leader, his daughter, and a "principal Indian" named Guat Utima, who claimed he knew "what was farther on, and gave very great news about it."[9] Armed with that news, the entrada marched on to the next village.

Scenes like this repeated themselves wherever Soto's men marched that autumn and for the three autumns that followed. Although it would not have much comforted the Timucuans, Hernando de Soto, governor of Cuba and governor and captain general of the Island and Province of Florida and its Annexes on the Mainland, would himself soon be dead, his diseased body buried at night to conceal his passing from the local Indians. Not long afterward, the downhearted survivors—barely half the number of men who marched into Aguacaleyquen—would turn their backs on La Florida and sail for home on seven hastily constructed ships, their grand entrada a failure. When they floated off down the Mississippi they left behind hundreds of Indian guides, porters, and other companions, some of whom held in their arms the half-Spanish children of the march. The mothers wept as the fathers of their babies drifted out of sight, but the path of Soto's march was everywhere wet with Native tears.

Soto and his martial counterparts on other entradas usually occupy the spotlight in the stories of the so-called Era of Conquest. But at every turn in the road, at every river crossing, in each village along the way, through each trackless swamp or hard-baked desert, and along every coast, it was Native knowledge which set the course, and Indigenous backs which carried the loads. Native food filled Iberian bellies, and Indian ways set the parameters of the march's possibilities. Marches like Soto's were almost literally borne on the coerced backs of the Native population, and it was Indians, and not Europeans, who almost wholly controlled the fates and paths of these explorations. And therein lies the great irony of this early landward phase of Europe's long colonial foray in North America. The great entradas were dependent on Native assistance in many forms at every level of the expedition. And yet, at the same time, these expeditions' heavy-handed means of securing that assistance ensured the enmity of those Indians the Spaniards most relied upon. On the great entradas, Europeans were at a disadvantage, their travel shaped more by the demands, desires, travel networks, and distance knowledge of their often-unwilling guides than by their own colonial ambitions. The result was a unique regime of travel relationships based on coercion, mistrust, and anxiety, creating a spiraling cycle of deception, fear, and violence.

It was not the best of plans, and in many respects one which was doomed to failure. Soto's march was the longest and largest of those of his contemporaries and consequently produced the largest number of accounts documenting these strained travel relationships, but he was by no means the only entrada leader to rely on this flawed scheme. Soto's La Florida predecessor, Pánfilo de Narváez, and Vázquez de Coronado, who trekked from northern Mexico through the southwest and onto the Great Plains in 1540, both relied on the same heavy hand in living off the bounty of well-maintained Indian landscapes. In their own ways, each of these three expeditions drew on the same basic strategies, goals, and assumptions, and even though the particulars varied between marches, in general the results were the same. Spaniards, usually unable to fully understand their Native guides, lived and marched enveloped in a pervasive and consuming fear of being tricked and misled. Native guides, in turn, many of whom lacked the basic knowledge to do as their captors demanded, often did in fact mislead, either intentionally through guile, or unintentionally, through ignorance of the landscape or incomprehension of the language. Each dead-end trail, misunderstood description, or hostile welcome confirmed to the Spaniards that their guides were not to be trusted and had to be dealt with in a violent punitive fashion in order to inspire a fealty and truthfulness through fear. But for Natives, each killing and maiming of a "lying" guide, each raid and torching of a native village, and each new group of cringing captive porters only increased their incentive to work against the interests of their captors. This ever-accelerating cycle of fear, miscomprehension, anger, deception, and violence typified the great entradas' travel relationships, while also undermining their viability.

It is not merely a coincidence that these marches were largely failures, achieving little of what they sought to do. They left behind no new colonial settlements and no new allies and they brought home no great wealth and not even much in the way of useful geographic information—Spanish understandings of the interior were fragmentary well into the seventeenth century. If the marches were imperially results poor, they were also personal disasters for their leaders and companies. Narváez and all but four of his 1528 entrada disappeared into the Gulf of Mexico after a desperate attempt to float to the nearest Spanish port on makeshift rafts. Soto died on the march in Arkansas, and soon thereafter his ragged survivors finally returned home in their own fleet of homemade "brigantines," without gold or glory. Coronado and his men made it back to Mexico in better form than others, but as with Soto's march, this entrada also failed to find what it sought and established little in the way of enduring colonial toeholds. Coronado himself—the only survivor of these three entrada leaders—came home weakened and dejected and facing a long list of charges, including having abused his Mexican Indian porters.[10]

The roots of these failures were partly buried deep in the entradas' organizational structure and the workings of Spain's American empire in its earliest days. The entradas were royally sanctioned speculative ventures, meaning that leaders and private backers could only profit through the acquisition of New World wealth and the establishment of colonies with governorships pre-awarded by the crown to the men leading the march. But in addition to being private business ventures, these marches were also paramilitary affairs led by newly designated governors or "captains general," with a staff of a maestro de campo, mounted captains, and sergeants, all of whose activities were recorded by official notaries and spiritually overseen by selected friars. Rules of march served as an entrada's laws, and letters granting titles made the expedition leaders the crown's representatives on the trail. Yet, despite the military patina and authority undergirded by official paperwork, the entradas' companies tended to be loose and volatile, and their enterprises prone to faction and dissolution.[11] Leaders had to be men of some charisma, with the ability to persuade as much as bully, in the full knowledge that each rebuked captain could become the leader of mutinous discontented party. The constant tension over maintaining order in the unruly ranks, coupled with the large risks entailed in a march into alien territory, went a long way toward fostering much of the fear and nervous rearward glancing which underscored these expeditions' violence. The entradas' volatility did not stem from an imagined malicious Spanish nature, as rival European powers liked to aver.[12] In fact, Spain's earliest North American travelers had no monopoly on cruelty and coercion. The crews of northern Europe's ships were also quick to "lay handes upon" and take "with maine force" the Native people they needed for any purpose on any shore either by impromptu demand or official order.[13] Instead, entradas took their shape due to an uncomfortable mix of the unnerving conditions they faced, the rules and internal tensions governing their marches, and the characters of the men who signed on. If France, England, and Holland had no great entradas of their own, it was not because they were incapable, but rather because Spain had already played out the viability of this type of travel and written extensively about the experience.

But explanations based on jealous, infighting conquistadors and the vicissitudes of imperial interest politics and colonial administration can only go so far in explaining what the these marches were and why they often failed so spectacularly. The great entradas were first and foremost creatures of the trail, and as such were almost wholly dependent on their travel relationships. Viewed that way, the strained relationships North American conquistadors formed with their Native companions—most particularly those they forced into guiding their expeditions—and the skills, knowledge, and desires of accompanying Indians are crucial to understanding what took place on these marches and why they unfolded as they did. The largest and best known of the early explorations were so thoroughly defined by their self-defeating attitude toward local Native populations that they became themselves a distinctive arena of early Indian-European travel relationships in which both Native and newcomer, and the conflicts between them, imprinted themselves on the paths and fates of these marches.

It is also no coincidence that the most enduring North American Spanish colonial enterprises did not grow out of the travel of men like Soto and Coronado. Instead, the Spanish missions and settlements in both La Florida and the northern reaches of New Spain followed the travel of post-1560 governors and friars who had largely abandoned the procurement tactics of the earlier generation of would-be conquerors. The abortive 1560s marches of Tristán de Luna and Juan Pardo were Spain's last old-style entradas into La Florida's interior. But even though both of these marches expected local Natives to supply food and aid along the trail, neither used the heavy-handed procurement style of their predecessors.[14] Likewise, the great southwestern marches of the likes of Juan de Oñate at the end of the century resorted only rarely to coercing Native guidance.

Several things had changed by the 1560s. For one thing, the imperial ground rules for traveling conquests shifted as the crown began to prefer smaller, missionary-led ventures to large, costly, and potentially troublesome entradas.[15] The so-called New Laws of 1542 sought to correct the excesses of the conquest's early years by curbing the ability to capture Natives and stating that Indians should not be laden with an "immoderate burthen."[16] A reiteration of these laws in 1573 further limited conquistadors' powers by specifically outlawing "conquests" and abuses of Indians, while insisting that only men of the best character march for Spain.[17] By the 1600s, the crown went so far as to outright bar soldiers from La Florida exploration.[18] Of course, enforcing such laws was harder than promulgating them, but such policy changes did force a shift in entrada practices and reporting.

Another change was that later entradas did not take on the large distances covered by Soto or Coronado. Pardo's 1567 march, for example, which went only from the Atlantic coast to the Appalachian Mountains, was one of the longest of its day. Not only were treks shorter, but the places were increasingly better known, having entered the Spanish colonial atlas via the sketchy fragmented reports from earlier entradas and subsequent visitors.[19] All of this made for a marked change in the travel relationships between early and later entradas. The key tasks of guidance and translation were, after 1560, generally in the hands of local allies or people with true and tested ties to the Spaniards, their rights clearly defined within the legal apparatus of the empire. Militarized marches were still part of the Iberian colonial plan into the seventeenth century, but after the 1560s, at least in North America, the callous and somewhat random seizures of Natives like those at Aguacaleyquen were no longer the norm. What had been a core plan of the march became instead a strategy saved for crises, meaning that post-1560 marches were less plagued by the paradox of their early counterparts. In short, the Spanish succeeded by abandoning the failed methods of their earliest travelers.

The tenor of the entradas' travel relationships shaped these marches from the moment they set off, if not earlier. Initially, the entrada's planners hoped to rely on the testimony, translation, and guidance of previously captured Natives brought back to colonial cities, interrogated, and taught Spanish especially to serve their new "friends." Coronado and other southwestern marchers had the best success with this plan. Unlike La Florida, the route to New Mexico was overland and there was no shortage of already-subject Indians in New Spain's northern reaches who could aid the expedition. Coronado's troubles began, however, when he tried to get beyond the lands familiar to his northern Mexico guides. King Charles V ordered Narváez to keep his kidnapping down to only a few Natives. Nevertheless, Narváez brought no guides of any tribe and thus immediately found himself virtually unable to communicate with local Indians except through crude "signs" and sometimes "threatening gestures."[20] Soto tried to avoid Narváez's error, and arrived in Florida with four guides previously captured just for this purpose.[21] But once landed, the Spaniards found that these four had little knowledge of the land, "lost their bearings somewhat," and led them in a "wandering and confused" fashion.[22] What is more, language became a barrier anyway, as the guides had trouble communicating with both the local Indians and the Spaniards themselves. The guides' lack of language skills, whether feigned or genuine, quickly became irrelevant, as most of them soon slipped off. Whether through bringing no guides, or the wrong ones, the marchers generally had to fend for themselves in alien territory and with no way to communicate efficiently with the locals. The result was a pattern of raiding and capturing which became essential to the entradas' survival and progress.

The early entradas simply took what they needed in the way of guides and Native porters to carry heavy loads of weapons, supplies, and plundered food. Soto's modus operandi was typical, if somewhat larger in scale than others. The preferred plan was to "place a guard" over chiefs in each new town or region "so that they might not go away." Once this was done, the men "took them along" until "leaving their land." The goal of this plan was simply stated by one witness: "for by taking them, the people would await in their towns and they would give a guide and Indians as carriers."[23] Entradas repeated this scheme in each area and the previous captives were set free and given "leave to return to their homes." The marchers were also quick to take people by force when none were offered. In one roundup, Soto's men netted "a hundred head among Indian men and women." These they "took along in chains and collars about their necks and they were used for carrying the baggage and grinding the maize" as well as "other services which so fastened in this manner they could perform." A hint as to what those "services" might have included lurked in the raiding party's division of the captured women. The captain leading the raid "selected one or two for the governor," and the rest they "divided amongst themselves and those who went with them."[24]

Good as this plan seemed to its enactors, it did not always function quite so smoothly. At Coosa in 1540, for example, Soto's riders scoured the landscape and "seized many Indians, men and women," including many of the town's most prominent men, placing the whole lot in chains. But many of the new "slaves" managed to "file off their chains at night," and others slipped off the trail "with their chains and with their loads and the clothes they were carrying."[25] Other captives went for a more direct challenge to their captors. In some cases a group might kill the "Christian who was leading them" and then run off, chains and all.[26] In one instance, a north Florida woman seized a singularly aggressive Spaniard "by the genitals" and refused to let him go until he became "very fatigued and submissive."[27] But in many cases no escape possibilities presented themselves, and oftentimes the tasks given captives proved to be simply too much to bear. Soto's Apalachee porters are one example of the fate many faced. Weighed down by heavy loads of corn on their bare backs, these captives were said to have simply "died because of the hard life they suffered" since their capture.[28]

A porter (or several dozen) might die or run off with a load of corn or clothes, but by and large entrada leaders regarded these losses as little more than the cost of doing business. As long as new backs would be offered by, or coerced from, the next chief, the march could continue apace. But the question of reliable guidance provided a bigger and more perilous problem, and one which touched the entradas' core goals and abilities to achieve them. Entrada leaders generally knew what they wanted—wealth, food, porters, and so on—but usually did not know where to find it.[29] Instead, the courses of these marches depended almost entirely on the skill, knowledge, and, most essentially, the goodwill of Indian guides. Of all the relationships entradas formed with Natives, few were as pivotal as those formed between captive guides and their captors. Yet despite the vital importance of gaining the best and most reliable information, the early entradas relied on the most haphazard and self-defeating means of gathering that information. Captors could slap a porter in irons and reasonably expect that however resentful and resistant the porter might be, he or she could still provide some measure of service. But guides were another story. In trusting either long-term or short-range guides, entrada leaders effectively let go of control of their fates, which now rested on the goodwill, knowledge, and skill of the individual guide. In this way, the path of these entradas became European reflections of the distribution of geographic knowledge within Indian societies, and the types of relationships travelers formed on the trail.[30]

Societies whose way of life required members to move over large territories pursuing game or trade produced men and women who were all, by necessity, highly skilled and informed travelers. By adolescence, every Montagnais, Cree, or Athabascan boy or girl had an expert's knowledge of a wide swath of land. Members of mobile Indian societies all had to be well skilled in how best to move over their landscapes, find ready food and build warm and dry shelter in a hurry, and survive the hardest of times. But the dazzling wealth of Aztec Tenochtitlán and Inca Cuzco was never far from any North American conquistador's mind, and migratory people, wherever they might live, did not possess the kind of wealth sought by every would-be Pizarro or aspiring Cortés. Only well-populated, settled states could yield the kind of quick haul that made men rich and drove other men to sign on to the next expedition. Consequently North American conquistadors always tried to steer themselves toward large villages, ever believing in the El Dorado over the next river or behind the next mountain.

This meant that the entradas most often marched into areas inhabited by Indians living in settled state societies. These societies best produced the wealth the entradas sought and were often tied into tribute networks and a centralized authority which the Spaniards could usurp and redirect. But unlike migratory bands, the members of state societies were not *all* skilled and experienced travelers. To be sure, these societies produced many Indians who traveled far to hunt, trade, or fight with distant foes. But there also were large numbers of villagers who rarely ventured more than a few dozen miles from their homes. In one instance, Soto's advance parties brought in "three or four" Natives to serve as guides or to provide information, but the seemingly most informed of them "did not know farther on from the town."[31] The four coastal Timucuans who "lost their bearing somewhat" while leading Soto's men northward in 1539 may well have been genuinely lost in the swamps dozens of miles from their homes, as indeed they claimed.[32] To be sure, claims of being lost may have been attempts to get away from captors as quickly as possible. But at the same time, many of these people indeed had simply no idea where they were. The Spaniards' undiscerning, wide-net strategy of guide procurement ensured that more than a few inexperienced travelers would ineffectively lead the march. The entradas' expansive territorial ambitions further meant that even experienced travelers would sometimes be forced to serve as guides well beyond the bounds of their geographical knowledge.[33] In this way the early entradas' course reflected less Iberian ambitions than the skills and willingness of specific Indian guides. The routes these marches took were themselves fragmented Europeanized versions of Indigenous landscape knowledge, shaped by and mapping the distribution of that knowledge within Native societies.

The randomness of this procurement strategy and its frequently accompanying brutality combined to create the worst possible situation for both guides and marchers. Spaniards were acutely aware of their vulnerability and were ever on the lookout for signs that their captives were deceiving them or leading them into disaster. Native guides, whose thoughts are harder to piece together, soon learned that their captors were quick to mete out violent retribution for perceived trickery. But little that the entradas did inspired much of a Native desire to cooperate with these strangers. Despite the risks, many captives lashed out against their captors and exploited the marchers' vulnerability and geographic ignorance to redirect, misdirect, or undermine these most unwanted guests. Far from being intrepid marches or a colonial vanguard, the early North American entradas were in reality half-blind, brutal, anxiety-ridden bands of Europeans led from place to place by coerced and terrified Natives themselves eagerly awaiting their chance to escape, ditch, or kill the men who held their chains.[34]

Entradas used a few basic tactics to procure guidance. The simplest and most repeated was to round up a few people at a new town and see what they knew. Sometimes captives fell into the hands of the main party, and other times small mounted "excursions" could ride away from the main line of march and "capture some Indians" who might reveal local details.[35] This allowed riders to see firsthand what the country held, while bringing back small groups of local Indian informants. Likewise, any chance meeting could also provide a possible guide. Narváez's trailside meeting and hand-sign discussion with about two hundred Indians resulted in an exchange of unfriendly gestures. Quickly, Narváez's men grabbed a half dozen of the natives and forced them to lead them to their nearby village.[36] It should have come as no surprise, then, that these parties might travel for days on end without seeing any Indians "who would venture to await" their arrival.[37] Indeed, one of Soto's men coolly noted that at Mabila one group of Indians "hanged themselves" in order to avoid Spanish capture—others threw themselves into the burning remnants of their homes.[38] The marches' frequent armed conflicts also provided chances to capture people who might prove effective guides. Early in his 1529 march through Florida, for example, a squad of Narváez's "cavalry" rode down a small group of Timucuan warriors and brought back "three or four, who thenceforth served as guides."[39] Such scenes repeated themselves again and again.

Even though guide procurement was often indiscriminate, taking whoever could be caught regardless of skill or knowledge, entrada leaders were well aware that some Indians made better guides than others. Chiefs, for example, provided perhaps the best easily identifiable source of geographic knowledge, as such men and women often had a keen understanding of their own lands and those of their neighboring friends and foes. Unsurprisingly, entradas were quick to exploit this rich source of indigenous knowledge and prestige when possible. For their part, chiefs had a host of reasons to cooperate with or deceive the strangers. Some leaders wanted little more than to get the Spaniards out of town as quickly as possible. Others saw in the line of march an opportunity to strike a blow against a Native foe, and in either case often gladly sent the intruders down the best road out of town, or even led them that way themselves. In the best of circumstances, these men, whom the Spaniards named for their villages, complied willingly, like the headmen of Cofaqui and Totofa who offered Soto gifts and "all the tamemes [porters] they had need of."[40] Likewise, the headmen at Ocute and Cofaqui offered up ample provisions, capable guides, and eight hundred of their own people to carry it all, once Soto made clear his intention to march against their traditional enemies at Cofitachique. At other times, a chief's recalcitrance over Spanish demands required some measure of coercion. At Tulla, for example, Soto's men captured a group of villagers and sent six back to their chief "with their right hands and noses cut off," threatening to do the same to more people if the headman did not come personally with guides and interpreters.[41] In one instance, the interrogation of possible cacique-guides resulted in a solid blow to Soto's mouth which "bathed" the governor's "teeth in blood," leaving him spitting out blood, and spitting mad. The assailant and his fellows quickly died "riddled with arrows."[42] This pugilistic cacique was not the only one to score a final, pyrrhic blow against the invaders. Some leaders preferred to burn their towns and supplies while inhabitants fled into the surrounding countryside, thus denying the newcomers what they most wanted. On more than few occasions marchers arrived to a find town in flames, "for the Indians had set fire to it."[43] While the entradas—particularly Soto's—were eager to coerce or win over local leaders, with an eye toward exploiting their knowledge and prestige, the task was not always easy, and chiefs did not always make compliant and reliable allies or guides.

Indigenous travelers were also a potentially useful source of geographic information when they could be found and identified. Obviously, such people had firsthand travel experiences and familiarity with distant communities, knowledge which could be quite valuable to wandering Spaniards. While chiefs' local prestige, when properly exploited, offered the possibility of moving through territories with relative ease, travelers offered what the Spaniards took to be reliable information about distant lands and wealth. But unlike chiefs, who, for better or worse, usually presented themselves directly to the invaders, experienced travelers were generally harder to come by. Given the interconnectedness of southeastern Native societies, there would have been no shortage of travelers on the roads and in the towns the entradas visited. Archaeological deposits all over North America confirm that Native trade networks conveyed all kinds of goods over very large distances. It follows that someone had to carry those goods, although it is unclear to what extent this distribution resulted from individual long-distance travelers or local peoples trading goods from village to village. In short, there were some Indians who did travel great distances from their settled homes, for any number of reasons. Entrada leaders, aware of travelers' unique skills, were ever on the lookout for anyone who told what seemed to be a convincing story of a place far away.

Traveler-guides were few and far between, but their significance, and the value the Spaniards attached to their specialized knowledge, is partly revealed by the fact that the two best-documented entrada captive guides both appear to have been Native travelers. No chronicler recorded their Indigenous names, so we must know them by the nicknames their captors gave them, names which reflected their roles in the entradas as well as no small amount of projected Iberian anxiety. Likewise, all we know of these two captives is what their captors thought worth recording. Their stories, and the intelligence they offered, come to us filtered through the fears and desires of people who spoke different languages and saw the world through very different eyes. But even with these limitations, the retold experiences of these two Indigenous travelers provides a glimpse of how such captives experienced and made sense of their plights and may have tried to turn bad situations to some advantage.

In northern Florida, Soto's men captured a young man claiming to be from a distant interior land "in the direction of the sunrise" called Yupaha, where a great ruling lady lived in a town of "wondrous size," collecting tribute of cloth and gold from neighboring chiefs.[44] The Spaniards, convinced by the youth's description of Native metal smelting, took the story as gospel and set off eastward directed by the boy from Yupaha. They named the boy "Perico," the Spanish word for "parrot," an appellation which simultaneously paid tribute to and denigrated the lad's language skills—he spoke Timucuan and Muskogean languages. The nickname also highlighted the vast language chasm then separating Iberian and Indian, and the anxieties this deafness created. Perico led the march northeast from the Florida panhandle into the Mississippian chiefdom of Cofitachequi in modern South Carolina.

But in the village of Patofa things took a turn for the worse. There Perico had a fit in which he "began to foam at the mouth and to throw himself at the ground."[45] So convinced of demonic activity was the aptly named missionary Fray Juan el Evanjelico that he immediately began to pray the "evangel" over the boy's writhing body. Rodrigo Rangel, however, believed that the youth "made himself out to be possessed" because he "did not know anymore of the land."[46] Perico had indeed had ample time to watch and learn about the Spaniards, and this fit may have been a well-planned ruse, designed to scare his captors into leaving him behind in Patofa. Yet the fit may also have had a more ingenuous purpose. Perico's knowledge of the path ahead may indeed have been failing him. Recognizing the dangers implicit in his failure at this important juncture, he perhaps turned to spiritual assistance through a ritual trance. Perico's writhing and "foam[ing] at the mouth" is consistent with numerous Native transcendent practices. What the Spaniards took to be either demonic possession or playacting may have been a search for guidance by a guide himself out of his depth. Whatever the fit's derivation, Perico emerged from his stupor with the news that Yupaha was now only "four day's thence toward the rising sun."[47]

The people of Patofa did not agree with Perico's trance-induced geography and told the Spaniards that they knew of no such place in that direction and at that distance. Nevertheless, Soto chose to follow Perico, taking with him hundreds of Patofan porters. But when the four days became nine, the provisions ran low, and the path "gradually grew narrower until it was all lost," trust turned to rage.[48] Soto ordered the young guide thrown to the dogs "because he had deceived them."[49] Only the intervention of the expedition's main translator, who knew all too well how vital Perico's language skills were, saved him for being torn apart by the governor's mastiffs. Lost and angry, Soto sent the Patofa porters back to the town so as not to have to feed them any longer. On April 26, 1540, Soto's men set off in a new direction for a town called Aymay, guided there by "an Indian woman and a boy" whom Juan de Añasco captured at a town a few leagues away.[50] Perico was no longer useful as a guide and so he was replaced, but his language skills made him still a needed part of the expedition. At some point later he joined those Indians who chose to become Christians like their captors. What experience or revelation brought him to that choice is unknown, but his baptism and his officially taking the Christian name "Pedro" not only granted him access to the Kingdom of Heaven, but also eased his travel, as "the Governor ordered him to be loosened from the chain in which he had gone until then."[51]

Coronado's traveler-guide's story was quite different. While visiting the buffalo-trodden dry plains northeast of the Pueblo village of Cíbola, an advance party of Coronado's men learned that one of their Pueblo guides in fact hailed from the eastern land of Harahey—the land of the Pawnees. Through a mix of hand signs and broken language the Spaniards understood this man to have told them that Harahey, and the closer land of Quivira, were full of "gold and silver." The story stirred the advance party's gold sense so much that they "did not care to look at cattle" any longer and quickly "turned back to report the rich news" to Coronado. Despite trusting this enticing story, the Spaniards mistrusted its teller and named him El Turco—the Turk—nominally "because he looked like one," perhaps a reference to a scalp lock or even a turban.[52] But the sixteenth-century implications of such a name are not subtle and perhaps less benignly descriptive. The nickname combined a range of Spanish fears and prejudices, ranging from perceived untrustworthiness to skin color. Marching eastward toward El Turco's homeland rhetorically cast the venture as a New World version of Christian Spain's long war with Muslim Spain. Heading eastward also alluded to the rising tide of Ottoman power, which by 1540 had already washed against the gates of Vienna.[53]

Coronado's time in Cíbola was ugly and bloody and its people and leaders could not have been sorry to see the Spaniards' armored back plates as they marched off into the sunrise and toward the promise of Native gold. But the Turco-led march to golden Quivira and Harahey of the east found only the endless grassy plains of the Midwest, inhabited by people who could not confirm Turco's tales of wealthy golden hordes. Cracks began to emerge in Turco's story soon after the party set off with visions of untold wealth in their heads and pounds of Indian corn in their saddlebags.[54] For one thing, Turco was not the only Native offering information to the Spaniards. Early on, Xabe, a Quiviran captive boy, related that "there was silver and gold" in Quivira, "but not in the quantities" Turco had suggested.[55] Soon afterward another source of doubt and tension arose. Turco set a course that took the marchers more toward the south than expected and another Quivira Native with the entrada, named Isopete, came forward and protested that Turco was leading them in the wrong direction.[56] At first the Spaniards dismissed Isopete's nay-saying, but his credibility grew as they cut deeper and deeper into their supplies and Turco's promises of only a few days' further march proved untrue. What is more, as they marched farther onto the Great Plains, local Querecho buffalo hunters corroborated Isopete's doubts. As the march progressed, the two guides Turco and Isopete fell into conflict over differing visions of the path ahead. Through hand signals Isopete indicated that he would "rather have his head cut off" than follow Turco's course. In response Turco called Isopete "a scoundrel" and assured the Spanish that his rival "did not know what he was talking about."[57] In the face of mounting evidence, Coronado lost faith in Turco and asked Isopete to lead the new course to Quivira. Isopete gladly consented but warned them that Turco had lied about both Quivira's wealth and its location.[58] Turco's star fell and he found himself confined to the rear of the column and in chains, with a hostile Isopete wanting him abandoned on the plains. Once in Quivira the bubble finally burst; "no gold nor silver nor information of any" as one disappointed marcher wrote.[59] Even the hope for more-distant wealthy lands were dashed by Quivirans reporting that "there was nothing beyond Quivira" except Harahey, which they said was pretty much the same kind of place.[60] The best the Spaniards saw was a chief's disappointing copper-plate medallion.

With Isopete vindicated and Turco's story proven untrue, the Spaniards turned on the journey's originator and demanded to know why he had misled them. In response Turco now claimed that the whole venture was a scheme to lead the metal men onto the plains where "through lack of provisions" they would gradually starve or become so weak as to be easy prey for Native warriors.[61] As with every aspect of Turco's communications, the reliability of this story, and the Spanish understanding of it, is uncertain. In one chronicler's version he was acting on behalf of the people of Cíbola. In other versions he called upon local Indians to rise up and kill the intruders once the plan had failed. Whatever the case, the price of Turco's last story was his life. To the reported great pleasure of Isopete, a Spanish soldier garroted their former guide.[62] Soon the marchers turned back for Cíbola, led by six new Quiviran guides. For his cooperation, Isopete was allowed to remain in Quivira with his own people.[63]

There are several parallels between Turco's and Perico's captivities, stemming from their own similarities and those between their captors. Both came to Spanish attention due to the enticing stories they related about distant wealth, built seemingly on the fact that both were strangers in the lands where they met the entradas. Both guides had traveled before they met the Spaniards. The Native world Soto traversed was a network of villages all tied together through bonds of friendship and hostility. Such a network provided numerous opportunities for people to move about for any number of reasons. Perico was young, raising questions about how he came to be so far from home. He may have been part of a group of travelers then visiting northern Florida; indeed, at least one of Soto's four chroniclers contended that Perico was part of a group of traders from Yupaha.[64] But Perico could just as likely have been a war captive, a part of a diplomatic exchange, or any number of other types of travelers moving between these villages. Turco appears to have been a Pawnee, and was probably a slave in Pueblo society, as were Isopete, Xabe, and the other men and women accompanying Coronado onto the plains. As in the Southeast, people in the Southwest moved along an extensive network of trails and villages for a vast array of reasons. People like Turco gained their distance knowledge as captives, over time moving from village to village, just as did any other "trade item."[65]

Perico and Turco both may have seen in their respective entradas a chance to return to their homelands and to do so at the head of a large body of men; in fact, such a motive may have been the spur in the Turco-Isopete rivalry. This meant that both told more than mere stories—they told the right kind of stories, even if, as may have been the case with Turco, those stories may have been more bait than reconnaissance. The conflict between Turco and Isopete suggests that some guides perhaps did see these marches as offering a sort of safe passage through alien lands. The fierceness of their argument over the entrada's course reveals that captives could also disagree dramatically over the nature of their shared plight and how to turn it best to advantage. The reliance on captive guides ensured that conflict between captor and hostage would shape the courses of marches. But the Turco-Isopete rivalry reveals that conflicts between captives themselves could also play a role in where entradas marched and did not march. This particular rivalry caught the chroniclers' attention; one wonders how many unnoticed conflicts governed other paths.

Since what brought Perico and Turco to Spanish attention were the stories they told, it is understandable that language also factored heavily in both guides' experiences. Perico served a vital role in the growing human chain of translation, which governed all communications between Soto and the people whose lands his men traversed. One of the best bits of good luck to befall Soto's entrada was their early meeting with Juan Ortiz, a young hidalgo left behind by a search party that was looking for clues to the fate of the Narváez expedition. Ortiz had spent the years between his early 1529 abandonment and his 1539 reunion living with the Timucuans, learning their languages, and doing some limited travel—by his own claim he had not been more than thirty miles from where he met his former countrymen. The tattooed and Nativized Ortiz could not offer much information about surrounding lands and their wealth potential, but the reclaimed Spaniard became an irreplaceable linguistic link between the entrada and local peoples. Until his death in Arkansas nearly two years later, Ortiz stood at the end of an ever-growing battalion of translators, each of whom would take a message from one language into another until it came to Ortiz to turn it into his rusty Castilian.[66]

But without native linguists and informants, Ortiz was of little use once beyond his thirty-mile limit. Although captured in northern Florida, Perico had some experience of other lands and spoke not only Timucuan but Muskogean languages as well, making the multilingual youth a vital language link as the entrada moved between language groups. This translation chain, like guide-procurement strategies, placed a considerable amount of influence in the hands and tongues of captive Indians like Perico. They controlled what and how the Spaniards learned about the land, carefully choosing a word here, editing some information there, and at all times understanding and translating through the uncertain and uneven lenses of their no doubt differing language abilities. The courses of the entradas were as much immersed in Native language as they were confined by the Native landscape. Perico and other translators may have seen power and prestige in their otherwise unenviable situation, partly for their unique ability to manipulate their captors. But the role also mirrored that of what Apalachees called an *atequi*, or a chief's official translator. Such people held considerable prestige in their social hierarchies throughout the Southeast, and Perico and other translators may have seen their own experiences in that light.[67]

Language saved Perico, but it contributed to Turco's demise. Thanks to Ortiz, Soto was able to gain a reasonably good idea of what Perico had to say. His story of Yupaha's tribute-rich headwoman, while being the stuff of entrada fantasy, was also plausible and jibed well with the Native world the marchers had already seen. But Turco had no Juan Ortiz to translate either the words or essence of what he related. Through an unreliable mix of hand signs and some Nahuatl—the Aztec tongue which had become a sort of a lingua franca throughout northern Mexico—Coronado heard the detailed credibility-straining story of distant wealth.[68] In conquistador Pedro de Castañeda's memory, Turco told of an eastern land of plains and rivers "two leagues wide" in which one could find "fish as large as horses." Chiefs in this land majestically rode at the stern of large gold-adorned canoes rowed by "more than twenty oarsmen on each side." When not gliding on the water, these chiefs rested under large shade trees, lulled to sleep by the tinkling of countless "golden jingle bells" and dining from "pitchers, dishes, and bowls" all made of gold. Commoners had to make due with a "common table service" which was "generally of wrought silver."[69]

In some of the details, Turco seems to have been describing a Mississippian high chiefdom, albeit filtered through Spanish fantasy and what may have been his own secondhand information.[70] The wide river, the plains, the large canoe, and the aura of nobility all accord with what we know of the Indian state societies that thrived in the fifteenth- and sixteenth-century Midwest. But other details strain belief, especially considering the formidable language barriers. Turco may have used hand signs so subtle and evocative that an impressed Casteñeda claimed that "it seemed as if they spoke."[71] But no hand signs could be trusted to have described things as detailed as "golden jingle bells" or silver dinner sets. Coronado's men satisfied themselves of the tale's veracity by quizzing the teller, presenting him with some tin which he "smelled" and identified as not being *acochis*—gold.⁷² The Spaniards translated this word as "gold," but some modern Indian linguists note that *acochis* sounds very much like a Hispanicized version of the Wichita word *ha:kwicis*, meaning "yellow metal, usually copper."⁷³ This linguistic parallel would also help confirm Turco's having been a traveler. But it also highlights the confusion arising between European and Native American metallurgical categories and the challenges presented by hasty, results-oriented entrada interrogations. Turco may have alluded to differences in the metals' color and workability, or merely meant that the proffered tin was unlike Harahey's copper. But whatever Turco may have said or meant to say, Coronado and company employed their own alchemy of wishful greed and poor communication, turning Native copper into golden bangles and silver baubles.

Perico's and Turco's captivities highlight the volatile mixture of fear and anxiety shaping these travel relationships and the paths they followed. Communicating through hand signs and large translation committees ensured the constant shaping and reshaping of information as it passed between languages, assumptions, and desires. The information itself became unstable as it was pushed and pulled, tweaked and twisted at each evocation. Anxious conquistadors reacted to this by dichotomizing Native information into categories of "lies" and "truth" and by acting accordingly in response to each, imposing a rough usable order on alien and incomprehensible cartographic and linguistic landscapes. For their part, captive Natives possessing little, some, or all of the skills and information their captors demanded reacted in an unknowable array of ways. Some fought back quickly and directly, but others found ways to endure their situations. Soon after visiting Cofitachequi, Perico, for example, asked to be baptized a Christian—a move which if real may have reflected sincere conversion, a crisis-driven identification with his captors, a shrewd calculated ruse (perhaps à la his Patofa fit), or any number of other lost meanings. Whatever the intent, soon afterward "the Governor ordered him to be loosed from the chain in which he had gone until then."⁷⁴

But as Turco's demise shows, deception, or at least the fear of deception, was ever present in the relationships between entradas and their guides. One of Soto's chroniclers voiced the sentiments of many early marchers when they discovered that a guide's garbled information about the near and distant riches proved untrue. The conclusion was simple: the guides "told us many great lies."⁷⁵ This assessment reflects what must have been the entradas' greatest raw nerve—the often justified fear that their guides were lying to them. Certainly some of these "lies" resulted from entradas' flawed communication regimes. Guides who could barely communicate with their captors, nontravelers whom marchers forced to serve as guides, and experienced wanderers pushed beyond the bounds of their geographical knowledge all ran the risk of being accused of "lying" when marchers' fantasies and misunderstandings failed to materialize in Indian villages. But sometimes paranoia is based on reality. The marchers knew that they were vulnerable to the hostile intentions of their unwilling guides and their power to mislead. Likewise, Indians too were often well aware of the entrada's soft underbelly, and many were ready to use their superior geographic knowledge to exact some revenge—regardless of the personal cost.

The depth of this fear was revealed in the Spaniards' violent reaction to Indian guides engendering their suspicion. When Soto and his men arrived at the recently abandoned Florida town of Oçita, the soldiers vented their anger over finding no people or supplies by torching the empty homes. Angered at having been led down a useless path, Soto allowed his large war dogs to tear the hapless guide limb from limb.[76] When Coronado's men "brought in food and a few Native prisoners" near Chiametla, they took the chance to revenge themselves for earlier grievances and "hanged" those captives they thought were from offending villages.[77] Whether tortured, killed by dogs, "hanged from a tree," or garroted like Turco, the costs of misleading entradas could be high.[78] The mangled and burnt corpses of captive Indians were grim testaments to conquistadors' self-perpetuating fears and misguided strategy for maintaining control over their guides.

Nevertheless, despite the risks, impressed guides did hatch plans to fight their captors by leading them away from towns and villages, walking them into an ambush in a trackless swamp, or guiding them onto some dry plateau, there to die of thirst. By carefully manipulating an entrada's core needs for food, information, porters' assistance, and mineral wealth, Indian guides could and did make misleading an effective defensive strategy. The extent of these plans and how frequently they cropped up is unknowable. Conquistadors were quick to punish anything that to them smacked of treachery, meaning that many plans may have been snuffed out in their early stages through a mix of internal dissention and Spanish hypervigilance.

If indeed Turco acted as a Cíbolan agent, he was not alone. In the eastern Texas flatlands, a Caddoan Indian from the town of Nondacoa told the Soto entrada's new leader, Luis Moscoso, that the people of another nearby town spoke of seeing other Spaniards not far away. Eager to reach New Spain or make contact with their countrymen, the Spaniards followed their friendly Caddoan guide southward and two days off the beaten trail. But Moscoso, fearing that his men would "get lost in some unpeopled region," suspected trickery and ordered the guide tortured.[79] At some point during his ordeal the guide revealed that he had been asked by the chief of Nondacoa to lead the dangerous strangers away from Nondacoa and hopefully toward where they might ultimately die of hunger.[80] This confession resulted in the guide's death at the jaws of the ever-ravenous Spanish war dogs.

Such stories soothed rattled Iberian nerves by reinforcing the idea that marchers could spot and thwart the misguider in their midst. The veracity of a torture-induced confession was less important than the illusion of control such actions bolstered. But entrada vigilance could not stop every deception. It is not surprising then that what was probably the single most successful Native misguidance plan seems to have come off without its victims fully understanding that they were being led to disaster—Spanish ignorance of the plan may have been what enabled its success. The plotters were the people of Apalachee in northern Florida, and the by-no-means-blameless victims were the men of Pánfilo de Narváez's 1528 La Florida entrada.

Narváez and his men landed near Tampa Bay in May of 1527 and spent the next few months on a northward march which ultimately led them to the Gulf Coast beaches near modern St. Marks, Florida. Like Soto, who would later follow his trail, Narváez was a veteran of the Spanish conquest. He had spearheaded the subjugation of Cuba and commanded the army Cuba's governor sent to bring to heel a rebellious Hernán Cortés when the latter slipped his imperial chain and decided to make the conquest of Mexico more his own venture. Like Soto, Narváez was the adelantado of the new province and conducted his march preparatory to establishing settlements. But Narváez's expedition would prove to be the largest failure in Spain's attempts to explore and colonize North America. Within a few months of landfall, all but four of Narváez's party were forever lost to their countrymen, either killed on the trail, drowned in the Gulf of Mexico, starved on makeshift rafts, or washed up on shore to be killed by Indians or absorbed into their villages—lost forever to their country and kinfolk.[81]

Most contemporary observers and subsequent scholars have attributed Narváez's failure to poor planning and provisioning, as well as to the character flaws of the man himself. Indeed, the character flaws abounded, and certainly all the above-mentioned factors played a part, but there was more at work. Hidden in the events' only extant firsthand retelling are muted clues pointing toward a seemingly carefully planned, very well-timed misguidance scheme which even the wary Spaniards missed. This plan, like so much of trying to understand Indian thinking through European documentation, is visible only in relief or through a sort of historical peripheral vision. Yet given how often Indians worked to deceive and undermine entradas, it is more than likely that what happened at Apalachee and along Narváez's road to the Gulf of Mexico was no accident, but instead the result of careful planning and coordination.

If true, then the Apalachee plan to destroy the Spaniards may have been the decisive factor in dooming the Narváez entrada, as well as an important moment in Indian-European travel relationships.[82]

Almost immediately after their landing, Narváez and his men fixated on the northern Florida town of Apalachee as the place where they would find the riches they sought. Their march northward from Tampa Bay was not easy, relying as it did on captive guides who led them through swamps and woods, which they "could not pass without making many detours and having great difficulty."[83] The men marched weary and hungry, their necks chafing from rusting armor, their backs sore from shouldering heavy weapons, their bellies grumbling from a lack of food. Spirits rose and they gave "many thanks to god" when they at last came within sight of Apalachee.[84] But their joy was short-lived. An advance party of riders and footmen cautiously entered the town only to find a double disappointment. Far from being the rich, gilded city they had dreamed of, this hamlet boasted only forty-odd thatch-covered huts, with no immediate signs of vast, appropriable wealth. Additionally, the town was nearly deserted, with just a few "women and children" darting over the dusty square.[85] But the Spaniards soon learned where the hidden men had been, as Native stone-tipped arrows poured in on them from the woods outside the town.[86] This welcome was an indication of things to come, as were the "very large fallen trees that form obstructions" which the Spaniards casually noted.[87] Once securely in the town, Narváez and his men found themselves again attacked, first by the villagers themselves, and then later by men from another village. But finally these attacks abated and Narváez and his men occupied the town for twenty-five days. During this month, the Indians exploited Iberian geographic ignorance and gradually constructed and enacted an elaborate plan combining deception, misguidance, warfare, and scorched earth.

Narváez and his men relied on two principal sources in learning about the surrounding countryside into which they intended to march. One was the local cacique, whom they captured and imprisoned early in their stay and who seemed eager to tell them what they wanted to know. The other source was an unspecified number of Indians whom they had "brought along" with them to the town: some of these may have been from Apalachee itself, others may have been from more distant places.[88] How the Spaniards communicated with these people in the absence of a good translator is a mystery, although "gestures" probably dominated the conversation.[89] But either by hand signs or drawings, "each one by himself" related that Apalachee was the region's largest town and that "ahead there were fewer people, who were much poorer than they, and that the land was poorly populated and its inhabitants widely dispersed." They added that "going forward there were great lagoons and dense woods and great empty and unpopulated areas"—the Spaniards had already followed their guides through similar terrain and were in no hurry to relive the experience.[90] Furthermore, three separate mounted reconnaissances, each one presumably led by a captive guide, seemed to confirm this picture. In this way the guides collectively offered the invaders the bleakest possible picture and the one most at odds with what Narváez most wanted to find, thus discouraging their advance.

The uniformity of the Natives' testimony was for the Spaniards a confirmation of their stories' validity. But most of what Narváez learned from his captives was probably a lie, and the uniformity was quite possibly evidence of the depth and skill of the Native plan. For one thing, the guides' portrayal of Apalachee as a wasteland is singularly at odds with what Soto found there a decade later, and indeed what archaeologists have learned as well. One of Soto's men later described the same region as being a place of "many towns" and a land of "plentiful food," while another noted that "within a league and a half league" of one town, the province held "other towns where there was an abundance of maize, pumpkins, beans, and dried plums native to the land."[91] Given the difficulty of communication, any number of mistakes and mishearings (or more accurately, mis-seeings) was possible. It may have been that the Spaniards confused town name for province name, or simply attached a much-heard place name to their current locale.[92] But the uniformity of Native information, however conveyed, and subsequent events suggest something quite different from what the entrada imagined to be taking place.

Each in their way, the guides made every path out of town seem to be a dead end, while, with the subtlety of a magician's card force, making one route—the southerly one—seem the best option. Nine days to the south, they claimed Narváez would find the friendly town of Aute, brimming with beans, corn, and squash as well as large supplies of fresh fish, since Aute was "so close to the sea."[93] Meanwhile, as the guides described the countryside, Indian bowmen hiding in surrounding swamps and thickets kept the Spanish under constant assault, "wounding the people and horses" whenever they wandered too far from the town. This leg of the plan kept up the military pressure on the Spaniards while also making it impossible for them to see much of the countryside and perhaps unmask the deception.[94] The message was clear—all directions led to more trouble, and staying in place was too dangerous to risk for long. Finally Narváez took the bait. Without any hint of awareness that they were being fooled, the expedition's treasurer wrote that "seeing the poverty of the land and the unfavorable reports that they gave us about the population and everything else, and since the Indians made war on us continually," the marchers "decided to depart from there and go seek the sea and that village of Aute about which they had told us."[95] The hook was set.

Once Narváez's men set off down the southerly path, the next phase of the plan was simple to enact. For the first day the entrada made its way through mires and swamps suspiciously unbothered and "without seeing a single Indian." But on the second day, Narváez and company found themselves "chest-high" in a particularly large and "difficult to traverse" lagoon.[96] Once the invaders were in the middle of this morass of black water and cypress knees, weighed down with soaked armor and clothes, and their matchlocks rendered useless by moistened match cords, the Indians attacked. From behind trees and downed logs the warriors loosed volley after volley of arrows with such force that a few fully pierced oak trees "as thick as a man's lower leg."[97] Arrows splashed into the water, slammed into armored plate, and skewered exposed Spanish arms, legs, and necks. With no ability to fight back where they stood, all the men could hope to do was escape the assault by forcing their way through the archers and out of the swamp. When, in this manner, the governor and his men at last freed themselves from this Native-selected killing ground, they could only watch as their assailants retreated into the safety of the swamp. Accompanying the victorious Indians were the guides the Spaniards brought along with them, leaving the entrada blinded, crippled, and even more vulnerable.

With no option left them, Narváez and his tired, wounded, and demoralized men trudged on toward the sea, here and there fighting the occasional skirmish with Native defenders. But at Aute they found only a burned-out abandoned village—the people of the Aute had burned all they had before it could fall into Spanish hands. After a few days spent gathering and eating the produce of Aute's still full fields, the weakened, wounded, and sick men headed for the sea. Unable to move farther on land and having failed to find the rich cities they sought, the party built themselves makeshift boats, sewed their shirts into sails, filled horse-skin bags with fresh drinking water, and floated off to their deaths.

The Apalachee swamp ambush effectively broke the back of the Narváez entrada. It left the diminished party weakened, ill, guideless, and lacking any knowledge of the land. Narváez now had no choice but to follow the path the Apalachees had described for them, regardless of where it led. An artful combination of deceptive geographical information and manipulation of the entrada's needs set the Spaniards on that trail, and it seems that careful coordinated planning up and down the path worked to corral the party and lead them to their doom. In this way the demise of the Narváez entrada stemmed directly from the coercive, hostile, alienating, and counterproductive relationships the marchers formed with their Native guides and informants.

And Narváez was not alone. Whenever and wherever the large, earliest North American entradas marched, they employed a self-defeating strategy. By taking by force of that which they needed from Native peoples, the entradas ensured more hostility than cooperation. By taking guides when they needed them in an ongoing pattern of random kidnappings, they ensured that many captive guides would lack the skills or knowledge to be effective guides. The large territorial ambitions of these marches—particularly Soto's and Coronado's—likewise ensured a large language gap between captor and captive, only adding to the fear and anxiety governing European and Indian travel relationships on these great marches. All of this combined to make these entradas uniquely vulnerable to the machinations of the people they simultaneously most needed and most alienated.

By the end of the sixteenth century, the style of Spanish marches had changed. A set of new laws officially brought the curtain down on the Era of Conquest, and required that would-be conquistadors keep out of Indian affairs, maintain decorum within their parties, and treat the people they met along the way fairly and with respect. Did it work? Not entirely. Many of the excesses seen on Soto's and Coronado's marches continued to be commonplace on North American marches. For example, during their 1580s march along Coronado's path, the Chamuscado-Rodríguez expedition seemed to be repeating past patterns. At one village, they marched in "carrying the cross in [their] hands" and demanded "corn flour" from the townsfolk. When none was forthcoming, the party's musketmen leveled their arms and fired a few shots at the crowd to make them "understand that they had to give it."[98] They took Indian guidance "either willing or by force." They "seized" one man whom they "bound" and brought back to camp.[99] Others they simply "took." When dreams of rich villages failed to materialize in the desert's rocks and scrub, and narrow paths through the cholla and mesquite led nowhere, the marchers were quick to conclude that "the Indians had deceived us."[100] Familiar pattern repeated once again.

Yet despite the strong resemblance to forty years earlier, things had changed in real ways. The tensions implicit in traveling in a strange land diminished as each wave of marchers brought back more and more information about what the next group could expect and created alliances with peoples who could provide guides without physical coercion. Spanish law and authority were less willing than before to turn a blind eye toward marchers' excesses, but, more importantly, the Indians themselves forced a change. The Indian-driven failures of Narváez, Soto, and Coronado show that Native people understood the nature of the threat these marches posed and were ready, willing, and able to undermine, mislead, and curtail even the best-laid Spanish plans. By the end of the 1500s, Spanish marchers were willing to take Native aid at times, but it was not the core strategy it was in the first half of the century. The growing number of allied Indians who could be brought onto a march with less physical coercion lessened the need for captives. But Spaniards also had ample example that captives could be more of a danger than a help.

2

"Upon Proper Terms"

The Rewards of Guidance

The roads of Iroquoia were well designed, by travelers, for travelers. Like all Native paths, they followed the easiest routes, snaking their way through passes between hills and crossing waterways at their shallowest fords. Pathfinders beyond memory had established these routes. As long as the path was clear, people could travel and visit, thus maintaining the bonds of trust and friendship tying together their network of villages—the Great Iroquois Longhouse. Keeping the path clear was both a metaphor for friendly relations and a real task which helped make the metaphor work. Iroquoia's many trails were dotted with cabins and resting spots suitable for intervillage travelers' needing a night's rest. At unfordable rivers, carefully stashed canoes often awaited those wishing to cross over. Along the trail, travelers could learn news and needed information by looking up at trees carved with the messages of previous passersby. It was the travelers themselves who cleaned and maintained these trail houses, repaired and secluded canoes, and left messages for fellow travelers. On Iroquoia's paths, as on other Native trail networks, part of being a good traveler was helping facilitate one's own and others' future travel along the same trail.

In the winter of 1634 a party of three Dutchmen from the Hudson River trade settlement of Fort Orange made good use of the Eastern Iroquois trails as they traversed the lands of the Mohawks and the Oneidas. Nominally, their reason for heading westward from their fort was to better strengthen the Dutch-Mohawk trade relationship. The Mohawks and the Dutch had been trading goods and furs for over a decade, but their friendship had been rocky. The Dutch had recently sided with the Mohawk's southern enemies and Fort Orange traders were not always on their best behavior. Making matters worse, French traders from the north and their Native emissaries had begun to turn up in Iroquois villages desiring to replace the Fort Orange traders as partners. The Dutchmen saw this rising trade rivalry through the lens of their economic and imperial models. The French were competitors nosing their way into what should be Dutch-allied fur supplies by offering better deals to Fort Orange's Native trade partners. Such a move jeopardized the viability of the Dutch presence along the Hudson River by threatening to siphon off the beaver pelts which provided needed economic gain, and by undermining the trade-based regional alliances which helped guarantee the colony's safety. The travelers went out that winter to secure Dutch alliances and see just how deep the French inroads were.

As the three emissaries made their way westward on the path connecting the eastern and western doors of the Great Iroquois Longhouse, the people they met and traveled with showed a range of attitudes. Their first group of travel companions—five Mohawks with whom they began the trip—tried to leave the Dutchmen in the predawn darkness on the second morning. Perhaps these men were still angered by the late Dutch alliance with their Mahican enemies. But they may also have been displeased with the Dutch habit of traveling too long before sunup and well after sundown, especially considering that the preferred river route was in flood, forcing a more arduous overland winter trek. Other people they met on the way were willing and even eager to help the small party make its way westward. In some villages people welcomed them with feasts and speeches. At others, particularly those outside Fort Orange's immediate orbit, villagers chastised them for showing insufficient generosity in their travels. But for the most part, the trail was easy, its footpath well traveled, and its cabins warm and dry—all thanks to Iroquoia's travelers.[1] Like countless other colonial travelers, at every turn of the trail the Dutchmen relied on Native assistance to show them the way, help them over physical and social obstacles, and keep them fed. Indian aid to Europeans took many forms, but it generally arose in two ways—it was either offered by Indians or solicited by Europeans. During their travels the Dutchmen built many travel relationships. But those which they formed with two specific Mohawks exemplify how the two paths of offering and soliciting brought many Indians and Europeans together on different terms and toward different ends.

While resting on the fifth day of their journey the small party met a Mohawk man named Sickaris, who was eager to build a friendship through travel and trade. The Dutchmen identified Sickaris as a "good hunter," a statement which may have reflected a source of Sickaris's community reputation, or perhaps what the travelers thought most useful about their new acquaintance.[2] Not only did his reputation tie him to travel, even Sickaris's name, meaning "bark cutter," alluded to the travel skills of canoe building or tree marking. This "good hunter" traveled through the snow to Onekahoncka, where the party was then resting, and invited the three men to his home at Canagere, a few miles distant. There they could stay as long as they wished and perhaps trade their goods for some of the 120 "pelts of marketable beaver" they would find waiting at Sickaris's home. They accepted the offer, but before any trade or travel began the Dutchmen presented Sickaris with "a knife and two awls" for his troubles and his kind offer. Along the way Sickaris made it a point to denigrate the smaller towns they passed, claiming that Canawarode's six houses were "not worth much" and that Schatsyerosy's twelve were not much better.[3]

At Canagere the connections between travel, goods, and the Dutch visitors seem to have been foremost in the minds of the few Mohawks who stayed behind in town during the winter hunt. When the Dutchmen showed off a sulfurous paper which burned blue in the cook fire, their hosts told them that they already had gained some in trade with "the foreign Indians."[4] The paper's acrid smoke, the Mohawks claimed, was good for soothing legs "very sore from traveling," a word of advice to visitors no doubt cold and stiff from the winter trail.[5] A group of western Iroquois women came through town with some salmon the finicky Netherlanders thought unpalatably pungent. Nevertheless, they bought a few fillets at one guilder each, but they also unwittingly bought more than fish. The trip's chronicler jotted an enigmatic line hinting that more was afoot than the Dutchmen either wanted or fully understood. He wrote that after the sale "we were supposed to travel with them when they returned."[6] Something in their trade created for the Iroquois the distinct impression that the Dutchmen were now obliged to travel some distance with these women. The Dutch travelers not only did not understand the nature and source of this seeming obligation, they also failed to act on it.

The next day the party thought it time to push ahead, so they sought out a guide to help them along. Most of Canagere's residents were off on the winter hunt, so there were few likely guides in town. In summer, finding aid would have been easy, as Iroquoia's paths would have been full of people coming and going. But winter was another story. The Dutchmen approached a man named Sqorhea and asked him to lead them westward. The request for aid came with a trove of goods which the Dutch chronicler recorded like a shopkeeper counting his stock; "one half piece of duffel, two axes, two knives, and two awls" was the price the travelers paid to "hire" Sqorhea.[7] The Dutch writer also noted that in winter the Indians "did not want to leave their country because it snowed there often a man's height deep." The chronicler's associating the list of goods (far more than Sickaris received for his time) with the offhand mention of winter hardships are not an accident, in fact they are probably connected—Sqorhea was up to something.

Sickaris appeared eager to have the Dutchmen accompany him to Canagere; after all, as a prominent man and "good hunter" he would have had a lot to gain by bringing the Dutchmen to his village and keeping them away from rival neighbors. But who was Sqorhea (a name which might mean "skeleton"), and why was he lingering in the nearly empty Canagere?[8] The Dutch wrote considerably less about him than they did about his presumably more respected fellow villager, leaving little from which to glean Sqorhea's character and motivations. Sqorhea was probably the source of the snow worries, given that the chronicler relates the anecdote amidst his discussion of "hiring" the man. To be sure, snow could be a hindrance to travel, but most of Canagere's male residents were off facing the same possible bad weather in their hunt for deer. Clearly if the rewards were great enough, one took the risk of winter travel, and Sqorhea would have known this. What we see here may be a negotiation over the price needed to make traveling with Europeans worthwhile for an Indian who would just as soon stay at home. The detail of head-high snow may have been Sqorhea's way of beating a good price out of the travelers by making sure they understood that their request was an imposition. If so, both sides got what they wanted in the end. The Dutchmen had a guide and Sqorhea got some nice stuff, including an additional pair of shoes given to him soon after they set off.[9]

Like almost all Europeans wandering beyond the small pale of colonial settlement, the Dutchmen needed Native aid in their travel. They needed places to stay, people to carry their bags and hunt down food, and, most importantly, people to guide them along the way. Earliest European travelers were willing to simply take what they wanted regardless of whether or not it alienated Indians. Fort Orange's close proximity to the Mohawks enmeshed Native and newcomer into an ever more complex interconnected social web, and the same happened all over North America, as colonial settlements and projects expanded and proliferated. Earlier less-than-successful heavy-handed strategies risked too much conflict and ill will between neighbors whose lives were increasingly more closely tied together in varieties of ways.[10] But at the same time, Europeans in ever greater numbers, and for ever more purposes, continued to need Indian aid in their wanderings. This need was a growing constant during the seventeenth and eighteenth centuries, as more and more Europeans took to the trail for trips of discovery, diplomacy, religion, trade, knowledge, and even simple wanderlust. The need for travel aid and the expansion of the numbers and types of Europeans seeking it out created numerous new opportunities and potential rewards for Indians with the desired skills and knowledge who chose to accompany colonial travelers. What replaced earlier regimes of coercion were networks of alliances, trade, and obligation—a sort of rough economics of common travel.

Sickaris and Sqorhea provide examples of the ways Europeans described acquiring Native travel assistance once the days of taking by force faded into the past. Indians who offered their aid or who received pay after being asked for it made frequent appearances in the annals of colonial travel. The two figures of the offerer and the "hired" companion reflect in part a European way of comprehending relations with Indians and in part the ways that these relationships played out on the trail. Chroniclers understood and described travel relationships in light of emerging capitalist ideas of wages, labor, and employment. By casting travel relationships in this light, chroniclers made an argument for the commercial nature of their activities, and the social hierarchy implied by this economics, and they also suggested that similar ideas lurked behind Native willingness to aid European travelers. For many Europeans, Indians accepting goods in exchange for travel aid was proof enough that a desire for the goods alone was sufficient to get Indians on the trail, that Native companions shared the logic of an exchange-based trade model, and that the rules of commerce and the social relations they engendered were in play. To be sure, many Indian travelers did use common travel as a low-investment means to acquire the goods which Europeans offered. But a willingness to trade services for goods did not always mean that Indian guides and other travel partners bought fully into the implied hierarchical relationship of employer (the one offering goods) and employee (the one providing service). In fact, in many cases travel companions saw this sort of trail-side exchange through very different lenses, and likewise engaged in the exchanges for very different ends.

The examples of Sickaris and Sqorhea also point to the ways many Indians travelers became guides or other aids and what these Natives gained from the services they provided on the trail. Offers of aid, particularly guidance, often came from men like Sickaris, who held some prominence in their communities and saw in common travel useful ways to build, transfer, or protect their status. The specifics of these rewards varied, depending local custom and on how closely certain Indian societies interacted with colonizing Europeans, but in many places and times, it was Native leaders who often made themselves vital facilitators of European travel. Therefore, the often obscured motivations, values, and intentions of these leaders were in their way just as formative of colonial travel as were the more easily disclosed goals of traveling explorers, missionaries, traders, and others. Furthermore, European requests for travel aid throughout the seventeenth and eighteenth centuries opened up numerous possibilities for Indians of all statuses, as travelers did not always restrict their requests to established leaders or authorities. In seeking out aid whenever and wherever they needed it and from whoever (with some restrictions) may be able to offer it, European travelers created opportunities for a variety of Indians companions to gain trade goods, some measure of status, and control over foreigners' travel which may otherwise have been unavailable. In this way, the opportunities of common travel could become a distinctive species of trade item which many Indians could provide themselves and benefit from directly.

The differences between those who offered help and those whom Europeans "hired," and the dynamics of the resulting relationships, do not form a clear-cut dichotomy. For example, while chiefs or other prominent individuals sometimes offered their aid in one form or another, they were also often the objects of European requests. Furthermore, Europeans offered goods in exchange for aid in many relationships regardless of whether Europeans understood themselves as having purchased a given companion's aid. But despite the imprecision of these models, offering or "hiring" seems to have called into play different relationships in a variety of trail settings, and in writing up these events later, European narratives highlight different aspects of travel relationships in their description of Native companions. Looking at the stories of a few of the best-documented guides—mostly Native men who accompanied seventeenth- and eighteenth-century European travelers—provides a window into why Natives agreed to serve as guides, hunters, and in other crucial roles.

In the spring of 1608 John Smith and about a dozen other Englishmen sailed a small ship's boat around the rivers and estuaries of the Chesapeake Bay. They visited numerous towns whose Algonquian inhabitants greeted them with varying degrees of fear and fascination. In some places the Natives welcomed them with gifts of tobacco, while at others villagers thought a show of force was the best strategy. Many of these villagers had seen strangers before in similar wooden vessels—indeed, Europeans had been sailing into this riverine world for over a generation. How Natives responded to the small party of Englishmen in their sailing "barge" depended in part on what they had seen before of other Europeans and how their neighbors—friends and foes alike—received the newcomers. Friendship with the Moraughtacunds made the Englishmen enemies of the Rappahannocks who would be less hostile if the English had good relations with the Mannahocks. The boat and its party sailed though a social world as well as a geographic one; both required careful navigation.

For some Natives, the strangers' presence signaled considerable danger. The boaters understood one Piedmont Indian, whom they had wounded, to tell them that many in his village feared that the English "were a people come from under the world, to take their world from them."[11] He was more right than he could have known. For others, the stranger's arrival offered opportunities to build friendships through kind acts and trades. One party of Nansemond Indians, for example, initially fled on sight of the boat, but lost their fear once the mariners left "divers toyes" at the riverside.[12] To the Nansemonds, the goods were a sign of the strangers' goodwill. In light of this gift, they returned to the waterside to lead the mariners to their villages, all the while with what Smith described as "all show of love that could be."[13] The act of giving goods was a social lubricant and an opener of paths.

On one northern foray to the fall line of the Potomac River, the Englishmen noted that a light metallic dust covered the river's rocks and shores, making "many bare places seeme as gilded."[14] The travelers began to dig in the sand, hoping to find buried riches ready for the taking. What they found was a clay-filled sandy soil mixed with "yeallow spangles" which reminded the English of the brass dust created by the grinding of pins.[15] With their curiosity piqued, the travelers turned to a nearby Potomac chief, asking him what he knew about this dust. The chief told them of a mine not too distant where his people acquired a similar powder, which they collected in bags and used to adorn themselves and their totems. The chief did more though. He offered the Englishmen guides to take them to the mine and went on the trip himself, allowing the strangers to see firsthand the source of an item the Potomacs prized and which they traded all over the region. For their troubles the Englishmen gave their companions a "small chaine," which the Potomacs gratefully received.

What took place along the Potomac was a simple exchange centering on the actions of a Native leader who, like Sickaris, used travel in building a relationship with the strangers. The combination of local geographic knowledge and social prestige, which had compelled the great entradas to capture chiefs and force them into guiding their marches, continued to draw European travelers to Native leaders even after kidnapping was no longer workable. During the seventeenth and eighteenth centuries numerous Native leaders offered to aid Europeans in their travels. While leaders offered supplies, shelter, and information, headmen appear frequently in European travel writing as guides of one type or another. It is easy to see what Europeans gained in these relationships; access to guidance, supplies, and a measure of travel security all made a chief's residence a worthwhile stop for travelers. But why did so many Native leaders prove willing—even eager—to lead Europeans through their territories? European travelers generally followed Smith's interpretive lead, and saw the goods they offered as the principal motivator, and thus emphasized the commercial side of these travel transactions. In some cases the stories of European travel interaction with various and varied Native leaders provide hints about the motivations of Natives seeking to use and even control the travel of Europeans. The Potomac chief's meeting with John Smith provides one example of the kind of choices arising from the arrival of strangers. In the Algonquian chiefdoms of what is now the eastern United States, heredity, martial skill, and diplomatic ability all played roles in determining who would be a chief and how effective a leader was.[16] The Potomac chief's actions show that he hoped to make friends with Smith and his Englishmen perhaps for diplomatic advantage, perhaps for trade, or perhaps for some other, forgotten reason. A leader could only be helped by being the source of beneficial alliances for his people, and the "small chaine" the Potomacs seemed to have esteemed so well was a symbol of the chief's abilities. It was his actions that led to the gift, and therefore the gift enhanced his prestige, even if it was the Englishmen who actually offered the item.[17]

Strangers wandering willy-nilly through a people's land constituted a number of threats, to both the people themselves and the prestige of their rulers. Even though the Potomac chief may have welcomed Smith's small party, he did not seem willing to let them have free run of his lands. The offer of guides, therefore, may also have been a way to maintain control over the wandering visitors. Smith, like so many exploration-minded Europeans, saw Native assistance of this type as the "kindly" actions of a "kinde king and his kinde people." In the invaders' logic, such leaders were motivated to offer assistance by a desire to please these manifestly superior Christian newcomers, and thus "did their best to content" the strangers.[18] Their "kindness" was in English eyes a sort of acquiescence to the will of the strangers, and the distribution of a few trinkets mirrored the largess of the European rich to the poor or a leader's to his followers. These interpretations of the Potomac exchange reinforced Smith's vision of himself as the travel-controlling leader. But the offer may to have carried a subtle message which the headstrong English failed to see. By offering guides, the chief reminded the English visitors that this was *his* land and that *he* controlled access to it. He effectively sanctioned English travel in his territory, but only on his own conditions and overseen by himself or men of his choosing. While the chief may have been impressed with Smith and his gun-toting, armor-bearing retinue, he may also have wished to lay down the geographic law and ensure that these freebooters understood who was the boss.

Observing the proper protocols governing the exchange of goods (whether intentionally or accidentally), and deferentially seeking distance guidance could also open a route into a chief's heart and land. Samuel Champlain, for example, discovered this when in 1610 the gift of a hatchet to an Ottawa chief made the man "as happy and pleased . . . as if I had made him some rich gift." The result was access to the chief's lands via a map of the land which he drew "with charcoal on a piece of tree-bark."[19] The members of René-Robert Cavelier Sieur de La Salle's southern exploration had a similar experience in

Texas in 1687. The Frenchmen's preparations for leaving one Gulf Coast village "much alarmed the natives, and especially the chief of them." To dissuade their travel the headman warned of the "immense dangers" ahead, including bloodthirsty enemies, "bad and impassable ways," and "many woods and rivers," all of which blocked the way.[20] The impasse was resolved when the Frenchmen asked for guides to lead the way. The unnamed chief provided three, and also received the promise of some future unspecified "rewards." The party left the next morning having, in the words of one member, "put ourselves entirely in the hands of divine providence." But this assessment overlooked that earning the chief's assistance was also part of the equation.[21]

Other Native leaders warned travelers of "bad and impassable ways," impenetrable woods with deep and wild rivers, and hostile locals who would break open heads "without any cause," or simply that the trip was long and that travelers would "get no vittailes and be tyred."[22] All of these warnings by headmen worked to keep strangers from seeing too much of their lands without some supervision. Europeans usually suspected that these chiefs tried to scare travelers because they did not want to see the benefits of trade and alliances slip through their fingers and go to their enemies. Sometimes they simply thought that these headmen were being spiteful or perfidious. But often European acceptance of specially offered guides allowed travel to continue, suggesting that maintaining control may have been, at least in part, what motivated chiefs to tell such elaborate horror stories.[23]

Hand-picked guides, and properly requested and formally granted maps, helped leaders control the course of outlanders' travel, but many headmen also offered to accompany European travelers themselves. Like the Potomac chief, joining a travel party simultaneously lent their own prestige to guests' wanderings and maintained their own control over territorial access and the distribution of geographic knowledge. In 1666 an Edisto headman in South Carolina offered his services as a pilot for an English coastal cruise, promising the ship's master "a broad deep entrance" for the ship and "a large welcome and plentiful entertainment and trade" for its party.[24] The Edisto Indian's actions assured favorable trading conditions for the people of his town. Prestigious travelers often warranted prestigious companions. Pierre Le Moyne d'Iberville's 1700 mapping trip in the endless, serpentine rivers of the Mississippi delta had the blessings and accompaniment of the local Bayogoula chief and a canoe "in which there were eight of his own men."[25] The same chief also sent guides to accompany the French on various other legs of their tour. The Oneida chief who wished to bring home Moravian missionaries John Cammerhoff and David Ziesberger in 1750 wanted to show these popular men that they were more than welcome in his country, and thereby to reap the social rewards that came from their friendship. The unnamed Oneida's desire was made more pressing by the fact that the German clergymen had already visited the Senecas, Cayugas, and Onondagas and the chief did not want his people to be left out of the missionaries' tour.[26] Halfway across the continent, and a decade earlier, when La Vérendrye took his leave of the Mandans, one village chief accompanied his party for the better part of a day, turning back only after "he made great demonstration of the regret he felt" at the traders' departure.[27] Some guests were simply too important to be attended by anyone but those of the highest status.

For the Onondaga headman Garakontié, that was true vis-à-vis the French traders and Jesuit missionaries who became frequent guests in Iroquoia in the 1660s. Garakontié used his voice and influence to aid French interests at a time when factional infighting tore at the stability and unity of many Iroquois villages.[28] Garakontié built on his domestic prestige and used the role of travel guide and aid to protect and enhance the status of his French allies. He also used his physical presence on the trail to indicate his colonial sympathies and to attach his prestige to his French friends. This francophile leader went out of way to accompany French travelers in and out of his own lands and used his skills in trailside diplomacy to turn enemy "hatchets in another direction" and to save the lives of French captives.[29] He escorted French parties to Montreal and in exchange was graciously treated to the finest the trade town had to offer. On one occasion in 1661, Garakontié and a group of elders went more than six miles down the trail to welcome an arriving Jesuit. The custom of welcoming visitors outside a town's enclosure was well established, but usually such rituals took place less than a mile from the gate posts. In an act that the priest saw as "an honor never, as a rule, paid to other ambassadors," Garakontié used travel and accompaniment as symbols of loyalty, ways to bestow prestige on the visitors, and a means to build an alliance.[30] The culmination of Garakontié's francophilia was his conversion to the Jesuit "black robes'" faith in an elaborate ceremony in Quebec in 1670.[31]

With colonial alliances came obligations. Colonial officials and missionaries quickly came to view providing guides and porters as the responsibility of allied tribes and villages, and that such services were a burden which frequently fell on leaders' shoulders. What men like Smith's Potomac chief, Garakontié, and others offered could be come an expectation on the part of needy European travelers. By the middle of the 1600s New France's Jesuit missionaries saw providing paddlers as a given by their upcountry allies. When colonial representatives of New York needed aid to get to a council at Oneida in the fall of 1700, they clearly expected it from the Mohawk sachems at the town of Canaedsishore. The sachems provided four men to carry their bags and help along the trail. Even though two of the guides ultimately proved unwilling, at least the sachems fulfilled their part of the bargain.³² Likewise, returning home could become a shared concern, and headmen also had to consider the realities of life with European neighbors. Supplying guides for return trips could be a good insurance policy against unforeseen disasters, and some offers of guides were simply to protect hapless European wanderers from harm in the recognition that when colonists wanted revenge they were often indiscriminate about their targets. The assigning of two Tuscaroras by their village headman to escort home a lost Baron Cristoph von Graffenried on the eve of the 1712 Tuscarora War smacks of exactly this kind of concern.³³

The Onondaga Garakontié's travel attached his own prestige to his friends and demonstrated his loyalties. But for some headmen, guiding Europeans played a central role in their own personal identities and in maintaining prestige with their own people and trade partners. One such man was the late-eighteenth-century Chipewyan leader and fur trade "captain" Matonabbee, who lived much of his life on western Canada's Shield and the flat tundras ominously named the "Barren Grounds." By the 1760s, Chipewyan life was deeply connected to the subarctic fur trade and the flow of goods from English supply points, and Indian, Englishman, and métis alike lived in a complex world of economic reliance and mutual obligation. Europe's voracious demand for beaver pelts facilitated sharp declines in eastern beaver populations. The result was that much of colonial trade history is the story of seeking ever more western sources of animals.³⁴ Forts located on the edges of Hudson Bay or on navigable rivers served as the trade centers in this world of exchange, and the Chipewyans were perfectly suited and situated to become the middlemen between coastal traders and western inland tribes.³⁵ These tribes, such as the Blackfeet, Dogribs, and Yellowknifes, did not want to make the long hard trips to English forts, fearing that they would starve or freeze along the way.³⁶ But many Chipewyan bands adapted their seasonal hunting way of life to the cycles and demands of the fur trade, and in doing so made themselves indispensable. The Chipewyans who trekked the arduous miles to distant peoples in order to bring the latter's furs to English traders were the vital connection between English ships and distant supplies of pelts.

In this world, alliances and prosperity went hand-in-hand. Forts, although nominally English, were often home to dozens of local Crees and Chipewyans—the "Home Guard" Indians—who performed the vital daily tasks of fort life and also played a key role in the trade by accompanying trade parties and even hunting. Close ties between English traders and local Indians were common, as lone Englishmen married Indian women and thus entered the Native kinship web.³⁷ Close ties to the trade could bring considerable material comfort in the form of warm, quick-drying woolens, metal tools, firearms, and numerous geegaws with which to acquire all and sundry. But this comfort came at a price: a powerful reliance on the trade and on trade partners. Good working alliances with Europeans were essential for group survival, and a headman who could deliver this diplomatic windfall was indeed a provider. Obviously, bringing furs to trade was one vital component of maintaining friendship. But providing other services, literally going the extra mile as a guide, for example, was a sure way for a leader to maintain his people's comfort and prosperity while ensuring his own prestige. Matonabbee was a master of this sort of politics and economics.

The Hudson's Bay Company traders on the bay's western edge came to rely on Matonabbee as conveyer and provider, and he played central roles as both planner and guide in several northern explorations. Samuel Hearne, who spent considerable time under Matonabbee's care and guidance, called him "the greatest man in the country," an assessment shared by many others.[38] Matonabbee was practically born for the role of fur captain, guide, and diplomat. He was the son of a Chipewyan father and a captive woman sold by the Crees. After his father's death, Matonabbee became the adopted son of English governor Richard Norton, who may even have arranged the marriage of the Indian boy's parents. Raised by the Home Guard Indians, Matonabbee spent his formative years in the shadow of Fort Prince of Wales at the mouth of Manitoba's Churchill River on the western edge of Hudson Bay. There he learned the Cree language spoken by the locals. He also learned English and came to understand the ways and beliefs of the fort's English occupants.[39] As the English sought to expand their trade base westward after the fall of New France, Matonabbee was a natural ally. As a headman he knew the mixture of placation and threat needed to maintain group cohesion in the loosely organized, often fractious, consensus-based world of Native politics. His travels taught him the fine art of tundra survival and afforded him extensive geographic knowledge, itself a source of prestige among Indians and English alike. In 1767 Matonabbee and another Chipewyan named Idotleezay traveled deep into Yellowknife and Eskimo territories and returned south with useful information about western Canada's Arctic coast and the region's waterways.[40] They also offered a route to the much-rumored copper mines on the coast, the possibility of which had intrigued the English since early in the century.[41] With English commercial interest piqued, Matonabbee offered to escort Englishmen across the forbidding Barren Grounds and onto a waterway optimistically dubbed the Coppermine River.

The Hudson's Bay Company traders at Fort Prince of Wales tried three times between 1769 and 1771 to get to the Coppermine River. Only the third attempt succeeded.[42] Winter is the best time for travel on western Canada's rocky tundra, as the snow smooths out endless miles of ankle-breaking rocks and pitfalls. But winter brings with it extreme weather which only the most expert traveler can navigate successfully. The Englishmen on the Coppermine trips were particularly dependent on the skills and cooperation of their Indian guides. The first attempt to reach the river's mouth barely got under way before the mostly Chipewyan Indian guides quickly lost faith in sailor-turned-Arctic-explorer Samuel Hearne and his two English companions, using the night's cover to slip off and go hunting on their own, which Hearne surmised was their real motivation for accompanying him in the first place. Although the head guide, Chawchinahaw, covered for his deserting friends, dwindling food supplies and the almost overpowering desire to set off on the winter's hunt finally forced the ill-equipped Englishmen and Home Guard Indians to turn back to the warmth and shelter of the fort's stone walls; the Chipewyan guides went off to hunt caribou. The whole failure took only forty-one days. Hearne set off on his second attempt about two months later, but again was thwarted from reaching his goal. A timely rescue by Matonabbee saved the lives of the second small group of English sailors and Home Guard Indians. Poor planning, the loss of Hearne's quadrant, and the region's unpredictable harsh weather left the party huddled together waiting to freeze to death—usually a short wait on the frosty Barren Grounds. But Matonabbee, who knew of the planned expedition, soon arrived at their makeshift camp with food and warm otter skins. Revived, taught how to make the essential snowshoes, and graciously fêted by Matonabbee and his northerners "in the southern style," the party lived to trek another day.[43]

The third expedition was the charm, and its success was in no small measure due to the active involvement of Matonabbee in the planning phase. The Chipewyan's skilled hand guided all aspects of the expedition's planning and execution. Matonabbee saw to it that the right people came along, and throughout the trip he was an authoritative presence, calling halts when needed, authorizing campsites, negotiating with Indians along the way, and keeping his own brand of order in the party. Hearne and the fort's mixed-blood governor, Moses Norton, wrote and spoke of the trip as if it were their doing, but in truth it was Matonabbee's hybrid hunting-exploration excursion with him in charge. Matonabbee took his group on the route he and Idotleezay followed a few years earlier. They went northwest through Manitoba and Saskatchewan to the edge of Lake Athabasca. From there they headed northward to the mouth of the shallow and rocky Coppermine River. The group left Fort Prince of Wales on December 7, 1770, and reached the mouth of the Coppermine River on July 13, 1771.

Matonabbee's status as "the greatest man in the country" owed a great deal to his successful association with his English friends and particularly the Hudson's Bay Company. His reputation as a man of great abilities brought him recognition among both the English and his own people. From the English perspective, he was a man who could deliver furs and keep other Indians coming to Hudson's Bay Company posts, and his role as guide reinforced their faith in him. To those who followed him, he was a man who could ensure prosperity. Within the eighteenth-century fur trade, these two sources of prestige blended and reinforced each other. Matonabbee was so aware that his fate, fortune, and manly status were all tightly enmeshed with company fortunes that when in 1782 American-allied French raiders captured Fort Prince of Wales and carted away its residents, a distraught Matonabbee tied a rope around his neck and hanged himself.[44] With his friends' reputation so damaged by their vulnerability to the French, and the fabric of his trading world torn apart, Matonabbee must have felt that his star would soon fall too. The quick snap of the rope sealed not only Matonabbee's fate but also those of his six wives and four children, who starved to death in the winter's chill of 1783.[45]

Nestabeck was another Chipewyan who used guiding to strengthen his prestigious connections with English fur traders.[46] Like Matonabbee, Nestabeck was a Native headman and fur captain. Although as a young man Nestabeck traded with the Hudson's Bay Company and even went to the Coppermine River with Matonabbee in 1770, his greater service was to the Montreal-based North West Company.[47] After Matonabbee killed himself, Nestabeck appears to have taken over his role as supreme Chipewyan headman—in English eyes at least. He also built up his own stature by shifting his people's alliance to the ambitious North West Company and then using his distance knowledge and organizational skills to help the company expand the scope of its trade network. If anything, Nestabeck had a greater reputation than Matonabbee among the English. In the last quarter of the eighteenth century he rubbed elbows with most of the big names in Canadian western exploration. Men like Peter Pond, Peter Fidler, Sir Alexander Mackenzie, and David Thompson all owed a portion of their reputation as adventurers to the aid, advice, and guidance of the "great Chepawyan Chief."[48]

Nestabeck's best-documented trip was the one he took to the Arctic coast with the Scots fur trader and hard charger Alexander Mackenzie, in 1789. The trip was a western version of the one Matonabbee led Hearne on in 1770. Their route passed through the western side of the Northwest Territories' Great Slave River, and from there northward along what is now the Mackenzie River to its delta. This land would have been only vaguely known to Nestabeck and his people. Consequently, Nestabeck was less a source of geographic information than a coordinator, negotiator, interpreter, and wilderness-skills expert. Throughout the trip Nestabeck worked to maintain cohesion in the group and to gain the best information possible from discussions with people met along the way. As was often the case, it was Nestabeck's skill and knowledge, his people, and other local Indian guides that allowed the forceful and demanding Mackenzie to perform the explorers' tasks of observation and measurement.[49]

Both Matonabbee and Nestabeck mixed the Chipewyans' traditional prestige of the great hunter and provider with the material wealth and titles available through the fur trade. They turned their familiarity with Canada's vast Northwest into prosperity and security for their people and status for themselves. At the forts these men were treated with the respect due men of stature. Dressed in status-reflecting red coats and showered with gifts of trinkets, rum, and tobacco, these fur captains were cocks of the walk—so much so that their carriage occasionally tweaked some English observers' sensibilities. With recognition came status, with status came followers, and with followers came more recognition, since bigger bands could carry more furs and earn greater rewards for all. Headmen such as Nestabeck and Matonabbee were the points through which wealth entered their communities, positions which made them indispensable men for their people. In order to hold onto this fine condition, Matonabbee and Nestabeck had to fend off jabs at their authority from aspiring members of their bands. They also were willing to push themselves and their people ever harder and farther. Guiding fit perfectly into this equation. Serving as a guide or planner on a trip like Hearne's or Mackenzie's was in itself a recognition of a headman's talents, value, and manliness.[50]

Trade considerations suffused almost every aspect of fur trade life, but men like Matonabbee and Nestabeck were far from being mere hirelings, even though some Englishmen may have seen them as such. True, these guides received material rewards—looking much like pay—for their services, but these remunerations came through different protocols. An employee provides labor in exchange for pay, but these guides received gifts in recognition of their status, friendship, and ability, and then they provided services as part of an exchange between friends and equals. These exchanges carried with them obligations of return, alliance, friendship, reliance, support, and so on, and Matonabbee and Nestabeck benefited from a long skein of gifts between friends.[51]

For men like the Potomac chief, guidance appears to have helped contain the travel of Smith and his English companions. For Garakontié, common travel served as a means to lend his existing prestige to foreign travelers, thus helping to build the alliances he supported. For Matonabbee and Nestabeck, common travel was a way to build alliances and maintain and enhance their domestic status. Guiding Europeans into and through their territories became part and parcel of what made these leaders great men in societies whose livelihood was intimately connected to trade with Europeans. As with the Mohawk Sickaris, the offer of guidance worked to reinforce prominent men's status in their communities. The specific circumstances of this status varied depending on local custom and how closely tied together specific Native communities were to colonial settlements and enterprises. But during the colonial era, Indian leaders entered into travel relationships because they saw in guidance and assistance the possibility of gaining a variety of advantages for themselves and their communities.

By 1680 New York City was already a pretty cosmopolitan place. Although politically English, the port city and its environs still bore the distinct stamp of a multinational colonial heritage. From Dutch burghers' brick row houses to English and Walloon villages, the New York area was a place where a traveler could expect to run into American-born Dutch farmers, Welsh immigrant craftsmen, English Calvinist fishermen, and French-speaking black slaves. Living in and around this mixed world were the descendants of the region's original Algonquian inhabitants. Most lived in small family-centered bands, sometimes occupying lands right in the shadows of European settlers' homes. These Indians lived lives that were socially and economically tied to those of their immigrant neighbors. Many spoke Dutch, French, or English in addition to their Native tongues, and knew the habits of Europeans well from long observation and experience.

The aged sagamore and healer whom the Dutch called Hans was one such man. Although he lived with his family on the New Jersey side of New York Harbor, he had friends and kinfolk all around the area and his duties regularly took him far from home to settle his people's disputes and cure their ills. On the morning of March 4, 1680, Hans was at home resting after returning from a visit to the small Indian town of Ackquekenonk, near present-day Paterson. His recuperation was interrupted by the unexpected arrival of a small group of Dutch travelers who had rowed across the bay in the company of Hans's sometime friend Gerrit Evertssen van Duyn. It was van Duyn who led the party to Hans's home in order to request his assistance in the travelers' planned visit to Ackquekenonk. Hans, after all, spoke Dutch "tolerably well," knew his way to all the local Indian settlements, and was a man the locals knew and trusted. But Hans was less than thrilled at the prospect of repeating the trip he had just taken. In refusing to accompany the travelers, Hans candidly voiced his opinion of the Dutchmen and their request in words of discontent that still sting even centuries later: "Would you Christians do as much for us Indians? If you had just been there and had come back tired and weary, and some Indians should come and ask you in the midst of your children, in your own houses, while busied with your occupation, would you be ready immediately to go back with them?" After thinking over Hans's soul-searching implication-rich question for a brief second, the Dutchmen answered that indeed they would be more than happy to drop what they were doing and set off with a hypothetical Indian if the situation were reversed. They would be willing, that is, "upon proper terms," meaning, if the price was right. The aged Hans, who had lived alongside the bustling center of Dutch and now English habitation in New York, had seen too much of his neighbors to believe these wide-eyed travelers' answer. "I do not think so," he told them. "I know well what you would do." But the travelers were relentless and insisted that they "would fully satisfy" Hans if he came with them, and in the end Hans did go on the two-day trip.[52]

Hans's speech showed a keen critical observer of European colonists, and an outspoken one at that. During the trip he went further, candidly speaking his mind about his colonial neighbors and the consequences of their arrival for his people. "We did not have so much sickness and death before the Christians came into the country," he told his companions, noting that Europeans have "taught the people debauchery and excess" and that the Natives were "more miserable than they were before."[53] Hans also revealed that he was a shrewd bargainer as well as colonial critic. Initially, the Dutchmen did not want to settle on a price for his time before the trip, preferring to see "whether he would earn anything" with his service, and then pay him accordingly. But Hans made it clear if he took off with the visitors he would "lose so much time" in his preparation of sewan beads for trade. In other words, compensation would have to be adequate, or as the Dutchmen themselves suggested, the "terms" would have to be "proper." Hans told them "I am very cold; you are all well clothed and do not feel the cold," having "nothing but a little worn-out blanket for my naked body." And with that sentence the price of his travel was set and agreed upon, although the chilly sagamore would have to wait till a later trip to New York to pick up his reward.

The event's recorder cast Hans and his "tolerable" Dutch as the witty colonial critic. Indeed, as is invariably the case, we must hear Hans's voice through the writing of others free to shape and mold his words as they chose. Nevertheless, a wide array of European travelers recorded similar negotiations between themselves and those Natives they wished to "hire." The Mohawk guide Sqorhea's negotiation was only hinted at in the writings of his Dutch companions, while Hans's was somewhat more carefully recorded. Hans may have had any number of his own reasons for returning to Ackquekenonk, but whatever his hidden motivations may have been, Hans's negotiation provides a small window into the world of men like himself and the Mohawk Sqorhea who appear to have "sold" their time, skill, and knowledge to European travelers. Few of the earliest European travelers wrote of "hiring" Indians—they did often use goods to reward travel companions, but the specific language of "hiring" was largely absent.[54] But by the late sixteenth century in the Southwest and early seventeenth century in eastern North America, European travelers of all nations described many of their Native companions as having been "hired," with many variations on the theme. Whether describing Mexican porters brought north, or guides like Sqorhea, the phrase "we hired" or "we engaged" appears repeatedly in seventeenth- and eighteenth-century travel records. The failures of earlier, more coercive procurement strategies and the growth of settlements with their alliance and trade connections opened up new possibilities for the underlying constitutive logic of travel relationships. As Natives were brought into European colonization's ever-expanding web of trade, binding Native villages and colonial towns, goods for trade became a staple of interaction between Indians and Europeans and proved one of the most far-reaching and enduring forms of Indian-European contact. This was true on the trail as well, where desire for goods, and connection to and operation within colonial economies made many Indians willing to use common travel as a means to acquire goods.

Europeans who "hired" guides saw themselves as taking on employees; and as the hirers, it would be they who set the pace and direction of travel. In most cases these relationships were short-term, usually the duration of a single trip or a portion of one. Sqorhea, for example, may not have traveled more than a day or so with his Dutch companions before he turned back. Likewise, Hans joined his party for a single, clearly defined, specific trip. "Hired" companions were rarely brought into the travel party as full members as were men like Matonabbee or Nestabeck. Instead, "hired" Native guides, hunters, interpreters, porters, and others lived at the margins of travel parties, frequently doing much of their work away from their "bosses," and often receiving little documentary attention. Most appear cryptically at best. Virginia explorers Batts and Fallam in the 1670s mentioned that they had "hired a Seping [Saponi] Indian to be our guide."[55] One French traveler remarked that a group of Canadian Indians agreed to travel with them "in exchange for a few trinkets."[56] New York diplomatists Hendrick Hansen and Major Cornelis van Brugh could only deliver their messages thanks to "an Indian which we hired who showed us the way."[57] Samuel Hearne wrote in 1770 that his increasing load on one trip "obliged me to engage another Indian."[58] One French Jesuit described his Iroquois travel companions as becoming his "menials."[59] And so the litany of passing references goes on, an anonymous Indian "hired" here, and unnamed man "engaged" there. The casually cajoling manner with which the colonists approached Hans, and the brief passing notation of Sqorhea compared with the textual attention paid to Sickaris, both suggest that these two groups of Dutchmen, like many others of many nations, indeed did see themselves and their "hired" Native companions as little more than employers and employees.

Europeans may have found the language of employment useful, albeit charged, but their frequent use of terms like "hired" begs the question: did their "hired" Indian companions also see their common travel in that light? Like many "hired" aids, Hans did not simply go when asked—he negotiated what he saw as a fair price for his efforts. The act of negotiation served several purposes. For one thing it ensured that Indians could make common travel worthwhile. This fact helped create locally specific ground rules for future travel relationships. Negotiation thus not only helped the individual Indian haggler, it also helped establish the idea that a marketplace surrounded travel aid. Europeans reified this assumption in their writing. European travelers came to know that they would have to be ready to pay for the Indian aid they needed. As one French traveler noted in planning a 1730s trip's finances, "the heaviest charge and a quite indispensable one would be for the savages employed as guides and for scouting."[60] But negotiations like Hans's also helped set the tone for specific relationships themselves. It was precisely these haggling moments which made Europeans so confident in their assessments that their companions were in fact "hired." Likewise, Indians negotiating the best deal before setting off on the trail also revealed the extent to which many Natives understood the depth of European need and their own ability to exploit it. The trail was a seller's market for Indians with skills or knowledge to sell, and many were quick to turn European need to Native advantage.

The Mohawk Sqorhea got desirable metal tools, as well as woolens and shoes, while his later parallel, Algonquian headman Hans, received a blanket for his pains. Many other Indian assistants also used their common travel as a way to gather similar typical items of Indian-European trade. The items that Indians received for their travel efforts reads like a short summary list of all the goods Indians sought through their trade networks all over North America. One group of Frenchmen in Louisiana, for example, received the guides they needed after offering "knives, glass beads, and axes."[61] A Spaniard recalled that he had provided "tobacco, knives, and other things to get them to guide us."[62] A Ute man "requested" a fee of "two hunting knives and sixteen strings of glass beads" in exchange for escorting Franciscan fathers Escalante and Dominguez through northern Colorado in the summer of 1776.[63] The French-allied Blackfoot leader Wappenessew wheedled a down payment of "a little powder and c." from the English fur trader Anthony Henday for promising to aid his return to Hudson Bay in 1755.[64] One of Henday's fellow traders recorded on another trip that he could persuade a pair of Chippewas to accompany him only by "promising them payment in rum" after the trip.[65]

Another paid his porters "three beavers" for each of the "bundles" they carried in his service.[66] For some Indians, particularly those most closely tied to colonial economies, cash made a worthy inducement. Cash fees could range considerably. Jasper Danckaerts, who during his 1670s travels through New York and New Jersey formed many pay-based travel relationships, offered one New Jersey man a fee of "one guilder" to get him to a local sachem's house.[67] It cost one English traveler "six dollars" to get a pair of Mohawks to carry his canoes some distance.[68] Another Englishman noted that during his mid-eighteenth-century trip the fare for guidance down the Ottawa River's Sault and Carrion Rapids was a full five dollars.[69] By comparison, John Bartram and friends seem to have done quite well by hiring a guide to Oswego in 1743 for the low rate of sixteen shillings.[70] From knives and coin to rum and skins, the type of payment Europeans offered travel companions was usually the same as one could find at a trade fair or in a trader's canoe. This fact situated travel exchanges within those larger economies by mirroring Indian-European commodity exchanges and by serving as a noncommodity, trade-based way of bringing goods into homes and communities.

The rewards Indians received varied, and so too did the negotiating strategies they employed. For some, like Sqorhea, reminding travelers of the trail's difficulty could be a way to get a good price. One Caddoan man told a party of French map makers that the road they wanted him to travel was "very difficult, the whole route being overland," agreeing to the trip only after the Gallic geographers "promised to pay him well."[71] Others simply denied their services until offered the right price. For example, a group of Spaniards who spent the spring of 1689 searching out the remains of La Salle's short-lived French colony on the Texas Gulf Coast learned from two local Indians that there were some Frenchmen at a settlement two days away. The men made no offer to help the Spaniards get there. But a fee of "some tobacco, knives, and other things" was good enough to get the two men to agree to be guides for the trip.[72] Another group of Frenchmen in 1690 found that an offer of some clothing was not enough to get one Texas Native to take to the trail. But for the gift of a horse the Indian was willing to do their bidding and have his family serve as the Frenchmen's guides.[73]

The terms mattered in the business of travel, and when a better deal came along. Some Indians were willing to follow the money. During his 1749 travels in the spring air of New York's Hudson Valley, Peter Kalm and friends discovered this as their plans halted when the Indian guides they had hired for thirty shillings abandoned them for "an Englishman who gave them more." The conscientious guides returned Kalm's fifteen-shilling deposit before trading employers.[74] When Frederick Post's Indian guides learned of the English defeat at Fort Ticonderoga in July 1758, the leader of Post's unnerved guides, a Delaware named Essoweyoualand, whom the English called "Shamokin Daniel," checked Post to make sure that "he should be satisfied for his trouble" in continuing the trip. With the assurance that "any service for the province" in Post's opinion "would be paid," the guides continued.[75] Essoweyoualand's concern about his pay reveals a problem that faced many Indian companions. He, and others of his acquaintance, had had the disappointing experience of *not* being rewarded at the end of the journey. Daniel's simple question showed that while there were material rewards in the travel business, actually receiving them sometimes was no sure thing, and guides and porters often knew it.[76]

Because of the possibility of being stiffed, there were some Indians who would not budge, despite travelers' cajoling and lavish promises. John Lawson and his companions discovered this when they tried to hire a seven-foot-tall Santee man with whom they had passed the night. The man "seem'd unwilling" to guide them through a nearby Carolina swamp, and recognizing that it would be unwise to anger a giant, they "press'd him no farther about it."[77] The same Dutch travelers who approached Hans fared less well in recruiting Native assistance at another turn in the trail. While traveling north of Philadelphia the small party met a "young Indian," probably a Delaware, who had earlier agreed to act as their guide. His price was a woolen blanket coat whose value the Dutchmen reckoned at five Holland guilders. But even so, the coat was not enough, and after going off to have his gun fixed, he never returned.[78] Fur traders, whose activities were often singularly dependent on Native aid in many forms, lamented that when Indians expressly hired as guides or porters did not wish to continue in their tasks, they simple took their leave or refused to carry their allotted load. Even worse was the habit of many porters of simply taking what they wanted out of the stores they were charged with porting when wages or conditions were not to their liking. Samuel Hearne, perhaps recalling his own abandonment at the hands of Chawchinahaw, was thus particularly concerned that the trade's reliance on Indian aid and a general lack of ability to enforce a satisfactory work ethic made his company the "game and laughingstock" of every other fur trade outfit.[79] Not only were "hired" Natives capable of negotiating the best terms for their labor, they were also able to control conditions of employment while on the trail.

There were some Native travelers who fully embraced the market for Indian skills and turned the guides' sure feet or the hunters' keen eyes into accompaniment careers of sorts. When John Lawson wandered through the marshes and rivers of lowland South Carolina at the turn of the eighteenth century, he was aided by a series of guides and hunters, all of whom seem to have had long experience in this growing trade. Men like Santee Jack, who Lawson noted had a reputation as a "good hunter and a well humour'd fellow," took Lawson and friends to the Congaree Indians. Another guide named Enoe Will was well known to the English as a man with an "agreeable temper," and reputedly was "always ready to serve the English, not out of gain, but real affection."[80] Reputation aside, Will was often paid for his services.

Enoe Will and others like him were shadowy figures at the periphery of colonies and documents alike. In many respects, Will resembled the Bayonne Algonquian Hans, in that European travelers described both as being leaders among their people and that both lived Native lives at the edge of European colonial settlement. For both, guiding wove together many of the circumstances, needs, and goods that motivated and rewarded other Native traveling companions. Men like Nestabeck and Matonabbee built their status and independence by controlling access to lands and riches. Men like Garakontié lived lives removed enough from European settlement that they could be beneficent with their people and their own persons and aid European travelers when they wished. But Will and Hans did not have the same control over goods, souls, or territory that propped up these other headmen. Life in the shadows of European roofs and spires meant that maintaining good relations with potentially troublesome neighbors was vital to survival. Guiding, and the reputation as men of "agreeable temper" it brought, were themselves ways to guard personal autonomy—a considerable reward, as Hans, Will, and countless others would have known. Will had a better knowledge of his territory than did John Lawson, but at the same time he could not have hoped to control access to it. Instead, the job of a guide for the pay of some cash or a blanket or some other item proved a good way to live on the edge and yet tap into the goods that were in the colonial era becoming as indispensable to Indians as they were to average colonists.

Ned Bearskin was another early-eighteenth-century man of stature who indulged in this sort of trailside jobbing while finding greater rewards in travel than simple pay. When William Byrd II and a group of surveyors, slaves, and gentry bon vivants set off to survey the line between Virginia and North Carolina during the fall of 1728, their plan was to travel light and live off the land. But Byrd, the party's leader and chronicler, soon found that his companions were "unfortunate gunners" and so made plans to hire Native hunters to make up the deficit.[81] He hired the Saponi Ned Bearskin, who was known as a "most able huntsman," and an unnamed companion to supply the company with meat during the trip. These Indians lived in the vicinity of Fort Christianna at Virginia's edge and on the Ocaneechee trade road. In 1717, in the wake of the Tuscarora War, the Saponis—already accustomed to moving back and forth between the dominions of Virginia and North Carolina—took up residence on the Meherrin River and placed themselves nominally under the protection of Virginia governor Alexander Spotswood. Spotswood had the fort built for their protection and armed it with five cannons; he also supplied his charges with missionaries, teachers, and European trade goods. In return, the Virginia-allied Saponis, Tutelos, and Ocaneechees of Fort Christianna would serve as a frontier guard, protecting English plantations from marauding bands of Southern Catawbas and Northern Iroquois. By 1728 Bearskin and his people lived as did many of Virginia's allied Indians: their fort was an important stop on the north-south trade route that kept a steady flow of goods moving into Saponi hands. Apart from the trade, they eked out a living on a tiny, six-square-mile reservation, which they could not leave without formal colonial permission. Restricted in movement, threatened with land reduction should their numbers dwindle, pressed by land-hungry settlers (the nearest English plantation was only three miles away), and reliant on sluggish and distant colonial authorities to redress their grievances, the Saponis at Fort Christianna became increasingly frustrated.

Byrd and company asked for Bearskin's assistance at a time when Saponi discontent with their domesticated life was coming to a head. That same year a delegation of Saponis went to see if the Catawbas would aid them in getting some of their people out of Virginia jails. Soon after the Saponis gave threatening voice to their discontent, claiming that if the colony executed one of their leaders—a man named Captain Tom—they would prepare for war and then wipe out the Virginians. Within a dozen years many of these same Saponis would be living in Cayuga villages in New York and Pennsylvania, having joined the migration northward, preferring to live with their onetime Native foes than with their sometime English friends.[82]

In this heated context, Byrd and his surveying party's very presence at the fort must have seemed like a bad portent to the Saponis. When the Saponis first moved to Fort Christianna, it was well removed from English habitations. But in the intervening years, little by little, farm by farm, the English had moved up almost to within shot of the fort's guns. Surveyors were the first harbingers of colonial expansion, and with a declining population and indifferent colonial authorities, the Saponis must have seen the future in the party's chains, rods, and transits.

But even so, the Virginians' desire for Native assistance provided an opportunity for travel too good to be passed up. The fact that the English knew Ned Bearskin as a good hunter suggests that he was used to seeking out official permission to take to the woods. If so, his familiarity with the colonial ways, laws, and language made him a natural choice to go with the party. And of course there were many significant rewards too. In return for his service, Bearskin received "a note" for 3 pounds sterling, "a pound of powder with shot in proportion," and the skins of all of the animals he killed, to be transported by the party's pack animals.[83] Byrd noted that another reward for Bearskin was "the great knowledge he had gain'd of the country."[84] Byrd's own wanderlust and sense of adventure may have made him sensitive to, or quick to project, similar desires in others. Indeed, the chance to take a westward trip of over 250 miles was not to be passed up, especially considering how restricted Saponi movements were at the time. The chance to travel a great distance in the legally secure company of Englishmen may well have been an intangible reward as great as the promise of piles of animal skins.[85]

And piles of animal skins there were. In just under two months, according to Byrd's accounting, Bearskin and partner killed at least 1 partridge, 8 turkeys, 7 bears, and 26 deer.[86] Most of their kills were made by stealth, but they also employed the time-honored method of "fire hunting," whereby a controlled blaze served to drive animals into a prearranged killing zone. The haul in skins from this protected jaunt was of considerable worth in colonial markets, and having a free pack train to carry them made the deal even sweeter for Bearskin. Given Virginia's restrictions on Saponi movements, it is hard to imagine that many other Saponi hunters could have boasted of such numbers that fall.

Bearskin was also more than a hunter during the surveying trip. He served as sort of mascot and role model for the would-be woodsmen, who went so far as to name their little band of brothers the "Order of Ma-ooty," employing the Saponi word for a turkey's "beard" and sporting the little trophies in their hat loops.[87] On at least one occasion Bearskin's geographic knowledge came into play when he identified a stream that the surveying line crossed over "no less than five times" as the Hyco Creek. Byrd wrote that the Saponi "mistook" the creek for the south branch of the Roanoke River, which Byrd thought "impossible, both by reason of its narrowness and the small quantity of water that came down it." Byrd went on to claim that Bearskin, "discovering his error soon after," assured the group that it was Hyco Creek.[88] In fact, despite Byrd's seeming joy at having caught his Indian companion in a geographic error, both of Bearskin's identifications were essentially correct; the Roanoke River forks in Halifax County, Virginia, where its fork again splits into three rivers, the Bansiter, the Dan, and the Hyco. The Hyco is the southernmost of the three and its waters mingle with the Roanoke's.

While perhaps not granted due respect for his geographic knowledge by Byrd and company, Bearskin nevertheless benefited considerably from his travels. The pile of fresh skins was one obvious gain. But perhaps more important than the hides' trade value was the boost the trip gave to his reputation as a hunter at time when most Saponis could travel only few miles from Fort Christianna's walls. The hides were tangible symbols of Bearskin's ability to hunt and navigate the woods successfully. The trip also allowed him to rub elbows with a few prominent Virginians at a time when tensions between his people and the still somewhat new Old Dominion were on the rise. How Bearskin felt about the diplomatic issues of his day is lost to time, but he may have believed his willingness to aid the Virginians could have been a salve for open political wounds. Perhaps, like Garakontié nearly sixty years earlier, Bearskin used his physical presence on the trail as a sign of alliance to be read by his own people. Whatever his views, Bearskin probably saw rewards in his accompaniment well beyond the much-desired skins. Byrd at least saw Bearskin as beaming his pride during his people's farewell to the English travelers after the trip. Standing alongside the leaders of his people, all of whom bore "an air of decency very uncommon," Bearskin the hunter, as traveler Byrd wrote, stood out as the "gravest of them."[89]

Byrd was not the only one to cast on his Native companion in this kind of positive light. The annals of travel are full of the "best" hunters, the most "respected" and the "most skillful" Indians, all of whom volunteered or were drafted to serve as guides and in other roles for European travelers. On one level, such claims worked to bolster a rhetorical superiority of the Europeans benefiting from these "great" men. But at the same time, skilled hunters and other sorts of socially influential people were not rare in the Native towns Europeans visited in their travels. Many of these Natives would have had a host of their own reasons to travel with Europeans. By praising Bearskin's "decency," Byrd implied both his own ability to pick the best guides for his travel, and also perhaps that he and his fellow Englishmen could even have a positive influence on the people with whom they traveled. He also suggested that he and colonial-era Indians and Europeans came together as guides and the guided through a variety of economic and alliance logics. The essential conditions of this form of intercultural relationship remained largely steady over the more or less two centuries following the earliest Spanish incursions—European travelers kept on needing the knowledge and skills of Indians through whose lands they traveled. Indians continued to hold the keys to territorial access for colonial travelers and were often willing to offer up their acumen in exchange for rewards both tangible and intangible. The 1630s examples the two Mohawk guides—Sikaris and Sqorhea—serve to put at least names (if not actual faces) to the two most prevalent ways that Europeans took on Native guides, either by Native offer or through what European travelers saw as having "hired" their companions. Indians were often able to leave or change undesirable situations on the trail and were quick so to do. Friendship, pay, or mutual convenience allowed both parties to get what they wanted on terms that made sense to them. Hans got his blanket and the Dutchmen got their guided trip; Matonabbee got to be the "greatest man in the country" and the Hudson's Bay Company got a regular supply of porters. Similarly, while the territorial messages lurking behind the assignment of guides by headmen may have been lost on European explorers, both adventurer and headman could walk away from the meeting having found something of value in their association.

3

"Quite Contrary to the Custom"

In 1700, naturalist John Lawson noticed that his Santee, Congaree, Toteros, and other eastern Carolina Native companions approached one minor travel obstacle in a singular way. Upon coming across a fallen tree lying astride the trail, these Native travelers always went around it, "quite contrary to the custom of the English, and other Europeans," who presumably moved the log or stepped over it.[1] Lawson also recorded numerous other differences between his and his companions' travel habits. His fellow travelers always kept "a constant pace," and used the moss growing on trees' north sides in place of a compass. They had what Lawson saw as an uncanny ability to locate the heads of rivers and journey to them despite having never made the trip before, and they also marked the trail with "certain hieroglyphicks" which record for all to see "the success or losses they have met withal."[2] Lawson further noted that Carolina Natives were fine cartographers, able to draw maps in "the ashes of the fire" or "upon a mat or a piece of bark," which in Lawson's estimation, "agree[ed] with a great deal of nicety." But Lawson also noted that one had to be "very much in their favour, otherwise they will never make these discoveries to you."[3]

Lawson's Native companions moved carefully along the trail, avoiding special obstacles and marking the path itself with the events which gave their travel meaning. As Lawson portrayed it, Carolina travel entailed at once moving successfully through the landscape and crafting the trail into an assiduously maintained space.[4] European and Indian travelers of all stripes used and simultaneously created the landscape through which they passed, imbuing it with meaning, defining its attributes, and marking the stories of their lives, loyalties, and cosmoses along the way. Consequently, how best to do this, and whose ways of travel should prevail, became an ongoing conflict between men like Lawson and the Natives who traveled with them. For Lawson, these differences were curiosities and markers of differences. But for others, travel habits could become outright battles shaping the course and outcomes of travel itself.[5] While travel was, for all travelers, a means of getting from one place to another, how to travel always sat within specific social contexts; people brought to the trail differing assumptions about the best way to travel. In describing how he and his Native companions diverged, Lawson's litany of differences tapped into a long conversation between Native and colonial travelers about what the trail was and how best to get along on it. This conversation was itself part of a larger process whereby Indians and Europeans noticed, created, and maintained differences in order to conceptualize each other and formulate their own identities. On the trail together, Indian and European travel companions could see each others' ways up close and evaluate them against their own travel habits. What resulted was an ongoing process of assessment, absorption, and rejection within an environment which often negated or overrode the dynamics of colonization which could come more powerfully into play out in other places where Europeans and Natives interacted.

Lawson was not alone. Many European travelers noted that they traveled on trails saturated with the experiences of their Native companions, and that embedded memories shaped their travel habits. Across Native America, trees were billboards announcing how many animals a hunter had killed nearby or how many nights he had spent in the area, or were "war archives," telling stories of raids and killings.[6] Native travelers carved signs into bark or the peeled-clean underlying wood. These signs could be simple pictographs of animals, men on horseback, guns, and even letters which had entered some Native tree markers' lexicons by the mid-1600s.[7] In some cases Indians "painted" their messages with stunning realism. One Frenchman was taken by the clarity of one illustration showing "six men hanged, with their heads and their feet cut off," in such detail that he could tell from the tonsure of one severed head that it had once belonged to a priest.[8] Sticks hanging from branches might mark the number killed by a war party, or serve as a commemoration for a lost kinsman.[9] Rocks and other trailside objects, too, conveyed stories to passersby. One German traveler remarked that a stone "memorial" of an Iroquois warrior was "so accurately executed as even to represent the lines cut in upon his face."[10] Colored sticks surrounding the stone all indicated to the initiated the details of the many fights in which the warrior had made his reputation.

Trails wended past rocks which were the remains of people changed to stone, and fields where deer no longer congregated, driven away by some past Indian quarrel.[11] Travelers passed places of historical import like the "Peace Point" on Alberta's Peace River, so named for having been the site where the Cree and the Beaver Indians ended a longstanding dispute over the name of the river.[12] They stopped at places like the one the Nippisings named the Lost Child, in memory of a child "suddenly pulled under water" right before his terrified helpless parents.[13] Trails also took travelers to places of personal significance, like the site of a onetime village, or the spot where a guide's child was born.[14]

Some of these places required special action each and every time travelers passed. Many European travelers noted that their Indian companions frequently stopped at a special rock, waterfall, or other spot to make offerings of tobacco, arrows, stones, food, animal skins or bones, or sometimes even trade goods like guns or fabric.[15] All of this commemorated long-gone people or placated the nonhuman powers that resided with considerable force in these special places. Samuel Champlain recorded how his Algonquian companions carried their canoes to the foot of the Ottawa River's Chaudière Falls. There, each traveler would place a small bit of tobacco in a wooden collection plate. After dancing around the full plate and hearing a speech recounting the history of the offering, the party's leader threw the plate and tobacco into the raging waters, followed by a collective "loud whoop."[16] Chippewa paddlers always threw tobacco and other gifts into the Lake Superior's waters when passing a "high rock, somewhat in the shape of a man," which they called the Kitchee Manitoo, the "Master of Life."[17] Illinois Indians showed several French travelers down the Mississippi River a large painted rock on "which the boldest savages dare not long rest their eyes," and to which they made tobacco offerings.[18] Pennsylvania Indians avoided a turn along the Susquehanna called Otzinachson, where dwelled and "revel[ed]" what one missionary called "evil spirits."[19] One French Jesuit noted that his Iroquois companions "never fail" to "pay homage" to what the disbelieving priest called "a race of invisible men" who live at the bottom of Lake George. The travelers made the ubiquitous tobacco offering, but also gave over a number of flints the "watermen's" special use.[20] Caution and respect were always used at such places in the certainty that "misfortune will befall" those failing to pay proper reverence.[21] Worse still, mistreating or even touching some trail sites could result in a person's "dying on the spot," as some 1700s Mobilians believed of an old sacrificial site.[22] The trail itself could sometimes carry special meanings. This was the case for the seventeenth-century Virginia Indians who commemorated a long-past fight between the Powhatans and the Chowans with a special trail ritual. Upon passing a certain pair of "remarkable trees," travelers each took care to clean a portion of the small trail between the trees. Indian passersby with a historic tie to the Powhatans cleaned one side of the path and those connected to the Chowans cleaned the other. In this way, travel parties refreshed the amity between past enemies and reified the significance of the trails which connected all peoples.[23]

In their way, early modern Europe's roads, and their ever-expanding colonial counterparts, were not that different from America's. They, too, were lined with ritual stopping places, usually called inns or taverns, and as in Native America, sacred sites, churches, and shrines marked a landscape rich with spiritual significance. At intervals travelers had to stop and make offerings to tolls, ticket takers, and paper checkers each exacting their due from travelers. Nevertheless, some European travelers were struck by how different American travel was to what they had previously known. One of James Madison's companions on the journey to Fort Stanwix, in 1784, was struck by the emptiness of the land he passed through and lamented how "really barbarous and wild" the roads they traveled were.[24] The Jesuit Gabriel Marest could have been speaking for many in writing that "the journeys that are made in this Country ought not to be compared with those that you make in Europe." Marest related that whereas in Europe one finds "from time to time, Towns and Villages, houses to receive you, bridges or boats for crossing rivers, beaten paths which conduct you to your destination, and people who put you on the right way if you are going astray," nothing of the sort was to be found in North America.[25] Marest traveled in the particularly harsh Hudson's Bay region in 1712. Had his wanderings brought him to a warmer clime or a more densely settled area his vision may have differed. But many European travelers thought as little of the Native trail as did this incommoded Jesuit.

Many European travelers were quick to deride Native "superstitions" about the landscapes through which they traveled. Upon seeing the Mississippi River's painted rocks, La Salle and his men "endeavored" to make their guides "understand that the said rock had no manner of virtue" and that the French instead "worshipped something above it."[26] Europeans sometimes went out of their way to flaunt their disrespect of Native place beliefs and rituals by touching things they should not or refusing to play by the rules.[27] But European travelers shaped their trails just as surely as did Natives—and in ways which must have seemed as arbitrary to Natives as Indian ways seemed to European eyes. Pious travelers scratched crosses onto trees or erected full sized ones where they could.[28] Buried lead plates, nailed-up engraved bronze plaques, whittled royal ciphers, and blazed trees were all ways in which European travelers tried to mark their own presence and bring the trail into line with their own idealized landscape visions.[29] Europeans collected plant specimens and drew pictures of novel animals. They blew horns and shot off guns to announce their arrivals or departures, and sang songs sacred and profane to frame their travels. They took careful measurements with quadrants or surveying equipment to plot and contain space. The act of recording travels in reports, essays, and memoirs was itself a means of making sense of travel and the trail, and containing and comprehending the experience of travel.

These varied acts were central to how travelers created meaning for and contextualized their travels, the trail, and themselves as travelers. Whether taking measurements or making offerings, travelers tried to move along the trail in ways which best ensured their safety and success in their journeys.

Lawson and others observed Native travel habits with curiosity, and in many cases were quick to adopt the elements that they saw as most useful, such as eating dried corn or wearing protective leggings or snowshoes in winter. But differences in travel practice, differences which touch on deeper logics of how best to travel, were likely to create conflict between travel partners unwilling or unable to give up their own ways of doing things and yield to practices which seemed alien, if not downright foolish or dangerous.

On a spring morning in 1652, Pierre Espirit Radisson, then the captive of a Mohawk family, tried to wake his new kinsmen. He shook his new brother, who blearily sat up and looked about. Everyone was still asleep, so the Mohawk lay back down and let his mind drift back to the real world of dreams.[30] In another place, nearly a century later, Ned Bearskin, the Saponi Indian hired in 1728 by William Byrd II and his party of Virginia surveyors, urged his companions not to mix in the same pot the deer and turkey meat he had brought in. He told them that to do so would "certainly spoil his luck in hunting" the next day.[31] In yet another place at the end of the eighteenth century, a group of Indian guides made it clear to their Scots companion that there was no point in burying bags of much-needed supplies along waterways that they would not see again this season. The Scotsman, Alexander Mackenzie, nevertheless cached "two bags of pemmican" for future use, despite the protests of his guides.[32]

In each of these varied instances, an Indian or a European traveler attempted to impose their own way of doing things on an alien partner. In Radisson's case, it was through the application of a sense of time which dictated that a workday began with the sun's first rays. For Ned Bearskin, the careless cooking habits of his companions jeopardized *his* ability to kill more game. After all, he had come along to hunt, and what was the point of hunting if English disrespect chased away all the game. For Mackenzie's guides, the trip they were on was a leg of their annual hunting trek through Canada's stony northern tundra. When on those treks, one always moved forward, following herds of caribou. Backtracking was not only pointless, it could be deadly, because it entailed moving back into territory already hunted. For Mackenzie, though, this was an exploration—a straight over-and-back proposition—and when one got to one's destination, one turned around and went back home via the most expeditious route possible. If everything had been planned and executed correctly, the best way back would be along the same route.

Once on the trail together, European travelers and their Native companions faced not only the rigors and hardships of colonial-era travel; they also faced the complex social dimensions inherent in traveling with people foreign from themselves. Shared travel entailed a considerable degree of cooperation, but tensions, differences, and conflicts were nevertheless a steady drumbeat behind these relationships. Indian and European travelers brought an array of skills and assumptions to the trail and often saw trailside events through very different lenses. The possible points of contention were in fact as numerous as the possible combinations of travelers. Discrepancies between the many reasons for, methods of, and rewards of travel blended with travelers' differing habits to ensure that personal conflicts, small and large, fleeting and consequential, would not only be a part of trail life, but would also in some cases significantly shape the course and results of travel.

Rules and practices were often at the core of these conflicts. Whether trying to get a sleepy party to their paddles or hoping to correct unwise cooking habits, travel companions operated from various sets of rules which defined and limited their actions. Each crisis and mundane travel decision opened up the question of whose rules to follow, and travelers were quick to assert the primacy of their own ways of doing things, through both overt and subtle means. At the same time, the grounds for conflict were ever changing, as colonial travelers developed new frameworks for understanding each other and became used to each others' ways of travel. But rather than building a shared culture of travel or gradually converging on a third way of getting by, one which was part Indian and part European, intercultural travelers instead contested and maintained their differences at every turn in the trail, even as the terrain of differences shifted. Challenging or critiquing alien travel habits, asserting the supremacy of one's own ways, and in some cases even appropriating and absorbing new ways of doing things were all tactics through which travelers defined themselves and the spaces in which they traveled. The conditions of early modern travel were long enduring and essentially leveling, subjecting travelers to an array of travel rigors which they had no choice but to share. Thus the creation, observation, and the constant maintenance of differences where and when they could be found was part of how travel companions defined themselves, each other, and the trail itself. In this way, the trail was a place of conflict, and its story one of contention and contest between travelers.

Early modern travel was no easy affair, and travelers of all backgrounds risked paying for mistakes, miscalculations, and simple bad luck with their lives. The colonial-era trail was a dangerous place and the shared risks and perils of even the shortest journeys set the stage for tensions between Indian and European travel partners. Seagoing ships frequently smashed to splinters on unseen shoals and shallow sand banks or were torn apart by other submerged obstacles.[33] Indian canoes, though well-designed and efficient craft, could become little more than flimsy toys when hit with the full force of bad weather or rushing waters. When a "storm suddenly arose," the light craft were tossed violently, upset, or even "split open," causing crew and cargo to be thrown into the roiling waters.[34] More than a few voyagers, both Native and European, drowned, sometimes even within sight of horrified friends and families, who watched "without it being possible to render them any assistance."[35] Winter travel on lakes and rivers could bring its own dangers. River ice frequently crushed canoes and small boats, leaving stranded boaters to drown or freeze or to float helplessly downstream on ice floes. Boats could become locked in ice, as did one French craft in 1758. The cold in the immobile boat was so severe that it caused nine of the crew's feet to became frostbitten, ultimately causing five of them to loose their feet entirely by amputation and two of those men to lose their lives as well.[36]

Negotiating rapids and canoeing near large waterfalls took special skills, but even the most experienced hands could only do so much in a crisis. Canoes got away from their handlers in the "violence of the current," only to break apart in the rocks below.[37] Upon seeing Niagara Falls' misty, vertiginous heights and hearing its "roaring" din in 1793, Jacob Lindley also learned the twin stories of a "white man" who "tumbled out of his canoe" and was "hurled down," and of an Indian who, asleep in his canoe, "glided down into the rapids." When the Indian realized his plight, he hopelessly "struck a few strokes with his paddle," but seeing that there was nothing wood and muscle could do to reverse his course toward the falls' high edge, he "wrapped his head in his blanket, and laid down in his canoe, to meet his horrid destiny." As Lindley's tale makes clear, this type of "horrid destiny" could await any unlucky traveler.[38]

Traveling by foot or on horseback was often no walk in the park, either. In winter, blowing snows covered narrow paths which, as one observer wrote, "frequently disappearing, leave the traveler in doubt and uncertainty as to the ways."[39] The unpredictable ice of frozen rivers and lakes sometimes "opened up" right beneath travelers' feet, causing them to be "swallowed up" and lost in the water beyond the possibility of rescue. Even far from water, winter travelers still ran the risk of freezing to death while huddled under a too-thin blanket or near a small campfire, even when snow and freezing rain did not "threaten to put out" the much-needed fire.[40] Winter could create a landscape devoid of food supplies, especially when hunting was poor or deep snow kept animals from moving about much. In such times, travelers had to forage for what they could find and eat anything they could keep down, such as shoe leather, dried sinews from snowshoes, the bark of trees, decayed animal carcasses, and, on rare occasions, even one another. But one European traveler noted that "when pressed with hunger" even the most unappealing fare could take on the "the taste of bread and the substantial quality of fish" in starving mouths.[41]

Warm weather and warmer climes had their own plagues. Southern heat could get so intense that one Illinois headman warned a southbound French traveler that it could be "so excessive that it would inevitably cause [their] death."[42] In the arid Southwest, regular water supplies were always an important concern. When rivers were dry, "a hollowed out depression in one of the crags" along the trail frequently provided the only available water.[43] Summer rains in other parts could be so heavy that animals and travelers became hopelessly "mired down" in thick, sticky mud.[44] In lowland and swampy areas, waters could rise so quickly that a party could find itself "in water up to the knees or belly and at times up to the neck" with little warning.[45] "Hords of mosquitoes" could become "so thick that they hardly allowed" travelers "to draw [their] breath."[46] Dangerous animals of all types, from well-hidden rattlesnakes to charging alligators, could kill a traveler or disrupt progress. The same was true of two-legged menaces, both friend and foe. The fear of ambush from one enemy or another was rarely far from most North American travelers' minds, but even one's own companions could be a hazard. A Huron traveler learned this costly lesson when one of his companion's muskets "went off against his leg."[47]

Coping with these risks was a high-stakes business, and in order to be safe, travelers attempted to bring their fellows' behavior in line with their own standards in an array of overt and covert ways. During their shared 1609 travels along the rivers south of Montreal, Samuel Champlain and his Algonquian, Montagnais, and Huron companions conflicted over the rules of travel and who was in fact leading their incursion against the Mohawks. While the Indian raiders cut the water in sleek canoes, Champlain and his retinue of French musketmen clunked along, rowing deep-draft shallops until the rocks at the mouth of Richelieu River forced most of the French to turn back. From then on, Champlain and a few companions were guests in Native canoes as the war party conducted its business according to time-honored patterns. The warriors divided into three groups to hunt for food, stay ready for ambush, and scout the path, while using down time to practice their maneuvers. At night they built walled encampments, and shamans in the party busied themselves trying to divine the upcoming battle's outcome. The Indians also continually questioned Champlain about the content of his dreams, both seeking good omens in his subconscious and effectively demonstrating whose rules were controlling the course and interpretive meanings of the raid. The allies were singularly pleased when the Frenchman revealed a dream in which he saw "in a lake near a mountain our enemies, the Iroquois, drowning before our eyes."[48] It must have seemed to the Indian warriors that Champlain was playing by their rules.

The resulting battle was a great success, with the Frenchmen's muskets playing a decisive role in their regional combat debut. But on the way home, Champlain began to kick at his Native traces. This tension came to a head during the torture of a captive after the battle. Despite his hosts having "begged" the Frenchman "repeatedly to take fire and do like them," Champlain refused.[49] This request probably made perfect sense to Champlain's companions. After all, the Frenchman had been more than eager to go on the raid, had revealed a propitious dream, and had played a prominent and active role in the fight. It only followed that he would also participate in the events flowing from the victory. But Champlain refused to indulge his companions' wishes, and somewhat disingenuously claimed that his people "did not commit such cruelties" but rather preferred to "kill people outright."[50] When the Indians declined the Frenchman's offer to shoot the poor captive as more mercy than the Mohawk deserved, Champlain sulked off. The allies in turn invited Champlain to fire the coup de grâce into the Mohawk to end the torture, which he did. From Champlain's perspective, it was his disapproval that led the Indians to ask him to finish off the bloody and burned warrior. Champlain believed that his "one shot caused [the Mohawk] to escape all the tortures he would have suffered" and thereby constituted an act of mercy.[51] He also believed that his actions ended the ritual, by bringing Indian rituals in line with French (or at least Champlain's) sensibilities.

But the whole incident may have had very different meanings for the allied Indian celebrants. Most of the best-documented torture rituals of eastern Indians ended when one or another participant—sometimes a warrior, sometimes a grieving villager—stepped forward to kill the victim, often by slitting his throat or cutting off his head.[52] By the time Champlain stepped in to kill the Mohawk, the torture was well advanced and the celebrants had long since moved from mere pain-causing to inflicting deep flesh wounds and burns that were life threatening. Since it was the Indians and not Champlain who selected the timing of the final shot, it may well have been that it was time to conclude the Mohawk's torture and the Indians turned to their new ally to perform the special task. Given the singular role that French firearms played in the raid, the use of the selfsame harquebus to finish off a torture victim—the only prisoner tortured by the whole war party (the rest of the dozen or so captives were divided up by tribe)—would have had a fitting poetry to it. Champlain had once again played the central part in a Native drama, only this time he was oblivious to it. The gap in communications and understanding between

Champlain and the allied Indians allowed each side to feel that they had controlled the timing and course of this important concluding ritual.[53]

The tensions between Champlain and his companions were a result of misreading codes of conduct, and thus both parties could walk away feeling that their ways had won the day. Furthermore, torture was a dramatic moment—always a lurid favorite for European writers' audiences at home, and, equally, a highly charged emotional moment for many Indians. But often it was more mundane moments which caused the most significant and telling flare-ups between fellow travelers. Seemingly simple acts like picking a campsite or setting the pace and duration of a day's travel could become occasions for disputes. For example, when Dutch traveler Harmen Meyndertsz van den Bogaert's Iroquois guides wanted to conclude a winter day's travel, they made their intentions known by building "a fire in the woods for they would go no farther." The Dutchman, on the other hand, was not satisfied with the distance covered and wanted to continue on despite his obstinate guides. And so he did, but without his Native companions. The price for his assertion of will was a night in a cold, abandoned cabin where he was "not able to start a fire."[54] In a 1700 reversal of roles, naturalist Lawson and his English companions "had a mind to have rested" but were thwarted by a guide who insisted that "the place we lay at, was not good to hunt in," and so in time the whole party moved on in search of a "more convenient place."[55] In this case, the guide's desire to hunt game trumped Lawson's, the putative employer's, plans. Likewise, Fray Silvestre Escalante became repeatedly "annoyed" at having to eat the southwestern dust of his fleet-footed guides as they traveled through the Four Corners region in 1776.[56] Similarly, in June 1793, Alexander Mackenzie was forced to abandon his planned campsite when a Native guide insisted that the site was "too cold etc."[57]

But it was not just when and where to rest that caused flare-ups. The most seemingly natural behaviors could also become the focus of a sudden dispute. Pennsylvania naturalist John Bartram's 1743 plan to climb a steep Susquehanna Valley hillside rattled the sensibilities of his Nanticoke companions. Once at the hill's crest, he looked back and saw how difficult his return would be because the hill was "full of great wild stinging nettles." In order to "make a path" for his "expeditious return," he took to rolling down "several loose stones," which tumbled down and crushed the worst of the painful shrubs in his way. For Bartram, this course of path-making action made perfect sense. But for his Native companions, Bartram's rock rolling had another meaning and a potentially troubling set of consequences. Such actions "would infallibly produce rain the next day," they told Bartram, who mockingly assured them that it was his "common practice to roll stones down from the top of every steep hill, and could not recollect that it ever rained the next day." The outcome allowed both the pro- and anti-rock-rolling factions to claim victory for their own beliefs. Indeed there was no rain the following day. But the day after, a morning shower drenched the party, which the Indians insisted was "caused by the stones." Bartram tried to argue that if indeed there was a connection, why did it take so long for the rain to come? One Nanticoke shrewdly replied however, that English "almanacks often prognosticated on a day, and yet the rain did not come within two days."[58]

Canadian fur trader Anthony Henday irritated his Cree tent mates when he insisted on discussing at length the many advantages of capturing wolves on the trail to help carry goods. His companions preferred to get pretrained dogs from the Archithinues in plenty of time for the return trip, and told him as much. But Henday became such a nuisance to his guides, both by prattling on about his plan and stopping to try and set traps, that finally one of the men curtly told him "to say no more about it."[59] The rebuke was effective enough to silence Henday. While Henday's chatter became an problem for his companions, it was Hendrick Hansen's silence in 1713 that made his guides feel insufficiently in control of their trip. Hansen persistently refused to tell his Mohawk guides the content of the diplomatic message he carried from New York's colonial rulers to the Onondagas. His companions were "troubled" about the message's content "lest it may be unwelcome news," and complained that they in turn should become unwelcome guests as a result. Nevertheless, Hansen refused to divulge all but the smallest amount of information, thereby using his guides' curiosity as a means to hold them with him for the whole trip.

Not all tussles were up-front. The first French Jesuits to make the long trip to the Hurons provide a good example of how acquiescing to companions' travel rules instead of challenging them could be an effective individual travel strategy as well as part of a larger colonial agenda. While, superficially, these priests showed no interest in challenging or manipulating their hosts' travel habits, their larger plans, and the success of their tactics, did in the long run effect significant changes in how Indians traveled. The Jesuit missions in seventeenth-century New France depended, to large extent, on the priests themselves being able to get to their would-be converts. Travel with Indian parties, either on the trail or in a canoe, was a regular part of their Christianizing activities. Although it was often hard work, the Huronia-bound Jesuits were willing to subject themselves to the canoe rules of their hosts, and, for their part, the paddlers were at first unwilling to let Jesuits into their crafts without considerable control over their conduct.

The paddlers made it clear that priests were to be timely and not keep the party waiting, were to take off their heavy leather shoes lest they puncture a canoe's thin bark skin, and were to lift up their thick woolen cassocks when getting into a canoe, to avoid tracking in cargo-drenching water or knee-scraping sand. Some priests found that they had to "paddle continually," keeping up with the strokes of their seasoned boatmates, and had to carry as much as any other party member at the portages between waterways. On top of the unaccustomed physical routine, early Jesuits also had to take care not to alienate any other party members, as an unkind word or gesture could result in their being ditched on shore or on an island to fend for themselves.[60] For Huron paddlers burdened with a peculiar and sometimes unwelcome guest, it made perfect sense to insist that these odd men in black function like every other party member. But Jesuits accepted this regime because it suited their long-term goals. Being the best guests could buy them time to gradually concentrate on other aspects of Native life which they in fact did want to change. As respect for the priests grew, along with an appreciation of the trade goods their presence ensured, the rules changed for black-robed travelers. As early as the 1630s, Jesuits were sitting happily on the floors of canoes, wearing their shoes the whole way upriver, and not being requested to paddle even a single stroke.[61]

In time, however, the Jesuit religious agenda did gradually work its way into the actual mechanics of travel. The same priests who could be such pliable canoe guests when they needed to be could also be tireless foes of other traditional practices, practices which for Indians were as much a part of traveling as canoeing was. When Algonquian hunters, for example, prepared to indulge in the mass consumption of all that they had killed, in what the French translated as the "eat-all feast," priests were quick to deride what they saw as simple gluttony. These condemnations infused an otherwise happy occurrence—a bountiful hunt—with conflict.

Converts changing their ways and beliefs could create or augment existing tensions within Native travel parties when these changes affected once-shared habits. One example is the simple Jesuit-retold morality tale involving a Native travel party made up of Christian Algonquians and pagan Atticameges. Upon spying two moose, the Atticameges taunted their Christian fellows, inquiring whether through prayer the Algonquians could ensure a successful kill. The Algonquian leader, a convert named Etienne, replied that "it is he who governs all; we hope in him, and not in our legs or in our drums," and with that ordered all of his party to fall to their knees and call upon God to "dispose the matter as he will." Meanwhile the Atticameges immediately set off after one of the two moose, only to return later empty-handed "after extreme fatigue."

Etienne's Christian Algonquians, on the other hand, waited and prayed until "toward the middle of the day," and then set out and soon killed not one but both moose.[62] The poor Atticameges were allegedly so impressed that they immediately asked to be baptized, thus accepting these new trailside habits.

When Jesuit priest Sébastien Râle traveled with his early-eighteenth-century Abenaki converts, his religious demands had other implications. Although the priest's goal was primarily spiritual control, he also radically altered the actual mechanics of neophyte Abenakis' travel. Most northeastern Indian travelers, upon coming to a new campsite, set about building shelters and getting things ready for the evening meal. But Râle had his converts first "set up poles at certain intervals, in the form of a chapel." In winter the first act was to clear the snow for the site of the temporary church. Every night in Râle's company included a mass over which the priest presided from a "smooth cedar board four feet long" which he "always ha[d] them" cut for him. The impromptu chapel's interior was always bedecked with "most beautiful silk fabric; a mat of rushes colored and well wrought, or perhaps a large bearskin, serve[ing] as a carpet." Râle's demands represented a considerable, if willingly accepted, departure from the traditional lighter marching order. All these sundries (poles and planks excepted) had to be carried along and "ready for use" by onetime lightly encumbered Natives.[63] Râle's message (intended or not) was that the demands of Christianity necessitated significant changes in traditional travel practices.

Questions of leadership lurked behind the Jesuits' travel relationships. By being good canoe passengers, the Jesuits did not challenge the leadership of their Huron hosts. But when it came to matters they perceived as spiritual, the priests were quick to impose their will on their companions and assert the primacy of their leadership in other matters as well. Their acquiescing in one part of travel gradually gained them credibility, and even some authority, which enabled them to make a powerful challenge about another aspect of trail life. Similar dynamics were at work in other travel relationships, though not always as well documented.

If pressed too far, travel partners could choose to separate. Although Indians were usually in the better position to exercise this option, occasionally it was the Europeans who chose to spurn Native guidance and set off on their own. In May of 1670, a mixed party of twenty-two Virginia horsemen and a few allied Indians left the Tidewater to scout the western mountains. The first stop on their way was a Piedmont Monacan village, where they sought supplies and information. Upon their arrival, the Monacans greeted the travelers with gunshots fired into the air, a practice which was becoming a common welcome in Indian villages. In the village, Monacan priests and elders shared information about the region in general and the local area in particular. Village priests told the party that a mound of stones they had passed earlier was a commemoration of past Native migrations which formed the current Monacan people. Each of the stones in the "pyramid" represented an individual who made the trip guided by "Monack, from whom they take the name Monakin."[64]

One "ancient man" continued the travelers' education by scratching out "with a staffe two paths on the ground."[65] This simple map charted both a social relationship and a geographical one.[66] The two paths led to two allied peoples, the Manahoacs in one direction and the Nahyssans in the other. Travel to the mountains entailed moving through a land full of Native history and enlivened by peoples' interactions. By sign and by word these priests and elders told their visitors how to travel well and sensibly through a landscape full of memories, rules, boundaries, and relationships.

But at the same time, these Englishmen had their own means for shaping their travel and making sense of the places in which they traveled. On this particular trip the differences between the Monacan and Virginian visions came to center on how to comprehend questions of direction. The Monacan elder's version of westward travel entailed moving through peoples and the places they gave meaning. Space, people, and history all combined as a traveler moved through lands enlivened by individual experiences of and within the landscape. The best way forward, then, was not only a geographic question, but also a social one, so much so that it was impossible to separate the human landscape from the physical one. The Virginians by and large saw it differently. Compass points were the principal constituents in their geography. They came from the eastern colonial heartland looking for places and peoples to the west; they had brought along an imported compass that would translate an alien topography into familiar and usable categories like north and west-northwest. Confronted with this choice in how to travel, all but the party's chronicler preferred following the English compass's rigid magnetic dictates to being led by the word of an old Indian and his scratching in the ground.

And so it was that they put their trust in technology and set off for the mountains. Lamenting the mistake of his comrade's choice, the event's chronicler wrote, "therefore it fell out with us, as it does with those Land Crabs, that crawling backwards in a direct line, avoid the Trees that stand in their way, climbing over their very tops, come down again on the other side, and so after a days labour gain not above two foot of ground."[67]

In time they reaped the consequences of their choice. The "steep and craggy cliffs" wore the horses so badly that they were "quite off the hoof." After a few days of this hard travel and finding "little sustenance for man and horse," the whole party found themselves dead tired and munching only "mouldy" biscuit which was wholly "unfit to be eaten."⁶⁸ The Englishmen had seen enough of the west. After convincing himself that a particular spur of the James River was really "an arm of the lake of Canada," the leader of the Compass Faction was ready to declare victory, raise a column marking the discovery, and head home. The rest of riders, "so weary of the enterprise," concurred, and "offered violence" to the one member of the party who advocated pushing ahead.⁶⁹ The solution was simple. Twenty-one of the party's riders turned back east, leaving their ambitious chronicler companion, German naturalist John Lederer (whom they now considered a "lost man"), to push on with a Susquehannock guide named Jackzetavon, some parched corn meal, and a gun.⁷⁰ Lederer and Jackzetavon did not fall "prey to Indians or savage beasts" as the riders expected, and made it back from the mountains to tell the story of their travels.

For Indians, choosing to stay with or quit a party was one simple way to assert control over their time and set personal tolerance limits when confronted by an overly demanding travel partner or an uncomfortable situation. Absenting one's self was also a challenge, a rebuke, and potentially a travel-altering moment for those left without guides, hunters, or porters. The annals of travel are full of Europeans lamenting that their Native companions had "failed" them in one way or another; leaving, or refusing to go ahead, were perhaps the most common types of "failure." The reasons are as varied as the travelers themselves. There are, however, a few general categories that at least offer a fleeting glimpse of the logic these Indians employed and reveal that what was to Europeans a vexing and perplexing letdown was for their Native companions a small part of a larger strategy to maintain control over travel.

Territorial boundaries offer one well-documented reason for Indians begging off. European travel plans—particularly those of explorers—often set out specifically to cross Native boundaries in hopes of seeing more land. But for Indian travelers, who not only may have been leaving their geographical comfort zone, but also may have been risking life and limb by entering hostile lands, crossing borders was frequently a dangerous gamble. "Our guides would go no further, for fear of falling into the hands of their enemies," reported one French traveler, and a Spaniard found that his interpreter "would not go beyond this place" when he arrived at a boundary. The interpreter was "very pleased" when he was released from his agreement and allowed to go home.⁷¹ An Algonquian man traveling in 1609 gave up his place in a French shallop because he was "afraid lest he shall be carried off" to distant lands by the far-ranging French and fall into the hands of the "enemies of his tribe."⁷² For Europeans, crossing these lines was part and parcel of exploration and travel; for their Native companions it was sometimes too risky an endeavor.

Other Indians found different reasons for leaving Europeans alone to fend for themselves, and European chroniclers recorded many, sometimes contradictory, reasons why their guides had "failed them." A young Caddoan man who promised to guide La Salle and his party to the town of Cahainihoua soon made himself scarce on the pretext of needing to return home, since he had "forgotten a piece of hard dried skin he had to make him shoes."[73] A Mohawk man who was to make a 1713 trip with New York colonial representatives demurred, claiming that "he was sick." His suspicious European would-be companions, however, "could not see it," and concluded that the man was just afraid to go on the trail.[74] A Cree interpreter left the French fur trader La Vérendrye in an awkward spot when the former chose to follow after "an Assiniboin woman of whom he was enamoured, but who had refused to remain with him." A party of eighteenth-century Englishmen had to leave a Santee village without a guide when their man Scipio became too drunk to continue.[75] Similarly, New York envoys Hendrick Hansen and Major Cornelis van Brugh had to seek out new travel aid when the Iroquois man who was to be their guide "was drunk, and so did not go."[76] Others offered no reason at all: they merely became literal manifestations of the vanishing Indian. Wenceslaus Linck, for one example, was troubled by guides who "knew how to elude" him and his party of Baja-bound missionaries, as night after night these unwilling guides stole away while the clergymen slept.[77]

The European travelers who were during the colonial era so often dependent on Native assistance for guidance and survival generally had a few simple explanations for why these Indians gave them the slip. They described Indians as having been either afraid of their enemies or afraid of their travel companions. Sometimes travelers thought their Indian companions were tired. Others ascribed guides' reluctance as resulting from as a duplicitous nature. Most European explanations generally fit into a framework that denigrated Indians and positioned Europeans as bold forward movers. But another possibility may lurk beneath the easy, chauvinistic explanations of colonial travelers. When the Scots Canadian explorer Alexander Mackenzie made two westward trips in the late eighteenth century, one to the Arctic Ocean and the other across the Rockies to the Pacific, he habitually insisted that his parties follow a rigorous course of early and long days. His demanding timetable irritated his Native guides to no small degree. Mackenzie wrote that, on both of his trips, his guides "complain[ed] much" about his preference for "hard marching" and on occasion made known their intention to leave the party because of its "mode of traveling." Similarly, when the Mississippi Delta's flood water got chest high in the spring of 1700, Iberville's Taensas guides decided enough was enough and left the French to muddle through the still chilly swamps themselves. Iberville bitterly wrote that "they do not like to wade naked through the water," as if he and his companions did![78] Though separated by nearly two centuries and most of North America, Mackenzie's and Iberville's different guides spoke their minds, and in so doing hinted at what might have been in the minds of countless Indians who saw no reason to travel farther with Europeans. The twin keys here are dissatisfaction with the relentless demands of some Europeans asserting their authority over a party, and the Indians' inability to control the pace, flow, direction, and meaning of travel in ways that made sense to them. Europeans rarely understood that their Native companions may have been uncomfortable in their company for myriad reasons. When faced with odd, uncomfortable, and dangerous situations, these Indians did what they could to beg out of their plight in the most face-saving way possible. Were the boundaries cited by so many travelers real, or only invented spontaneously to escape an undesirable trip? Was the shallop-bound Indian really afraid of where the Frenchmen might take him, or did he simply not enjoy or see value in pulling at a French oar all day long? By citing his fear, he may have been using the world's physical and social order as a way to get out of the trip. If so, this was a fairly powerful argument, and at least an effective way to maintain control over his own time while insisting on his vision of what was appropriate travel.

And what about guides whose drunkenness kept them from being useful guides and companions? Did the Englishmen leave without Scipio because he was too drunk to go, or did Scipio become too drunk so as not to *have* to go? Were New York emissaries Hansen and Brugh, two men who never seemed too popular in the Iroquois villages they visited, passed off by a man who did not want to travel in their company? There are no clear answers to these questions, but there are clues. Take the case of the Delaware man named Willamegicken. Willamegicken had some experience traveling with Englishmen in the service of Pennsylvania during the Seven Years War, and had a reputation as a prominent man among his people and his English neighbors. In July 1758, he was hired to accompany Frederick Post from Philadelphia to the Ohio for the price of one horse. But he never made the trip. After keeping Post waiting for some time, Willamegicken met Post, but "being very drunk, he could proceed no further." With war all throughout the backcountry, this kind of travel was a real risk and Post had difficulty persuading other Indians to go with him, despite some well-practiced persuasion techniques and the ability to bestow the province's bounty on his companions. No less a figure than Delaware leader and diplomatist Teedyuscung warned Post that he "was afraid that the Indians would kill" the Moravian or even that "the French would get" him.[79] In light of Teedyuscung's words of warning, it is possible that Willamegicken drank excessively to get out of the trip without an argument from Post, and perhaps also to avoid the often painful accusation of cowardice from his friends, both Native and English. Just as violence or destruction wrought while on a bender was to be excused and blamed on the liquor, getting drunk also may have served as an at least momentarily irrefutable excuse for unhappy guides wishing to get out of undesired travel agreements with Europeans.[80]

Whether through possibly calculated drunkenness or by insisting on specific schedules and travel practices, the relationships between colonial-era European travelers and their Native companions and the shape of their shared travel was molded by travelers' numerous conflicts over how best to get down the trail. All travelers came to the trail armed with a host of assumptions, practices, and expectations, which informed their actions and shaped the results of their travel. By entwining travelers' fates, sharing the trail gave sting to the choices travelers had to make when their visions of effective travel and the trail itself collided. In short, common travel made the logic of a host of culturally specific choices have very real consequences for people not sharing that logic. One result was that travelers worked to bring one another in line with their own standards and travel habits.

4

None but the Rattlesnakes!

In June 1764, a group of Ojibwa Indians en route to Fort Niagara unexpectedly encountered their grandfather. This meeting provided an opportunity to seek the grandfather's aid and advice in their travels. Certainly it was a dangerous time. War had replaced France's open hand with Britain's tight fist, and people like the Ojibwas, who had become wealthy and influential playing one European power off the other, found themselves weakened, hungry, and angry. Some Great Lakes Indians—including many Ojibwas—went to war against the stingy English, but the result was more death and more danger. Indian tribes and alliances divided and re-formed themselves in new ways, and war's shadow darkened the landscape. Leaving home to trade and build new alliances was risky business, and whatever message or advice the grandfather offered the travelers would be welcome.

One by one, each of the party's members took deep drafts on their tobacco pipes and then blew smoke offerings to the grandfather, who received them with apparent calm and satisfaction. After a full half hour of these quiet and respectful devotions, the travelers began to ask for favors. They first asked the grandfather to safeguard the families they had left behind at Sault Sainte Marie. They then asked that he "be pleased to open the heart" of Sir William Johnson, the English superintendent of Indian affairs, ensuring that he would be generous and "fill their canoe with rum" at the end of their journey. The grandfather's "visible good humor" was a tonic to the Indians, who now traveled along waterways so recently engulfed in international conflict. The good fortune and potential meaning of the encounter so occupied the travelers that they would talk of little else over the next few days.[1]

Before the grandfather left them to return to the woods, one of the party's leaders took care to implore the powerful being to overlook the insulting actions of their white fur trader companion and the moment's chronicler, Alexander Henry. It was Henry who first found the grandfather while gathering wood for an evening's fire. After nearly stepping on the grandfather, Henry ran back to the beached canoes to fetch his gun as fast as his naked legs could carry him. The Indians, busy building their night's lodgings, saw Henry rummaging through the lightly packed canoes and had the good sense to ask him what he was up to. Had they not able to intercede and stop Henry, he would have gone back into the woods and shot the grandfather to death. A powerful force—the Manitou Kinibic—would have been angered, a fortuitous opportunity lost, a sign not heeded, and a risky trip made potentially more dangerous.[2]

It was confusion, not bloodlust, that lay at the heart of Henry's murderous intentions. What the Ojibwas respectfully called Grandfather, Henry saw only as a dangerous hissing rattlesnake. When Henry unwittingly put his bare foot down "not more than two feet" from the coiled snake, he reacted with the fear and horror that typified European travelers' reactions to these alarming and dangerous reptiles. On the other hand, many Indians travelers, like Henry's Ojibwa companions, reacted to a seemingly chance trailside encounter with a rattlesnake in a variety of ways, ranging from deep respect to bold daring. Travelers encountered a host of perils while on the trail, and roaring rapids, poor weather, and short provisions were all common enough problems. But travelers' reactions to one particular peril—rattlesnakes—provide a unique glimpse into the social tensions which underscored the relationships between many colonial-era Indian and European travel companions. There may have been more common occurrences, but few are as well documented, as eye catching, or as suffused with meaning as rattlesnake encounters. Because snake encounters were memorable moments for many travelers, they generated a richer documentary record than did other perils. Such stories made good copy, many travel writers made use of these sensational moments, and all over North America rattlesnakes were in no short supply. Nevertheless, a close examination of the worlds of meaning which swirled around these beasts and informed how travel companions reacted to the snakes themselves, and to each other's reactions, reveals how tensions between travelers took shape, and how snake-related ideas, meanings, and practices affected each other.

The success of a trip, the health of the travelers, and even their spiritual well-being could depend on how one dealt with the snake in the path. But Native and Europeans travel companions often had different—even diametrically opposed—visions of what constituted the best, safest, and most efficient way to deal with snakes. Travelers' different responses to snakes highlighted their various approaches to travel and the world in which travel took place. Exploring the beliefs travelers brought to these snake encounters and the roles that these beasts played in European and Indian societies lays the groundwork for seeing how these ideas interacted on the trail.

Indians and Europeans alike generally saw rattlesnakes as dangerous animals requiring special care when encountered. Likewise, many Native and colonial societies saw snakes as being deeply symbolic and tied to big questions of cosmic order and personal well-being. But that is where similarities usually ended. Whereas Europeans travelers generally preferred to kill rattlesnakes as expeditiously as possible, their Indian companions just as often preferred to leave the animals as unpestered as they could. Each behavior was intended to avoid conflict and create a perfected safer trail for all travelers. For their respective adherents, each behavior also seemed to be the only logical approach to a risky moment. But since so much was at stake in these provocatively dichotomous responses, snake encounters became showdowns between larger worldviews with consequences well beyond the life or death of given snake. Like many aspects of common travel, snake killing or handling were part of how travelers created familiar, usable spaces on the trail, and were among the ways travel partners enacted their own identities for themselves, and for people different from themselves. Performances like these served to maintain travelers' identities amidst the trail's potentially dangerous unfamiliarity, by allowing them to imprint their own meanings on nonhuman places and creatures. They also allowed travel partners to witness and evaluate the merit of practices and ideas different from their own. Over time, Natives and Europeans appropriated elements of each other's snake habits, but always fitted these into their own contexts, rather than move toward a shared approach. Travelers' prolonged discussions about their own habits and those of their fellows on the trail, like those surrounding rattlesnakes, for example, take on a special import because they served crucial roles in the location, formation, and maintenance of differences. Common travel allowed travelers the freedom to witness, evaluate, and perhaps adopt each other's practices, all with an eye toward being the best and most efficient travelers they could be on their own terms. Intercultural travelers worked hard to maintain distinctions between each other's identities and habits, even if doing so meant using cultural elements not their own in origin. These seemingly small moments within the larger cultural encounter were, in fact, places where cultural difference was created, maintained, and reinvented. Distinctions between Indian and European travelers survived through the colonial era because individuals actively maintained them, using whatever cultural tools were available to them. Rattlesnake encounters were one of many travel moments which brought into focus the location, uses, and implications of Native and European travel companions' differing habits.

Over time, Europeans had attached many meanings to snakes. Ancient symbols like the caduceus and stories like that of the serpent-haired Medusa revealed a range of powerful possibilities for snakes. And although some of this sensibility survived in folk beliefs, for most of early modern Europe the snakes' images were fairly well fixed and informed by Christianity. From the Garden of Eden's notorious enticing serpent, to map-adorning ship-devouring sea beasts, to the polluting and transforming snakes of the *Malleus Maleficarum*, snakes were physically and spiritually dangerous creatures noted for their stealth and tinged with demonic slyness and malice.[3] Europeans feared that a snake might sneak into a sleeper's open mouth and eat away the victim's insides. They dreaded the tiny, red-eyed serpent that could kill at a glance, and they venerated the bold deeds of serpent killers, whose courage was made greater by the belief that a snake's poison could climb up a spear or lance and thereby do in the would-be slayer.[4] Snakes' reputations were so bad that sometimes even simple contact with one could bring on an accusation of witchcraft. In 1607–the same year as the founding of Jamestown and Santa Fe—a Kentish woman found herself in court accused of having had her neighbors kneel and worship a dead snake. She defended herself by claiming that all she did was point out the curiosity near her home. The court was worried about the use of a black-arts-tinged folk belief, holding that "if one see[s] a dead snake in the beginning of the year he shall overcome his enemies."[5] A snake's power to kill or to implicate made them dangerous indeed.

Europeans generally viewed America's many snakes through the lens of Old World fear and belief. Few of North America's manifold "horrors" could turn a European traveler as white with fear as the sight of snake slithering across the path, or worse even, the sound of a rattler's menacing clatter emanating from some undetermined, but unnervingly close, covering. The rattlesnake, in particular, held a special terror for Europeans. No such snakes lived in Europe, while America must have seemed to be literally crawling with the rattlesnakes' many varieties. Poisonous snakes were not new to Europeans, but ones that exhibited large fangs accompanied by a loud and unmistakable rattling were a wholly new terror. The rattlesnake so captured Europeans' fevered imaginations that they no doubt identified no small number of other only half-seen serpents as rattlers, thereby unfairly enlarging this particular animal's fearsome reputation.

Early European observers went to great lengths to describe the powers and attributes of this new and especially fearsome viper. Dutch traveler Rev. Johannes Megapolensis wrote in 1644 of sharp-toothed brutes who would "dare to bite at dogs" and would "make way for neither man nor beast, but fall on and bite them." The Dutch divine seemed as alarmed at the snakes' particular impudence as he was by their poisonous and "commonly even deadly" bite.[6] In 1656, the Jesuit priest Jean Du Quen listed the rattlesnake as one of the Saguenay region's marvels. The length and sharpness of the snakes' teeth and the speed with which their poison could kill a person captured the black robe's imagination. But it was the rattler's unique sound that most occupied him. Du Quen mistakenly believed that the snakes made their sound as they moved along the ground, but noted that the sound was audible at "twenty paces."[7] For Du Quen, the sound held a special purpose. He proposed that God himself had given the snake its sound so that "men may be on their guard at the approach of so dangerous an animal."[8] In Du Quen's zoology, such menacing creatures wandered the world equipped with their own natural leper bells to alert the unwary of their approach. John Josselyn thought New England's rattlesnakes—the "captain" of all the region's reptiles—made their sound with "nothing but a hollow shelly business jointed." If the snake's sound making tail did not impress Josselyn, one specimen's ability to swallow "a live chicken, as big as the one they give 4 pence four in England," certainly did.[9] French Sulpician and explorer René de Bréhant de Galinée described the rattler's sound as being a "noise like that which a number of melon or squash seeds would make, if shut up in a box." But it was the snake's cold-blooded boldness that really impressed Galinée. He noted that the rattler was "not timid like other serpents." Rather than darting for cover and avoiding human contact, these intrepid monsters commonly coiled themselves up in a "posture of defense" and then would "wait for a man."[10] Other travelers claimed that the rattlesnake generally avoided a confrontation until provoked by a misplaced foot or hoof. But the price of such a misstep was frightening.[11]

The fear of a dangerous encounter was often strong enough to warrant travel delay. A naturalist, traveler, and author of his own treatise on rattlesnakes, Peter Kalm, dared not climb over path-blocking logs which were "the chief retreat of rattlesnakes during the intense heat of the day."[12] Similarly, John Ettwein and fellows cautiously approached a portion of a Susquehanna-side trail where "rattlesnakes seemed to hold undisputed sway."[13] Despite their best attempt to make it past the lair unscathed, a well-placed bite on the nose of one party's horses ended up killing the animal, and thus deprived the travelers of a needed pack carrier. In 1745, along another portion of the Susquehanna, a small party of Moravian missionaries took time out to hunt down a varmint whose telltale rattle had spooked Bishop Spangenberg.[14]

As if avoiding a potential hiding spot or dodging a rattler's extended fangs were not stressful enough, some European travelers still held to the older folk wisdom that the mere sight of one of these serpents could cause harm. At a Niagara River portage, the otherwise stalwart seventeenth-century French Canadian explorer La Salle reportedly succumbed to fever "at the sight of three large rattlesnakes" sitting directly in his path. Of course, La Salle had already been feeling poorly after a brief hunting side trip, but few of his travel companions would have doubted that the snakes played some role in his illness.[15] In a similar vein Pierre de Charlevoix was no doubt glad that his 1721 travels did not take him onto a group of islands called the "Rattlesnake Islands," because the place was so "infested" that some claimed that "the air is infected with them."[16]

In the face of such terrifyingly dangerous creatures, European travelers generally had one response: they killed them, and preferably as quickly as possible. Certainly, when Bishop Spangenberg called back to his brother Moravians and Indian guides to come up and kill a heard-but-not-yet-seen rattler, a terror-colored caution was his principal motivation. But not all European snake killers showed such fear. One English writer noted that colonial militias "carr[ied] on a war with the snakes" and made killing them a regular part of their activities.[17]

The methodical nature of European snake killing suggests the degree to which these herpecides saw their actions as a form of public service—especially for travelers. Killing snakes served to decrease the animals' overall number and make the trail a safer place. Travelers facing a two-way trip knew that they could potentially run into the same snakes on the return. A dead snake that could not harm one's own party also protected others who might travel that way. Peter Kalm noted that colonists would seek out rattler's dens in the springtime when the animals ended their hibernation. As the animals came out of the ground the ready colonials quickly dispatched them. One "old Swede" told Kalm that he had killed as many as sixteen of them "with one shot" as the still-sluggish snakes relaxed and warmed themselves in the sun's rays.[18] In the fall of 1733, William Byrd II and his companions killed two "fat" rattlesnakes along the Virginia-Carolina border. Although the snakes' rattles were objects of some interest to them, none of the men really felt the desire to bring the "two very large" specimens back to camp to eat them.[19] Instead, they just left them to rot. Their reason for the killing was simply to rid the trail of dangers. Similarly, John Ettwein and party devoted some time to killing the snakes they encountered "at all points" along their Susquehanna trail, and Richard Blome summarily killed both of the rattlesnakes he met in his late-seventeenth-century Pennsylvania travels.[20] The preventative component of snake killing was especially pronounced when one ran across snakes near one's lodgings, as John Josselyn did in 1639. Josselyn killed off "above four score" of the brutes, who had had the temerity to come "within a stones throw" of his rustic New England home.[21] One Virginia planter surprised a rattlesnake, which rewarded him with a deep and painful bite. In his fear, pain, and rage, he killed the offending beast and then returned home, threw the dead snake on the floor, and told his no-doubt-shocked family "I am killed, and there is my murderer!"[22] The planter's emotional mix effectively expressed the terror and hatred that drove many colonial snake killers.

Snake killing provided travelers the therapeutic opportunity to take action against one of the many perils they faced while traveling. Many trail risks were simply unavoidable; storms, enemy ambushes, swollen rivers, and dangerous paths were just part of travel, and the only way to avoid them was to stay home. But snakes were vulnerable. One could not avoid the possibility of an encounter and even the risk of death at the fangs of a secreted rattling monster. But a traveler could fight back in a way that one could not fight the rain or a rock fall. Killing a snake—or a large number of them—provided the chance to master one element of a strange and often dangerous environment. Furthermore, snake killing fit into a larger pattern of exterminating animals that Europeans saw as dangerous or otherwise undesirable. Colonial wolf bounties and collective squirrel kills testify to the degree to which a perfected environment relied on animal slaughter.[23] Unlike squirrels, moles, and sparrows, which wandered into European colonial towns and farmsteads, snakes tended to stay in the woods, making their wholesale extermination impractical. The snakes' long-standing association with evil and their woods habitat combined in travelers' minds. Fear of the dark unfamiliarity of American woodlands and dread of a waiting serpent swirled together, each fear augmenting and validating the other. As John Smith claimed, folks returning to England complained that "the country is all woods," and some cited fear of "the danger of the rattell Snake."[24] Given this combination of fears and beliefs, it is not surprising that so many of the early European travelers who took the time to offer detailed descriptions of snakes were clergymen.

Acting out against snakes did not always require killing. In some cases, just interfering with a snake's evil plans gave satisfaction. Louis Hennepin reported seeing a snake "about six feet long crawling up a straight and precipitous mountain"[25] in order to steal some vulnerable chicks from a hapless swallow's nest. Feathers and debris from previous successful raids littered the ground at the foot of the hill. Hennepin and his companions took it upon themselves to intercede, and pelted the snake with stones until it lost its purchase and fell. In a similar incident in 1788, Samuel Kirkland and his New York State traveling companions saw a large snake slowly making its way up a tree to eat the young birds in a nest. Kirkland described the snake's actions in language better suited to a theatrical production than a woodland feeding incident. The snake reached the cavity in the tree which sheltered the nest and then "raised her head in a lofty manner and looked in upon the little harmless and helpless creatures."[26] In this little drama, Kirkland and company cast themselves as the heroes, and promptly chopped down the tree and killed the villain. Fur trader John Long encountered a large snake while traveling up the St. Lawrence River in 1781. The snake had a fish in its mouth, so Long took his rifle and with a single "fortunate" shot managed to "release the prisoner from the jaws of death."[27] Many of these tales take similar shape and, indeed, may have been informing one another as travelers recast their memories in a solidifying literary style. Nevertheless, they do reflect the fascination and horror Europeans felt toward snakes in general and rattlesnakes in particular. A long European tradition of fear and distrust of snakes informed these actions and their subsequent retelling. By thwarting a snake's plans, the do-good traveler struck a small blow against evil in all of its many forms.

In the eighteenth century, the language of science and the stance of the curious observer began to shape Europeans' travel descriptions. But the eighteenth-century naturalist's response to snakes differed little from the clergyman's. Killing a beast was still the best way to interact with one. Naturalists were perhaps less motivated by a biblical vision of snakes than were clergymen, but this did not decrease the number of animals killed. Killing a snaked provided naturalists (or a traveler adopting the stance of the naturalist) with the opportunity for a close examination of the creature. Although William Bartram preferred to see himself as above the brutality so many colonists showed toward snakes, he nevertheless killed and interfered with his fair share of them.[28] William Byrd and his companions paid special attention their dead trophy's rattles. Mark Catesby and William Bartram both painted fine portraits of rattlers based on dead specimens. Catesby was so taken with the rattler that he devoted more text to this type of snake in his writings than to all others combined.[29] Peter Kalm, who saw rattlesnakes firsthand during his American travels, wrote a full treatise on the topic, claiming that "the flame in [a rattlesnake's] eyes, particularly when irritated and killed no painter can imitate."[30]

Observers offered dozens of conflicting and overlapping anecdotes, and made authoritative pronouncements about the snakes' habits and customs. Some claimed them to be fast, aggressive, and vicious, while others thought them slow and passive. Some claimed that the number of rattles told a snake's age, while others denied the assertion.[31] Naturally enough, the snake's mouth was always a source of nervous attention. Jonathan Carver offered a detailed description of a rattler's teeth and a "small bag full of venom," a description which could only have been based on close examination of a dead specimen.[32] What is more, Carver went so far as to bait snakes by waving a "rag fastened at the end of a stick" in their faces just to see how the angered animal would attempt to bite at it.[33] Experiments like these provided a chance to watch these snakes in action. In the early 1720s, one curious South Carolinian killed upwards of five dogs and one bull frog by placing them before a tied and fired-up rattler, in order to study the snake's bite.[34] Similar observers took a keen interest in the rattlesnake's body and functioning, and wrote several detailed studies of dissected animals. Although these experimenters might have been a bit bolder than those who swooned at the mere sight of a large snake, they still believed that the best snakes were dead and distant.

European travelers sought to avoid snakes at all costs and generally killed them in the event of a sudden encounter. Their various Native companions, however, saw snakes very differently and consequently viewed their encounters with the animals in quite a different light. Like so many Europeans, Indians also saw rattlers as dangerous animals and did not relish a surprise run-in. But unlike the Europeans with whom they traveled, Indian travelers generally conceptualized the danger differently, and consequently arrived at different solutions to an otherwise similar problem. Snakes held a great range of possible meanings in Native America and especially along the trail. A given snake could be an incarnation or representation of an animal spirit bearing a specific encoded message, a powerful force holding the keys to a trip's success or failure, or a lost friend or family member bearing news or advice. As Alexander Henry discovered, an encounter with a snake could require special actions, rituals, and extensive discussion in order to be fully comprehended and effectively used.

Henry's Ojibwa companions called their rattlesnake "Grandfather," referring not so much to a narrow familial relationship but rather using the term as one of respect, alluding to distant kinship. Snakes were the nonhuman ancestors of many Indian clans, and European travelers found that relationship celebrated in the form of serpent images gracing the front of Iroquoian longhouses and elaborately carved snakes guarding the remains of the Natchez dead.[35] Snakes could also be closer kin, however. A Huron named Isonnaat, suffering through the epidemics of the 1630s, left his town of Anouatea to seek out his half-sister, who "had been changed into a serpent."[36] He may have been seeking his half-sister's aid for his very ill daughter. In a similar incident a Piankashaw Indian flew into a rage when a French soldier killed the snake living in the man's Illinois country home. The man told the Frenchman that the snake had been his manitou and the soul of his father, who had died a year earlier, "shortly after having shot two snakes which were mating on a rock."[37]

Snakes adorned the bodies of Indians, both in and out of legend. The Iroquois central story—the Deganawidah epic—tells of Atatarho, a powerful sorcerer driven mad by his rage and hatred for mankind. A knot of hissing serpents in place of hair was the physical manifestation of his insanity.[38] Jean-Bernard Bossu, during his 1756 Arkansas travels, met a well-traveled Osage man who had made his reputation by killing an enormous snake. A large tattoo of the snake on the man's body memorialized the bold act, and the snake became his village's chief manitou.[39] The snake's killing and the subsequent tattoo may also have been a commemoration of a spiritual journey during which the man saw a snake as his animal benefactor and guardian. Some Virginia Algonquians took the snake-as-ornament idea one step further by wearing a live snake through a pierced ear, with the snake "lapping himself about his neck oftentymes familiarly he suffers to kisse his lipps."[40]

A snake's body was often a useful and lucky object. Snakeskins made fine offerings to Gods; a snake found in a bear's or similarly brave animal's stomach was seen as the source of its courage, and became a powerful totem; and some Indians reportedly employed a defanged snake tied around the neck as a protective talisman in war.[41] Shamans employed snakes' powers and bodies in healing and religious rituals. Some cures required that the attending shaman take venomous snakes in hand while ministering to an infirm patient.[42] In some cases, a specially defanged snake wrapped around a patient's torso could also cure the illness.[43] In one early-eighteenth-century North Carolina case, an Indian healer cured a reluctant Englishman's "distemper" by wrapping a rattler around the planter's belly. By morning the illness had transferred to the now-dead snake and the planter was well on the way to full recovery.[44] Pueblo Indian shamans practiced a form of snake handling that included the markedly sexual imagery of priests putting serpents in their mouths and rubbing them on their genitals.[45] A Missouri Indian woman shaman carried a large living rattlesnake coiled around her body as friend, advisor, and a kind of live chain of office. French observers were both shocked and incredulous when she seemed to be able converse with the beast and even to sense its emotions. At one point she said to the animal, "I see [that] you are bored here. Go home and I shall meet you there when I return."[46] The snake then took its leave.

Snake images could sometimes have as much power as the genuine article, and parts of snakes themselves also had considerable power. An ill Huron had a brother who dreamed that a serpent-shaped stick could heal the disease. The ill man's friends and family immediately set about making the dream real.[47] Pictures of snakes painted or tattooed on the body could in some cases ward off a dangerous snakebite.[48] While rituals involving live snakes or effigies were usually the province of trained specialists, snake parts had many curative powers that common folk could put to their own use. Snake parts were key ingredients in ointments and balms for curing a variety of conditions, and a rattler's teeth made fine devices for administering medicine or for pricking the skin.[49] A rattlesnake's tail could cure a toothache, and biting a green snake around its body could prevent future tooth pains. In many Native societies, women knew that snake blood could ease labor pains, as could eating a powdered rattle. Some even asserted that simply shaking a rattlesnake's tail could make childbirth less painful. Cherokee healers used an oil made from the rattlesnake's lower body to soothe sore joints.[50] A rattlesnake's fat could ease bruises, sprains, and swollen limbs, although for some peoples a specialist had to ritualistically render the fat.[51]

In much of Native America, powerful nonhuman forces in the form of animals or objects were not divided into fixed good and evil forces like the Europeans' God-Satan dichotomy. Power could work for good or ill; it was up to the user to maintain the best possible relationship with it. But even a careful following of rituals and ceremonies could not guarantee that autonomous power-possessing forces would not cause harm for their own obscure reasons. Furthermore, just as a skillful shaman could implore, cajole, or manipulate spirits to act in a supplicant's interest, people could also employ these forces for ill. As new and seemingly uncontrollable diseases swept through their towns, some Hurons became suspicious that the illness may have been the work of their resident French priests employing snakes in some new and unfamiliar way. This fear was plausible enough that some Indians thought priest-owned artistic renderings of the terrors of hell were in fact pictures of the very serpents which the Jesuits used to "poison" the people.[52] For one Canadian Indian, snake images in a chapel tapestry were fearful enough to send him fleeing to his kin, warning them that the priests had "exposed the souls on figures of serpents and snakes" and urging them not to go into the church building, "for it is all surrounded with robes and garments of demons."[53] Snake power in the wrong hands was indeed something to fear.

Snakes appeared in Indian stories explaining the world and how it worked, and occasionally played the central role in rituals for keeping the world in balance. Some of these reptiles were essentially the same as the ones Indians encountered daily. For example, the Tobacco Nation Indians of the Erie Peninsula told of a god figure named Onditachiae, who would come to earth to get a supply of snakes to feed upon.[54] The Hurons connected snakes with celestial activity. They informed Father Paul Le Jeune that thunder was the sound of a god—perhaps Onditachiae—vomiting up snakes he had swallowed. Lightning was the god-eaten snakes as they flew to earth. This belief was well grounded in empirical observation. The Indians told of finding the remains of the celestial snakes in the ground at the feet of lightning-struck trees. Such objects are on display in many modern natural science museums bearing the rather dry explanation that they are fulgurites, which are heat-fused soil minerals resulting from lightning strikes.[55] The Pueblo Indians had their own version of the snake-sky connection, as revealed in their Snake Dance for ensuring rains. They portrayed the water's spiritual power in the form of a snake, and kept special snakes specifically for the ritual. The dance was the purview of the Rain Chiefs, who would handle the snakes and use them in seemingly sexually suggestive ways, which did not fail to catch European eyes.[56] Pueblo thought and ritual blended snakes with rain and water and the renewing forces they together unleashed. Cherokee Indians also saw a connection between the rain and snakes. They knew to take care and ensure that a freshly killed rattlesnake's body was securely hidden in the ground or in a log; otherwise the other snakes, angry over this lack of respect, would send so much rain that the streams and rivers would flood.[57]

Many Indians' worlds also contained snakes whose sizes, attributes, and powers transcended the abilities of their more quotidian cousins. These marvelous snakes were often the ancient progenitors of the snake tribe whose contemporary descendants threatened Indian travel plans and general wellbeing. European travelers heard from their Native companions a variety of stories about enormous snakes with unusual physical attributes and unnerving powers. In the Ojibwa Midewiwin medicine society, members practiced cures once learned from a giant serpent.[58] For New England Algonquians, a large, horned serpent of considerable power lived under the water and land. This beast, which they portrayed in stone and on amulet, was often paired with its celestial analog and inveterate foe, the thunderbird.[59] The Dakotas told Jonathan Carver of an enormous beast which they knew as Tautongo Omlishco—the Buffalo Snake. This large creature mixed a variety of physical traits—it reportedly had a snake's body of nearly eighteen feet in length, four feet with claws like a bear's, and a ridge of fins running down its red back.[60] Seneca travelers told of a small lake inhabited by a snake of indeterminate size which had the terrifying ability to shoot "balls of liquid fire" out of its eyes.[61] Huron Indians described a kind of scaled snake called Onniont, which had the power to pierce "everything that it meets in its way."[62] Cherokee Indians told stories of a large man-turned-snake called Uktena, "the Keen-Eyed." Uktena was as thick as a tree trunk and had horns like the northern Horned Serpent. Like the Senecas' snake, Uktena and its descendants lived in deep pools, but were also known to haunt lonely mountain passes. Uktena had the ability to dazzle its prey or an enemy with a flash of light from a large glittering stone in its forehead. The Cherokees claimed that this light could hypnotize and cause an unfortunate victim to run toward Uktena when the better choice would have been to run away.[63] The jewel in the snake's crown was a source of considerable power for those who had the courage and good fortune to possess one. Healers used these objects in medical rituals and for general good luck. Cherokee Indians told trader James Adair of one local healer, who had an Uktena stone "near as big as an egg" which he found "where a great rattlesnake lay dead."[64] European traders attempting to purchase one of these stones met with strong resistance from Indians, who feared that losing the stone would "prejudice their health or affairs."[65]

But snakes were also potentially dangerous animals, regardless of their larger cosmological connections. Indian travelers needed an array of skills and knowledge to get by on the trail, and knowing how to protect against and cure snakebites had life-saving importance. Travelers were in a singular bind vis-à-vis the snakes: they were more likely than stay-at-homes to have snake encounters, and travelers' remoteness from home, family, and healers augmented the danger from a snakebite. But simultaneously, the rituals needed to keep on the reptiles' good side frequently required close contact with a snake. Angered snakes might bite a person in revenge for improperly following the appropriate rituals, killing a snake rashly, or showing disrespect toward other members of the snake tribe. Rattlesnakes possessed a form of collective consciousness, so that offending one rattler meant offending them all. Similarly, rattlers enforced collective responsibility for humans who may have angered the snakes: the misdeeds of one human could be avenged on any human. Consequently, vulnerable travelers might have to pay the price for the sins of many others.

Given snakes' special association with water and the weather, an offended snake might avenge itself by bringing about a sudden and dangerous turn in the weather. As with bites, travelers were at special risk, since they could easily fall victim to an unexpected storm while on the water, or become isolated on a blocked trail by a swollen river or stream. Angered snake spirits could also avenge themselves in any number of creative ways, ranging from accidents to illness. But most often rattlers took revenge with their fangs. Therefore, Indian travelers had to pay special care to avoid giving offense to snakes, while simultaneously being prepared to handle the almost unavoidable snakebite.

Indian snakebite cures fell into two broad categories: those that one could perform on one's self, and those that had to be administered by an expert healer. Native travelers relied heavily on transportable cures, and were masters of a variety of herbal and surgical remedies. One way to protect against snakebites was to treat the animals with due respect by making offerings to special sites and to the animals themselves. But the means of doing so often called for close contact with the dangerous beasts; therefore a snakebite was always a possibility, and even the most respectful traveler could still find himself or herself bitten by an angered snake.

When a bite occurred, many Indian travelers practiced an early form of triage. Deep bites that hit major veins were far more dangerous than lighter bites or bites in artery-free muscular parts. The deepest bites were beyond the healing reach of herbal cures and required surgical procedures, such as cutting the wound and sucking out the poison. When a young Indian boy traveling with Pierre Espirit Radisson found himself badly bitten, he immediately took out his knife and cut off the entire affected area before the poison could spread too far.[66] If done quickly and properly, this draconian surgical practice could remove the poison before it moved too far into the bloodstream. Of course, such a cure was not only disfiguring, but also ran the risk of opening up a vein in a way that could cause severe blood loss or lead to a dangerous infection. Radisson did not record whether the procedure worked. When presented with this dilemma, many an Indian traveler simply recognized that his or her race was run and, refusing treatment of any kind, just waited to die.

But most Indian travelers relied on special roots and herbs to protect themselves against snake poisons. These herbal cures could be effective against light bites and were consequently a standard part of a traveler's kit. Snakeroot, whose English name suggests its principal use, grew throughout the North American woodlands, and was well known to many Indian people under many different names. "Snake root" may in fact have been a catch-all name for many types of herbs and plants with curative powers; surveyor and naturalist John Lawson noted the existence of at least four healing roots in North Carolina alone, while Mark Catesby listed at least three.[67] Plants including golden rod, dittany, and devil's bit all reportedly had curative powers.[68] Eastern Algonquians had a reddish root called *pocoon*, which had protective qualities, and when rubbed on a traveler's body could either repel a snake or neutralize the effect of its venom.[69] Southeastern Indians knew to chew on a piece of "Senecka" root to allay the effects of a bad bite.[70] Some Indians asserted that simply carrying a piece of the right stuff in a pouch or neck bag could provide enough protection to allow the bearer to sleep under a tree without fear of a nocturnal bite—a fear that kept some European travelers far from deep sleep.[71] Curative roots and herbs made into "decoctions" or boiled into a tea could serve as a preventative drink or be consumed after a bite. Chewing the root or applying it mashed to a fresh bite could effect an almost miraculous cure. One impressed English traveler had high praise for his Native companions' "thorough and speedy cure," which called for the victim's chewing of the proper root and swallowing the resulting saliva. After he had swallowed enough, he then applied the chewed root to the wound itself. The combination of antidote and poison caused a "terrible conflict throughout the body," but in the end the poison was "repelled through the same channels it entered and the patient was cured."[72] Proof over time demonstrated the effectiveness of these cures, and confident in their ability to stop a poisonous bite, Indians approached snakes with respect but not the outright terror exhibited by European travelers.

Experienced Indian travelers knew how to placate snakes with offerings and kind words, but, to be sure, they also took care to avoid places that held special risk, such as islands or ponds inhabited by snakes, snake spirits, or giant serpents. Failure to so do held grave potential consequences, since angered or wronged snakes might be avenged by the bites of their fellow snakes. Most travelers carried their own stashes of snakeroot or some similar herb so that a supply would be on hand should the need arise. Confidence in one's ability to heal a bite melded with the need to act respectfully toward snakes. After all, fear of a bite would make it difficult to approach a snake and show the proper respect while making offerings. The bodily security that cures offered made possible the kind of physical closeness that enabled the larger spiritual benefits to be gained through offerings.

When European and Indian travel companions encountered a snake on the path, these different ways of interacting with the reptiles came into conflict. The different courses of action, the one based on cautious interaction, the other on preferring distance or even killing, were entirely incompatible and necessitated a choice. For Indians travelers, knowing how to placate a snake was one of many travel skills that, while informed by larger worldviews, were nevertheless employed as simply as one would employ any other technology or labor saver. Indians paddling a canoe, building a fire, or setting a snare all had time-honored, localized methods, and dealing with a snake was no different. The connection between mistreating a snake (or any other powerful force) and the resulting disaster on the trail was as real as the connection between improperly tarring a canoe and later seeing it take on water. Like every other aspect of travel, the Indian way to deal with snakes was proper, efficient, and time-tested.

Europeans were quick to recognize the efficacy of Indian travel methods, especially when those methods involved recognizable skills which Europeans themselves could master and use. European travelers all over the continent had high praise for Indians' abilities to steer a canoe, find food in the woods, and build ingenious shelters from local materials. Within a short period, traders and missionaries whose designs depended on backwoods skills became competent travelers in the Indian mold. Europeans adopted the use of herbal cures and in some cases carried the root with them just as Indians did. Nicholas Cresswell learned of snakeroot not from an Indian but from an experienced English traveler, and Father Marquette himself taught his fellow Jesuit travelers in the use of the protective roots. William Byrd saw the "strong antidote" as essential travel equipment, and one English rattlesnake scholar claimed that English traders "know this root and keep it always about them."[73]

But while adopting Indian curing techniques, Europeans generally failed to see Indian methods of snake placating as a useful corollary. Different worldviews and centuries of snake fear and hatred made this nearly impossible. Utility in European eyes ended with the root itself. Europeans quickly adopted Indians' herbal cures and preventatives, but they did not adopt the idealized relationship with snakes that went with cures in Native practice. In appropriating Indian herbal cures, Europeans recontextualized the cure itself. For Indians, the cure for the bite and the veneration of the biting snake were tied. The ability to cure gave one the ability to make close contact with a being of considerable power. An encounter with a snake was a moment ripe with potential, and Native travelers wanted to be in the best position to understand the meaning behind the meeting. Doing so was a necessary part of traveling because of the dangerous ramifications of angering or not heeding a snake. Confidence in one's ability to cure or protect against a bite was a sine qua non of being able to make close and respectful contact with a dangerous animal. Therefore, snakebite cures were an intrinsic part of showing snakes proper respect and being a good and successful traveler. But for Europeans, Native herbal cures became a last-ditch defense against animals that were better avoided or killed.

Many European travelers were able to use and appreciate Indians' ability to cure snakebites, but most could not or would not share in the larger Native vision of snakes and the uses of the cure. Therefore dealing with snakes could take on a superficial similarity, such as the widespread use of special curative roots, while remaining a revealing simmering impasse in many travel relationships. Indian travelers appeared to have learned little of practical use about the snakes from their European fellows, travel chroniclers recorded a high degree of continuity and stability in what they saw of Native ways of coping with rattlers. These long-lasting methods worked well and were proven to protect travelers who followed them. For their part, Europeans were confident that their own methods were invariably the best way to rid the trail of a malicious danger. For them as well as for Indian travelers, failure to take proper action was risky. Problems naturally arose when these different and incompatible visions of how to handle a snake came to bear on the same animal, with consequences for all members of a party.

James Adair learned this lesson. During one of his mid-eighteenth-century travels, a Chickasaw chief companion chewed a piece of snakeroot, blew the protective spittle over his hands, and picked up a rattlesnake they had encountered. The Chickasaw feared that Adair would do something foolish to harm the animal, so he removed it from danger by placing it gingerly in a hollow tree. Although Adair did not hear the message, the actions of the Chickasaw were simultaneously a rebuke to Adair, a loving act toward a powerful animal, and a convincing demonstration of the right way to handle such encounters.[74] Apparently Adair did not heed the lesson, as a subsequent trip showed. On that trip, sometime before 1745, on the Chickasaw trade road, one of Adair's Native companions covered himself in snakeroot and sat down to remove the herb-smeared fangs of a rattlesnake. Like this bold soul, some Indians took it upon themselves to defang snakes in order to keep them as pets or leave them in places slightly less dangerous. One stunned observer wrote that his Indian companions had made the rattlesnakes so tame "as to carry them in their bosoms" and have them "come and go as they bid."[75] While it is impossible to tell for sure, it is most likely that these pets were of the defanged variety.

After Adair's Indian companion had carefully pulled the snake's fangs from its sockets, he then set the animal on the ground "tenderly at a distance."[76] Adair's response to the scene was to kill the snake forthwith. His rationalization for this act was that now that the animal had no more fangs, "common pity should induce one to put it out of its misery."[77] But the old Indian saw it differently and made his anger and objections known to Adair, warning that such a disrespectful action would "occasion misfortunes" for both of them. Indian travelers knew that such snakes required and deserved respect, and that to impiously kill one would result in bad luck in hunting, war, and travel.[78] The problem for this man was that his fate was now mixed up with Adair's. The rash and unthinking actions of the one held potential danger for the other. The old trader and Adair continued their acquaintance, bickering about the right ways to travel until the Indian's death in 1745 on the Old Chickasaw path.

Knowing how to handle a snake could also provide the opportunity to take advantage of generally less-snake-savvy European companions. During a mid-eighteenth-century trip, an unnamed Menominie Indian left his rattlesnake grandfather at a Fox River portage with the intention of picking him back up on the return trip. A Frenchman named Pinneshon traveling with the party thought the whole proposal ridiculous and made his skepticism known. In response the Menominie offered a small wager, claiming that within eight days of their spring return to the same spot he would call and retrieve the snake, which would enter the box the Menominie carried him in "of his own accord."[79] When all this came to pass, as the Indian was confident it would, Pinneshon would owe him several gallons of rum. Pinneshon agreed, saying that the Indian "would never see [the snake] anymore."[80] The following spring the snake did not return to his box within the agreed upon eight days. A no-doubt happy Pinneshon agreed to double-or-nothing the bet and gave the snake four more days to enter his box. On the last allotted day the snake arrived and calmly entered its box, just as the Menominie claimed he would. Pinneshon was out a considerable amount of rum. Luck? Perhaps. What is more likely, though, is that the Indian had mastered the snake's migration pattern and had trained the animal to winter in the box rather than in a den. Certainly, experience had shown the Menominie Indian that a snake well-treated was a reliable friend and good ally. It is also possible that the Indian originally understated the number of days he expected before the snake's return and thereby set a sly trap for his French travel partner. Whether or not the Menominie employed such shrewd planning, he appeared able to profit by pitting his understanding, knowledge, and familiarity with rattlesnakes and their migratory patterns against the confident ignorance of his companion.

The Menominie knew his rattlesnakes. But the snakes he and other Indians knew could be very different from those known by European travelers. For Indians, the powers of the great legendary serpents like the Cherokee Uktena, and their children or fellow snake tribe members—the snakes on the trail—could overlap and merge, a logical occurrence, considering the close relationship Indians saw between the great and small beasts. When John Lederer killed a rattlesnake in the Virginia woods in 1669, he was astonished to see a whole squirrel in the snake's belly, and wondered how a creature as slow moving as the snake could catch one so fleet-footed. His three Chickahominy companions explained that the snakes climbed to the tops of the trees, fixed "their eye steadfastly" upon a small victim, and through the "horrour" of their gaze struck "such an affrightment into the little beast, that he had no power to hinder himself from tumbling into the jaws of his enemy."[81] Similarly, Carolina traveler John Lawson learned from his Indian companions that rattlesnakes have the ability to "charm" animals so that they "run directly into their mouths."[82] Lawson claimed to have witnessed just such an incident. Although Mark Catesby did not claim to be a living witness, he too offered anecdotal evidence of the charming snake, claiming that birds and squirrels would "skip from spray to spray hovering and approaching gradually nearer their enemy." The seemingly unnerved creatures' fates finally came when they lighted into the snakes' open mouth. While Catesby did not reveal where he learned of this hunting technique, it sounds very much like a version of the stories Lederer and Lawson heard before him.[83]

When discussing these snakes with European traveling companions (often across a deep language chasm), Indian informants explained the behavior of individual snakes with reference to the behavior of legendary beasts like the Uktena, which had the ability to freeze its prey in their tracks. For these Indians, the distinction between the habits of the legendary beasts and the snake in hand was unclear, if it existed at all. The creatures were all tied together, and the Indians themselves were also connected to them. Understanding this interconnected corpus of beliefs—and knowing how to act on it properly—was an important part of being a good traveler. Whether a given snake captured a given squirrel by stealth or by charming mattered less than the lessons and connections the moment presented. When Lederer asked about the dead and flayed rattlesnake before him, it made perfect sense to his travel companions to offer him a lesson about the world of snakes writ large. Their explanations carried with them a slight rebuke for the perhaps unwise killing of a rattlesnake. Adair's companions, perhaps aided by an ability to speak the same language, told Adair that it was unwise to kill a rattlesnake. Lederer's companions, speaking a language not known to us in translation to an English colonist of German birth, chose to relate Native natural history with an implicit lesson. Their relating their stories suggested that in their eyes, had Lederer been better aware of the rattlesnake's cosmological connections, he might have shown greater respect for the animal. By cluing their travel companion in to the powers of snakes, they in part may have hoped to make him a better traveler, and thereby protect themselves from possible blunders, by helping the Lederer see why these animals demanded respect rather than violence.[84]

Lederer himself reacted with incredulity toward his companions' explanation, preferring to believe that snakes climb trees to "surprise their prey in the nest."[85] So did French officer Pierre-Joseph Celeron when he heard "a thousand marvelous things" about rattlesnakes from the Indians accompanying him into the Ohio Country. Peter Kalm believed in snakes' powers of fascination and William Bartram recounted the fascinating allegations but chose to avoid confirming or denying them.[86] John Lawson, on the other hand, gave the snake's charming abilities credence. For many Europeans who accepted and retold the stories, these beliefs jibed well with traditional European snake lore and a general willingness to believe the worst about these beasts, and served as an allegorical vehicle for expressing Europeans' anxieties about and even fascination with the American woodlands and its many seeming wonders.[87]

Naturalists and interested physicians debated the question of the snakes' ability to charm its prey in books, medical reports, and popular publications, with partisans both supporting and denying the allegation. Modern herpetologists deny that rattlesnakes hunt in this fashion, but the number of Europeans who accepted the Indian explanation suggests the degree to which European travelers relied on and related the testimony of Native informants or recycled Native lore. Europeans during the colonial era increasingly divided the natural world from the world of traditional myths and origin stories. European travelers, particularly those with a naturalist bent, wanted to know about the habits of these snakes, on what they saw as a strictly material plane. For them, acquisition of this type of knowledge was itself an important goal of their travel.

Understanding the snakes and their habits enabled better prediction of where and when one would encounter a snake. This predictability made the snakes less dangerous. Like Native travelers, Europeans saw knowledge of snakes as a necessary part of travel. But the difference was twofold. First, Europeans preferred a knowledge that they saw as being free from what they deemed myth. The second difference was that an important goal of the Europeans' studies was to render the snakes harmless by demystifying their behavior and making their actions predictable and thereby avoidable. Killing snakes was an explicit part of the acquisition of this knowledge.

Understanding a snake's message was vital to successful travel. The Ojibwas traveling with Henry saw their meeting with the grandfather as exactly the kind of meaning-laden encounter that required using an experienced traveler's full acumen. Such snakes, they told the fur trader, rarely traveled so far north; therefore, the snake had gone out of its way to convey a message to the travelers. The grandfather had come to tell the Ojibwas not to proceed on this dangerous trip. This was not good news for Henry. As a Montreal-based English trader, he, of course, thought it was vital that the trip continue as planned. His livelihood and personal safety, and the success of the ascendant English fur trade, depended on his and his colleagues' ability to keep Indian trade partners connected, hunting, and coming to English trade posts. Therefore, Henry made the case for continuing as forcefully as he could. The Indians had a choice: listen to the meaning of the grandfather's visit and turn back, or heed Henry's promises and forge ahead. Small wonder that the meaning of the meeting dominated their conversation.

They chose to continue as planned but soon came to regret the choice. While in the midst of a time-saving detour across open water, the party was swept up in sudden storm. Immediately the Ojibwas' thoughts turned to the grandfather. They called out to him to spare them and offered him more tobacco. But the storm did not cease, so the party turned to the other traditional Ojibwa sacrifice to placate the water gods and other angry forces.[88] The leaders of the party tied up the legs of their dogs and threw the squirming animals into the water, hoping that the Manitou Kinibic would "satisfy his hunger" with the bodies of the bound hounds. When the wind refused to die down, it became clear that the Manitou had not forgiven Henry's insulting behavior. One of the principal Ojibwas called out to the angered god and begged him not to harm the Indians for the sake of Henry's foolish blunder. After all, Henry was "absolutely an Englishman, and of kin neither to him nor to them."[89]

For the Ojibwas, Henry's European-style method of dealing with snakes had yielded dangerous consequences. Henry may have been able to paddle a canoe well, live on travel rations with little complaint, wear the same light and easy attire of his Indian companions, and even speak their language. But his inability or unwillingness to relate to the world around them in safest and most appropriate manner made him a liability.

In renouncing their connection to this inconvenient party member, the Ojibwa leader echoed, however intentionally or unintentionally the rhetoric of contemporary Nativist prophets. During the war years of the 1750s and 1760s, Nativist messages of spiritual revival and renewal blazed through Indian communities west of the English Atlantic settlements.[90] Like other tribes, the Ojibwas of Sault Sainte Marie heard the messages of Indians' separation from the Whites and spiritual revival and in varying degrees took them to heart and acted on them. When the Indians made their offering to the snake, they also asked him to stay in their country and "not return among the English."[91] This last request perhaps hints that these people were feeling a little uneasy about their new English alliance. By labeling Henry "absolutely an Englishman," the Ojibwa headman seems to have alluded to deep and perhaps even unconquerable differences between Indians and Whites, as preached by many Great Lakes' Nativists. But these prophets also decried the consumption of the alcohol these Ojibwas clearly hoped to get at the end of their trip. It is impossible to know whether the members of the party were themselves Nativists, however conflicted, or whether they were perhaps divided over this highly charged issue of the day. By this possible use of logic of Nativism, the Ojibwa leader may have offered a creative solution to a thorny problem.

The argument that Henry, by dint of his "absolute" Englishness, was indeed not part of the group—or at this point part of the grandfather's or the Indians' family—suggested that the protocols governing snake encounters could apply unevenly to members of a travel party. The Ojibwa headman essentially reversed the unified vision he acted on when he earlier asked the grandfather to overlook Henry's disrespect. At that moment, the same snake protocols applied to every member of the party. But the crisis-driven water-bound renunciation of Henry as kin—quite a step considering that other Ojibwas recognized Henry as an adopted kinsman—effectively recognized that there could be more than one way to approach a snake and that the ramifications could fall on party members differently. This was a marked departure from the anxiety exhibited by James Adair's snake-protecting companions, and a form of accommodation that held the potential to allow Indians to live their lives as they chose in a universe they could still control despite White interference.

If Henry's Ojibwa companion was willing to envision a way of travel that included different snake protocols, some Indians went so far as to adopt aspects of European preferences. A few European travelers reported instances of their Native companions killing rattlesnakes in ways that were quite at odds with the care and deliberation so often described by European travelers. In his 1752 rattlesnake essay, Peter Kalm claimed that some Indians of his experience had begun to kill the animals as Europeans did.[92] Kalm's observation may serve in part to explain the actions of a group of French-allied Algonquians and Senecas traveling with François Picquet and party on the great Niagara Portage Path in July 1751. The party encountered a "throng of rattlesnakes" in a pit near the road. It was too late in the season for the snakes to have been in a winter den, but these may have been hiding together to avoid the day's heat. Whereas the Ojibwas traveling with Alexander Henry in the same area saw their encounter as a chance to commune, the Indians with Picquet saw these snakes as providing the opportunity for some good sport. The young men in the party, "even though many [were] bare-legged," quickly jumped into the throng and began to kill the snakes as fast as they could. The combined din of shouting "animated" Indians and fiercely hissing rattlers terrified the Frenchmen. By the time the dust settled, the score was Indians forty-two, snakes zero; the snakes did not even manage to land a single bite.[93]

There had always been Indians who killed snakes. But the actions of these young men seem out of kilter with the attitudes of other contemporary Native travelers. There are many possible explanations for this uncharacteristic bout of Indian snake killing. The French-allied Natives may have been acting to please or protect their French companions, they may have acted on an obscure and undocumented protocol missed by Europeans, or perhaps Picquet, in his fear, misidentified the snakes as rattlers rather than some other snake not deserving of the same respect. Certainly, the profligate killing by these young men better resembles the work of Kalm's "old Swede" and other European herpecides than it does the respect of Adair's and Henry's Indian companions. Superficially, it supports Kalm's assertion that by the 1750s some Indians had adopted the European stance toward rattlesnakes.

Recognizing that Indian Christianity took many varied and often unpredictable forms, a Christian Indian would theoretically have broken with the cosmology that informed the traditional respectful attitude toward these snakes. If one accepted the prevailing Christian vision of the universe, then snakes could not be grandfathers or other kin, and they could not be powerful manitous or messengers from other planes. Instead, they would be simply animals put on earth for man's use and as vulnerable as any other. Seen in the light of religious conversion, the snake killing may have been the act of Indians who shared a view of the cosmos with their French companions. But this is not to say that these eager snake killers may have adopted the Europeans' longstanding fear of snakes. In fact, the glee and mirth with which these Indians jumped into the snake pit contrasts sharply with what Picquet and his cowering companions were feeling. These Indians may have wanted to kill the snakes, but they did so showing the same lack of fear that reverential Indian snake handlers exhibited while employing the same body of snake knowledge. Their skillful ducking and dodging, and the unevenness of the conflict's death tally, demonstrate that while these men may have been snake killers in the European fashion, they did so in their own way and with a seeming familiarity with the beasts.

Rattlesnake killing served as an opportunity to show off to friends, both Native and French. Like the Osage man tattooed with his prize snake, these young men may have sought to prove their bravery in combat with a respected and worthy foe. The confidence of their actions and the close nature of their combat differ dramatically from the European snake killers' tension and distance. There were Europeans who took great manly pride in snake killing; a Dr. Alexander Hamilton claimed that his having killed a rattlesnake entitled him to a colonel's commission because it was the custom that "a man has no right to that dignity until he has killed a rattlesnake."[94] But even the snake murders of William Byrd—a man singularly concerned with the being the hardy traveler—did not involve jumping into a pit of snakes to kill them by hand. Even while killing rattlesnakes, as the Europeans would, these Indian travelers employed a fearlessness and intimacy beyond that of their European fellows.

Indian and European travelers alike approached snakes in ways that accorded with their overall understanding of the beasts, their powers and habits, and the world and cosmos in which they acted. Travelers saw their own methods of coping with snakes as the best way to ensure a safe and healthy trip for themselves and for others. But like many aspects of the colonial encounter, these differing methods came into conflict when only one of the many competing visions could prevail in a given situation. Travel partners borrowed and appropriated aspects of each other's snake-handling methods, but this borrowing was generally somewhat one-sided and largely limited to Europeans taking on the use of protective roots, accepting some elements of Native explanations of the snakes' hunting techniques, and seeing dealing with the snakes as a form of manly bravery or, in Revolutionary hands, a symbol of defiance. Even so, this borrowing fell far short of creating a shared, hybridized style of snake interaction or melded meanings, and throughout the colonial era, dealing with rattlesnakes was an occasion for conflict between native and European travel companions. Europeans used Indian snakebite cures, but separated them from the larger body of belief from which they derived. Similarly, some Indians may have taken up European-style snake killing, as Peter Kalm suggested and Picquet may have observed. But even if some Indians copied herpecidal logic, they did so with a confidence and fearlessness that defied the original European reasons for killing the beasts in the first place. For some Indians, like the Ojibwa headman traveling with Alexander Henry, a snake encounter provided the opportunity to explore the possibility of a travel world divided—a world in which one set of rules applied to some travelers and a different set to another group. For Henry, though, and so many Europeans before and after him, the best answer was to kill the snakes as soon as possible, and his determination showed him ready and willing to force that logic on all concerned. In all of these cases, travelers clashed over their differences, while also on occasion learning from each other and even appropriating what they saw as most useful within their own travel paradigms. But most importantly, rattlesnake encounters show how the trail's unique conditions brought out the larger tensions often underlying the relationships between Indian and European travel companions.

5

Sex, Difference, and the Ideal Traveler

While on a 1733 jaunt to visit his south Virginia land holdings and perhaps scout out some new ones and a mine or two, William Byrd II had a small accident with his horse. Lumbering along the narrow, well-wooded paths of Virginia's Southside, the horse knocked its rider into a tree. The result was a knee injury which "pained" Byrd "very much." Despite his throbbing knee, Byrd noted with some satisfaction that he "broke not the laws of traveling by uttering the least complaint."[1] At another point in the trip, Byrd derided one of his companions, noting the man's "impatient and peevish temper, equally unfit both for a traveler and a husband."[2] At yet another turn in the trail, the party discovered that a "very careless servant" had lost one of their axes. Once it was discovered, the miscreant was subjected to the dizzying effects of a blanket toss, whereby he was repeatedly thrown into the air and caught by his comrades by means of an outstretched blanket. Byrd wrote that by inflicting such a punishment he and his party "exercised the discipline of the woods."[3]

Throughout the trip, the lord of Westover seemed to be referring to a set of rules that defined the ideal traveler's temperament, sentiments, and behavior. These unwritten "laws of traveling," with their "discipline of the woods," were hardly a codified, universally accepted body of knowledge. Instead, they were part of the way Byrd fashioned his own ideal traveler, and himself as one, by sanctioning certain behaviors and prohibiting others. His vision of this ideal traveler grew from his values as a wealthy Tidewater Virginia planter, and in turn these rules helped to shape exactly what it was to be a member of that singular society. By noting who did and did not fit the bill, Byrd marked insiders from outsiders, the vulgar from the refined, the gentry from the lower orders, and himself from others. For Byrd and others of his background, the ideal traveler was male. His overt connection of "traveler" and "husband" makes clear that a traveler must be an independent *man*, able to dominate both wife and woods.[4] He must be able to keep a stoic and stolid outward appearance, neither showing too much weakness nor bothering his companions with his own petty sufferings. He must endure pain well, whether it be a bashed knee or a rotted tooth—like the one Byrd removed on the trail by tying it to a heavy log with a short string and then jumping forcefully into the air.[5] A traveler must be reserved and not "impatient" or "peevish," both of which were womanly or childish characteristics against which manliness was defined. Travelers, according to Byrd's rules, should be industrious, yet devout enough to respect the Sabbath. A traveler must also be ready and willing to submit himself to the "discipline of the woods" and subject his behavior to the scrutiny of his fellows, and to take his lumps as need be. In this travel regime, derision and competition served to both test travelers' limits and stigmatize those found wanting.

In addition to his flawed English companions, a small group of Tuscarora guides and hunters accompanied Byrd's party. These men also earned some comment from their planter companion. Byrd claimed that the Indians "have no distinction of days, but everyday a Sabbath." Byrd employed that old colonial canard (used against almost everyone and every class at one time or another) to claim that Indians were essentially lazy. They were, in Byrd's estimation, capable of extreme exertion when the need arose, such as when they went to war or "a-hunting," but exhibited a marked inclination toward "idleness and doing nothing to the purpose."[6]

Byrd's Indian companions left no journal or musings behind as a testament to how they evaluated their English companions and each other. But they did not appear completely silent in Byrd's writings, either. For example, when the Englishmen took Sunday off from their rigors in respect of the Sabbath, they still needed to eat. The Indian hunters went out on one Sunday and "brought a young doe back with them."[7] The contrast of reclining English and hunting Natives amused the hunters, who laughingly commented to their colonial fellows that it seemed the height of sloth and wastefulness to make a habit of "losing one day in seven."[8] On another Sunday, both English and Indian travel companions took time out to bathe in a nearby brook. When the Englishmen took to swimming, they did so in an awkward fashion involving striking out with "both hands together," resulting in a considerable amount of noise and splashing and producing very little in the way of forward motion.[9] The Tuscaroras, no doubt amused and a bit taken aback by this display, quickly stepped in to show the Virginians their own more efficient means of swimming, a technique that involved using their hands "alternately one after another." Even the proud Byrd had to admit that this method allowed the Indians "to swim both farther and faster than we do."[10] When the Virginians did not live up to what the Indian hunters saw as the standards of the ideal traveler, the Natives were quick to offer a correction.

Through following the "laws of traveling" or critiquing the loss of "one day in seven," Byrd and his Native companions constructed their identities as travelers and challenged their fellows. By enacting their rules and codes—however they defined them—they put their travel theories into action and created a context in which to judge themselves and their travel. Rules and codes also provided benchmarks against which travelers could gauge one another's merits and worth, through their own lenses, of course. Just as Native and European travelers tussled over whose vision should set the pace, course, and style of common travel, they also clashed over who was the better traveler and what standards should go into that judgment. These personal competitions took many forms. Travelers insulted each other, they argued over worldviews, and sometimes they came to blows over various rivalries. They also challenged each other to contests involving physical skill, all with an eye toward establishing who could best whom. In challenging one another in a variety of endeavors, common travelers both tested each others' limits, and outlined what they most prized in themselves, as travelers. Byrd's and the Tuscaroras' mutual criticism that the other was lazy, for example, revealed how both parties prized industriousness on the trail, yet failed to see that trait in their fellows. Such moments show what elements went into the construction of Indians' and Europeans' ideal traveler.

A specific type of travel-related manliness was a theme that came up in many of these competitions, in part because so many of the best-documented travelers and their guides were men. Strength, courage, adroitness, and useful knowledge were all manly virtues celebrated in many ways on all sides of the colonial divide, and these values took special form and had special value on the trail. Many travelers were quick to show that they had these traits and that their fellows lacked them.[11] Assertions of manliness were also products of anxiety over the possible merits of fellow travelers, or the possibilities of one's own failings, or about the rigors of travel itself. A gendered anxiety surfaced in the writings of several European travelers, which manifested itself in how they approached travel challenges, and most especially in how they marginalized Native women's participation on their travels.

When travelers ridiculed one another, demeaned the other's manliness, or competed over skills, they revealed what they most valued in their own ideal travelers. But common travel added a special sting to weakness and inability. One traveler's mistakes and foolishness ultimately presented a risk for all members of the party; therefore, pointing out errors and correcting them could be more than academic—it could mean the difference between life and death. Throughout the colonial era, Indians and Europeans located and discussed the differences between them. Physicality, attire, cosmology, and skin color all served as categories through which differences could be codified and comprehended, each one blending in time with other seemingly defining traits. On the seventeenth- and eighteenth-century trail, though, what often mattered most were those habits and traits which bore the most direct effect on travel. Byrd's concern at his Tuscarora companions' "idleness," and their perception of Virginian laziness and poor swimming skills, were the kinds of differences which seemed most relevant. To be sure, these were part of much larger explorations of difference as Europeans' theories of race gradually hardened and Indian peoples refined and built new conceptions of who these strangers were. When Native and European travel companions competed with and ridiculed each other, they teased out the differences which mattered most, and thus created outlines of selves and others. All told, the trail created both the close contact and context for Native and European contests over the fundamental elements of personal identities. Whether through contest, ridicule, or competition, Native and European travel companions formed opinions about each other, and in so doing showed in relief the traveler's traits they most prized in themselves.[12]

Many Indian travelers made it clear that in their eyes, some Europeans lacked the traveler's fundamental skills, like knowing how and what to eat on the trail. A priest's need to blow on his portion of piping-hot cornmeal porridge elicited great laughter from his companions, who, according to the burned cleric, overlooked the fact that "neither my tongue nor my palate was iron-clad and hardened like theirs."[13] English travelers in the company of Chickasaws were likely to be called *shúkàpa* or *akanggàpa*, meaning "swine eater" and "eater of dunghill fouls," respectively, for their habit of eating dirty barnyard animals rather than good clean wild ones.[14] A Frenchman's preference for shooting quail seemed absurd to his Naansis companions when there were "fat young turkeys" to be had at every bend in the road.[15] A European neophyte's inability to walk well on snowshoes caused considerable amusement among his fellows when he "rolled to the bottom" of a slope and came up covered head-to-toe in snow.[16] The weakness of a Jesuit forced to "carry as heavy burdens as [he] could" resulted in a torrent of laughter and derision from his Native escorts, who suggested that perhaps they should "call a child" to carry both the priest and his burdens.[17] After an English fur trader and his Chipewyan guides survived a harrowing canoe wreck in which they lost almost all of their possessions, the Englishman pulled out his small pocketknife to use it as a striker for starting a much-needed fire. The Chipewyans were astounded to see that he had saved such an item and remarked upon "how avaricious a white man must be, who rushing on death takes care of his little knife."[18] A French priest, unaccustomed to the close sleeping quarters of a trailside bivouac, showed that he had "no sense" when he started hitting one of his slumbering companions after the man had inadvertently rolled onto the sleeping cleric. The father immediately began "crying out *aché aché*," thinking the man to be one of the party's many dogs. The bewildered Native simply replied, "It is not a dog, it is I."[19]

Common travel also allowed some Indians to solidify their views of some European travelers as being disorganized and imperceptive. When chaos erupted in Nicholas Cresswell's 1775 party of Ohio River paddlers, the reaction of Native observers was laughter. In the midst of a June day's travel, the party believed themselves about to be attacked by several oncoming canoes full of Indians, whose paddles became guns in the British travelers' terrified imaginations. They fumbled for their own guns, only to find them "unfit for use by the wet," and in their haste to get "prepared for an engagement," all of their equipment and a "great part" of their provisions were hastily "hoved overboard."[20] Adding to the confusion was the response of the more fatalistic party members, one of whom, much to Cresswell's anti-Catholic chagrin, "laid down in the bottom of the canoe, begun to tell his rosaries, and howled in Irish," while another began "weeping, praying, said ave Mary's in abundance at the same time hugging a little wooden crucifix he pulled from his bosom most heartily."[21] Once the Indian canoes glided close enough, the unnerved colonials saw that they had misread the intentions of this group of Delaware men and women, and realized that their fears were groundless. Cresswell recorded the amused Delawares' reaction to the jittery Europeans' preparations; "they had seen our confusion and laughed at us for our fears."[22]

The inabilities of the French priests and inexperienced explorers traveling to the Mississippi with Pierre Espirit Radisson annoyed rather than amused the party's fourteen French-allied Algonquians, who "complained much that the French could not swim."[23] They could not have been too pleased, either, at their untutored companions' insistence upon marking each arrival and departure with an inadvertently enemy-alerting gunshot or trumpet blast. When the Frenchmen were not busy broadcasting their position via song and horn to the feared Iroquois, they were trying to hamper the Indians' hunting. At one point early in the trip the Frenchmen warned a group of hunters to "look to themselves" with care as they set off to get some game. The Indians laughed at this misplaced caution and shot back that the French "were women," and that the Iroquois would "durst not set on them."[24] A little while later, the bulk of the French finally turned back, finding the trip simply too much for them. Radisson and his brother-in-law, Jean Baptiste des Groseilliers, both seasoned travelers in the Indian style, opted to continue the trek, and noted with some satisfaction that the Indians had no criticism of their travel skills. Radisson also noted that when the rest of the French left, the Indians were "not sorry for their departure."[25] When Europeans mastered some or many of the Native ideal-traveler's skills, they could be valued companions, but, more often, Indians saw them as ill-mannered stumblebums.

For their part, Europeans were quick to mock and deride Indian travel habits and skills when they differed from their own, or made them look foolish in European eyes. European observations, like Native ones, reveal the degree to which the trail served as a place for sustained close observation. Radisson himself offered a critique of his Algonquian companions' swimming abilities which, unlike Byrd's recounting, seemed to suggest that it was the Indians who were the poorer swimmers. He noted that his companion swam "like a water dog" and that "all the wildmen swim like water dogs, not as we swim."[26] Radisson did not offer an explanation of his own swimming technique, but his allusion to a widespread practice of dog paddling seems less than flattering at best, and bestializing at worst. Although many Indians quickly became superb horsemen soon after the animals first pounded American ground, some Europeans, no doubt more proud of their abilities when mounted than when riding shank's mare, did not miss the chance to poke fun at those Indians who failed to exhibit the best dressage. William Byrd, for example, found the sight of an Indian mounted on a horse laughable—a harsh critique indeed, given eighteenth-century Virginians' close association of horsemanship and social status. Upon witnessing the arrival of a group of Saponi "grandees," Byrd recorded that the well-respected tribal leaders rode their mounts "more awkwardly than sailors, and the women who sat astride." Byrd went on to suggest that the Saponis themselves may have felt uncomfortable with the beasts because they refused to "mount their ponys" until they were far from English eyes and ridicule.[27] The Huguenot traveler John Fontaine also noted that his Indian companions, in 1716, were "not accustomed to ride" the horses he and his party took for granted as a means of transportation. Fontaine and his well-heeled Virginian fellows took great joy in watching one "Indian chief" strip naked at the banks of the Meherrin River and lead his horse across the ford, rather than riding high and dry in English fashion. This different approach to crossing the river made the travelers "all merry for a while."[28]

When crossing the Hudson River in the fall of 1679, Jasper Danckaerts and his companions had a good laugh at the expense of a local Indian who, in their view, did not properly understand the economics of ferry usage. Just as a full ferry was about to put in for the far shore, an Indian came up and "asked the skipper if he might go over with him." What resulted was an odd exchange over the price of the ride. The ferryman replied that he was too laden with "freight" and could not fit the man on board. But the Indian quickly inquired how much people paid for their rides. Upon learning that the price was "six stivers" in locally produced strings of shell beads (one of the many currencies in use in Dutch New York), the Indian responded "I will give you seven." This struck the Dutch travelers as a ludicrous bargain. As they saw it, the Indian had "valued himself less" by offering more money for the same service, yet had "bound himself to pay more than the others."[29]

The inability to ride a horse, cross a river, or swim well could all be the basis for one traveler laughing at or chiding another for not living up to one's model of the ideal traveler. From these varied instances, intercultural travel companions learned valuable lessons about who they were traveling with, but they also revealed a few elements of different Native and imported versions of the ideal traveler. Ideal Native travelers should be hardened to the trail's conditions and cuisine; they should be able to tell the good from the bad and know which game to take and which to avoid; they should be strong and able to carry their share of a group's burden with ease; and they should be easy to be with, either asleep or awake. European travelers also prized skill and savvy, although perhaps with different emphasis than their Native companions. "Fat turkeys" may have been the better catch in Native eyes, but a gentleman's fowling piece was better employed on more delicate game. Keeping one's possessions on or nearby at all times ensured that they would be there later when most needed. And when one was so reliant on such items, it only made sense to do all one could to keep them clean and dry both on water and at fords. Likewise, trumpet blasts and singing were signs of good military order and hearty comradeship and were to be prized. A good traveler should also be ready to cut a shrewd bargain whenever entering into commerce for goods or services.

But if versions of the ideal traveler diverged over the particulars of horsemanship and ferry fares, they could also converge on some common ideas. When Byrd condemned his companion for exhibiting traits unbecoming both a "traveler" and a "husband," he unambiguously suggested that travel was a manly endeavor.[30] In many respects, his Tuscarora companions might have agreed, although their version of manliness may have focused less on Virginia-style domination and refinement than did Byrd's. Travel demanded physical skill and courage, a keen eye for opportunities and potential problems, and an understanding of the world and how it worked. These demands made the trail an optimal place for male travelers to test their manliness against both the demands of travel and against other travelers often quite different from themselves. When visions of traveling differed, travel companions were left to fight for the supremacy of their own visions or to scratch their heads at the oddness, stupidity, or ungainliness of their fellows. When manliness was on the line, the result was often direct competition to see who was the better traveler and the better man. As with other conflicts over how best to travel, manly competition contributed to the tenor of travel relationships, and in some dramatic cases, competing gendered visions for better or worse played into how a given trip took shape. But these types of competitions, occurring as they did within the intimate context of shared travel, were also part of the process of observing, testing, and evaluating which took place wherever and whenever Indians and Europeans met.

Both Indian and European travelers alike often enjoyed certain elementary forms of manly competition which could easily be played out on the trail. Indeed, an interest in some elemental contests came into play in some of the earliest North American encounters. John Davis's crew, in 1586, for example, interpreted the Davis Straight Eskimo custom of leaping in greeting as a form of physical challenge, and Davis immediately set his own men "to leape with them." He noted with some pride that his men "did over-leape them." Davis recorded that "from leaping they went to wrestling," where the English sea dogs discovered the Eskimos to be "strong and nimble" and to have such "skill in wrestling" that the Natives were able to "cast" some of the crew's best competitors.[31]

Davis's readiness to interpret Native behavior as challenge may have been a misread, but other travel incidents reveal how competition could serve as two-way means of assessment. And given the trail's demands and the basis of so many intercultural travel relationships, it is not surprising that practical skills like running and shooting should come into focus. In 1636, a young Frenchman named Godefoy beat a Huron companion in a footrace. Although the priest who recorded the incident noted that Godefoy was "of light and agile body," the Hurons themselves were astounded to see a Frenchman run so fast, as they had come to see the French as "turtles in comparison" with themselves.[32] On returning from a raid into Iroquoia, "all the young men" of the mixed Algonquian and French party were challenged by a captive Iroquoian to "a race, either with snowshoes on their feet, or without snowshoes." Several men in the party "entered the lists against him," but in the end the Iroquois warrior, soon to be burned to death near Quebec, "carried off the victory."[33] That Indians were speedy runners with remarkable endurance became something of a truism among Europeans, many of whom had considerable trouble keeping up. As one traveler wrote, his companions could run for upwards of a dozen miles, and "without any seeming toil, they would stretch on, leave us out of sight, and out wind any horse."[34] But Native speed was not always envied, and such compliments were also roundabout ways of saying that Indians were in many ways no better than the horse they could "out wind." Likewise, one 1673 English traveler in Virginia claimed that "Indians vallour consists most in their heeles for he that can run best is accounted ye the best man."

Good runners, yes, but to this observer, speed was the handmaiden of cowardice, as he insinuated that "vallour" consisted of standing up to a threat.[35] But in the long run, such value-laden dismissals were cold comfort for European travelers huffing and puffing in an Indian companion's wake.

As Indians became masters of firearms in their own right, guns themselves could be used to see who was the better man. One late-eighteenth-century Ojibwa man, for example, was much amused to watch a group of Englishmen try repeatedly to take down a loon which sat about 150 yards from them. As shot after shot missed its mark, the Ojibwa laughed at the hunters "and told them they were old women." The Englishmen, their manhood impugned, challenged their ridiculer to try his own luck at the obstinate bird, "which he instantly did." First "taking his gun and resting it against a tree," he then fired a well-aimed shot, which pierced "the loon right through the neck." The feat of arms was made all the more impressive by the loon's reputation among Europeans as a singularly difficult bird to hit; Frenchmen had even adopted the bird's Ojibwa name *maunk* and nicknamed the bird with the French verb *manquer*, meaning "to fail."[36]

In a few cases, travel companions even turned singing into a competition. A group of Algonquians dining with Gabriel Sagard and some Hurons went out of their way to show the priest and his allies that they could "sing and fence as well as our men."[37] A group of Frenchmen, camped near a party of Abenakis in Maine's backwoods, took the Indians' singing and dancing as a sort of challenge. Led by a priest, the French began to sing hymns in an attempt to outdo the musical Natives. After running through their hymn repertoire, the French choir turned to secular songs "with which they were familiar." When these too were finally exhausted without any visible impact on the Native revelers, the French "began to mimic the singing and dancing" of their Abenaki neighbors. This last performance did the trick, and the startled Indians stopped their own vocalizations and "began to listen" to their French imitators. But no sooner had the Indians stopped singing than the French did the same, waiting until the Indians began again to restart their parody. The attending priest admitted that this schoolyard prank was "really very comical"; no one recorded whether the Indians enjoyed the joke.[38]

Singing was also a vehicle for the 1700 French Mississippi mapping party, led by Pierre LeMoyne d'Iberville, to show their mettle to their Indian companions. Bad timing and perhaps some poor or mischievous guiding led the party into a region flooded with cold water up to their "bellies and armpits." In such fatiguing travel conditions, a number of the Frenchmen "were so seized with chills in the water that they climbed into trees to get some relief."[39] Throughout their soggy ordeal, the French did not stop "singing and laughing," partially to keep up their morale but also because, as their leader noted, "We wish to show our guide that fatigue does not distress us."[40] He might have added that he probably also did not want his reading audience to think the less of them either.

For the most part these small contests over running, jumping, shooting, singing, and knowledge were good-natured, or at least not motivated by anger. Competitors certainly took each others' measure through these contests and tried their best to win the day, but whether winners or losers in these instances, the parties let the matter drop. But it was not always thus. In some travel relationships, personal competition, different versions of the ideal traveler, and the trail's hardships combined and became the basis of outright hostility.

When tensions were high between travel companions, the simplest actions could lead to a fight. Perceived and intended slights could become real issues between travel companions. When some Chipewyan Indians accompanying Alexander Mackenzie to the Arctic Ocean, in 1789, began to make fun of the way that his Canadian "foreman" used his paddle, the result was an angry exchange of words.[41] While passing time with the Sioux in 1767, Jonathan Carver set about some routine maintenance on the canoe he would soon need to take from the Mississippi's headwaters to the trading post at Michilmacinac. While he was busy, a group of young women approached him and inquired as to whether their "sweethearts" could use the vessel to cross the river from the far bank. The boat being in poor shape, Carver refused. The women then set about finding another vessel in which to ferry their paramours across the river. This took some time, and when the young men inquired about the delay, they were informed that the "white man would not let them have his canoe." Incensed at the seeming selfishness of this act, and no doubt a bit fired up over their unwanted wait, one of the young men "in a great passion" ran up to the canoe "and with his hatchet gave it several strokes which damaged it greatly."[42]

Despite Carver's unfulfilled demand that the offender be beaten, no blows were exchanged. But some confrontations went much further. Radisson found that the "long familiarity" he had with one Iroquois canoe mate "breeded contempt." The two would "take nothing from one another," and it became a common sight on that 1656 trip for Radisson and his partner to "go together by the ears" and fight "very often" until both were fully "covered in blood." The rest of the party enjoyed the drama and only interceded when they saw one of the combatants "take either gun or sword." Their fights were so unremitting that even the hard work of moving their boat through the water offered no respite. On more than one occasion, the rest of the travelers were treated to the scene of their own Punch and Judy flailing away with their paddles, "flying water at one another."[43] A Soussaki man traveling with a French Jesuit and some traders, in 1672, took a beating from one of the more-skilled Frenchmen when the two engaged in "fisticuffs." Later the Indian tried to use his skills as a marksman to best his companions. He boasted that he "could shoot better" than the French, and challenged the black robe to a shooting match. The priest demurred, claiming that as a priest he "did not pride [him]self upon being a hunter or a soldier; and that he could address himself" to other members of the party if he wished to fight." Remembering his earlier drubbing, the man backed off and "put an end to his chatter."[44]

Time together on the trail also provided opportunities to ask questions about how other people understood their world. Some of these were friendly and respectful exchanges.[45] For example, William Byrd used the quiet of an October night in 1728 to chat with his Saponi hunter, Ned Bearskin, about the latter's religious beliefs. Bearskin outlined, and Byrd recorded, a vision of the afterlife that mixed traditional and Christian elements, including divided paths leading to lands where "every month is May" and "the earth brings forth corn spontaneously without labour" to be eaten by people eternally young and strong, or to a place guarded by a "hideous old woman whose head is cover'd with rattle-snakes instead of tyresses" where "'tis always winter," and "all the people are old, have no teeth and yet are very hungry."[46] What was most surprising to Byrd was not the details of Bearskin's cosmology but rather the "freedom" with which he related it.[47] The closeness of travel had allowed Bearskin to let his guard down and share some of his most deeply held beliefs with his fellows. But for some who did the same, the result was merciless ridicule and confrontation. When fur trader David Thompson asked his Cree companion why he always guarded closely the elements of his faith, the man bluntly replied, "you white men always laugh and treat with contempt what we have heard and learned from our fathers; why should we expose ourselves to be laughed at."[48] Thompson protested his own innocence of this charge, evidently forgetting that he had earlier lambasted the "pretensions" of his guides when they claimed that their singing had calmed a three-day-long steady wind. "If you possess such power," Thompson had demanded, "why did you not sing on the first day of our being here?"[49]

The shoe fit just as well on the other foot. When Thompson wanted to take scientific measurements of a freshly killed moose, his guides made it clear that they did not approve of such activity and would not allow it "for fear" that the animals' "Manitou would be angry."[50] The same hunters also heaped scorn on Thompson's explanation for what motivated animals' behavior. The fur trader explained that "instinct" or "the free and voluntary actions of an animal for its self preservation" was driving these beasts' conduct. His companions were not persuaded and replied, "Oh, oh, then you think this herd of deer rushed forward over deep swamps, in which some perished, the other ran over them; down steep banks to break their necks; swam across rivers, where the strong drowned the weak; went a long way through the woods where they had nothing to eat, merely to take care of themselves." When faced with the explanation, the Crees came to their own conclusion about the reasoning power of their companion and his people: "you white people, you look like wise men, and talk like fools."[51]

Practical jokes were also a way that travelers could test boundaries and win small victories over their companions. Some japes were simple tricks which preyed on the ignorance of a companion. For example, when, in 1661, Radisson and Groseilliers met with a group of Sioux near Lake Superior, their companions' unfamiliarity with gunpowder occasioned a startling trick. As was true of many Native travelers, the Sioux were in the habit of making small offerings of powdered tobacco by sprinkling it on a fire. For reasons unstated, the Frenchmen decided to surprise their new friends by pouring some black powder on the council fire, intending to make them believe that was some of their tobacco. The resulting explosion and cloud of sulfurous white smoke "made the brands fly from one side to the other." It also made the Sioux fly away from the fire "without any further delay," having never seen "a sacrifice of tobacco so violent." The Sioux were so shocked that they concluded that the two French travelers were "the devils of the earth."[52] Several decades later a group of Missouri Indians, impressed by gunpowder's capabilities, asked some French traders in their company "how the French came by this powder?" The hunters disingenuously answered that it was specially cultivated in fields and "harvested like indigo and millet in America." The industrious Missouris, believing they had found the key to end their reliance on French powder suppliers, saw to it that some was carefully planted in a well-tended, specially guarded field. When in time no powder plants bloomed, the Indians presumably realized that they had been hoodwinked. But as the Frenchman who recorded this tale of deception noted, "it should be remembered that Indians are fooled just once and they never forget it." The next French trader to pass through the area was robbed blind by the Missouris in retaliation. When he complained to the local headman, he was simply told that he would have to wait to receive justice until "the Indians had harvested the powder planted upon the advice of his countryman."[53]

Hudson's Bay man Samuel Hearne became the brunt of a singularly grim joke during his Arctic coastal trip, in 1771. His guides had planned to raid an Eskimo encampment near the mouth of the Coppermine River, despite

Hearne's objections that the "scheme" was fraught with dangers as well as "trouble and fatigue."⁵⁴ They reacted to Hearne's caution with "great marks of derision" and accused him of being "afraid of the Eskimaux." Hearne protested that for all he cared his companions could "render the name and race of the Eskimaux extinct," and ultimately had to realize that it was more in his interest to say nothing more about the raid, which finally went off as planned.⁵⁵ But during the raid, two of the Indians found a grim moment to tease Hearne about his initial reluctance to attack the Eskimos.

In his journal, Hearne distanced himself from the raiders' "barbarity," but at the time he was right in the thick of it, watching in horror as naked Eskimo men, women, and children fled their tents and ran anywhere they could to escape the violent, surprise assault. At one point a "young girl, seemingly about eighteen years of age," ran straight at him in her frantic desire to escape her pursuers. To Hearne's shock, two of his companions speared the young woman in her side and she fell at Hearne's feet and "twisted round" the Englishman's legs so that he could not "disengage" himself from her "dying grasps." The whole scene was too much for Hearne, who immediately "solicited very hard for her life," thus breaking his vow and once again risking his esteem in his companions' eyes. The two warriors "stuck both their spears through her body, and transfixed her to the ground." They then turned their attentions to Hearne. With the shrieks and screams of war all around and the dying exertions of a young woman "twining around their spears like an eel," the two men looked Hearne "sternly in the face" and began to make fun of his apparent weakness, suggesting that perhaps their companion "wanted an Eskimaux wife."⁵⁶

The Chipewyan taunts touch on a gendered anxiety which underscored many of these very personal contests. Implicit in the Chipewyans' words was a critique of their surveyor companion's bravery; after all, Hearne not only refused to participate in the raid, but also tried to stop it—it was logical to conclude that he was weak-kneed. The Chipewyans tellingly couched their gibes in a way that combined manliness and sexuality and bundled Hearne's unwillingness to fight with his compassion for the fatally skewered Eskimo girl, and turning them into an allegation of sexual desire. The Chipewyans thus brought questions about Hearne's sexuality into their small dispute, and did so in a way which maximized Hearne's discomfort with the situation.

Discomfort, awkwardness, and singling out like that which Hearne suffered all could bring out an underlying anxiety which many European men felt while on the trail with Native companions. Another meaning-rich example of this is the way European travelers reacted to a perceived, but often unintended, challenge, implicit in the widespread Native practice of welcoming guests by bodily carrying them.⁵⁷ Being carried by an Indian physically incommoded European travelers, but also forced them into a situation which in a subtle but very real way, suggested a diminution of European manhood. Teetering awkwardly on an Indian's shoulders, Native head wedged firmly between European thighs, or being carried like a child in Native arms, suggested for many Europeans an uncomfortably diminished manliness in a variety of ways.

Indians who carried did so with a few different techniques, ranging from "grasping" a guest "under the arms as though to help [him] walk" to picking travelers up and carrying them "bodily in their arms."⁵⁸ Recording such acts allowed writers to both flatter and bestialize Indians by expounding upon the "bignesse and stature" of America's Natives, which rendered such attention small exertions.⁵⁹ But many European travelers had mixed reactions when the same strong Native arms reached out to carry a new arrival into a village, over a rushing stream, out of a canoe, or into a council meeting. Some travelers did not seem to mind, and perhaps enjoyed the chance to rest their legs. Certainly the Native connection between carrying and honored-status flattered the egos of the carried, and writing about these moments allowed Europeans to portray themselves as men of great stature in Native eyes. Also, the natural European analogy to horse and rider served to elevate the European rider and denigrate the Native beast. Etienne Bourgomont, for example, showed no objection to being carried "into the dwellings" of Kansas Indian chiefs. Likewise, Jean Baptiste Bienville went quietly when Natchitoches men "carried [him] on their shoulders" to visit their headman; as did Robert Salford also, who had no complaints when a South Carolina Native carried him "on his shoulders over any of the branches of creekes or plashy corners of marshes in our way."⁶⁰

But while some Europeans were glad to take the proffered ride, there were others who found it too uncomfortable, too undignified, or even too demeaning to endure and so "would not suffer" to be carried in their Native companions' arms.⁶¹

The only times European travelers physically carried others were those when the human cargo was very young, very aged, as when Louis Hennepin carried a sixty-five-year-old Father Gabriel, or when they were ill or wounded as when Alexander Mackenzie carried an ailing young guide on his back in order to get across a river.⁶² These associations of illness, incapacity, and infancy must have swirled in a European traveler's mind as he reeled on an Indian's shoulders. When Father St. Cosme's Arkansas guides insisted on carrying him and his fellows into town during their 1698 visit, the priest teetered on his porters' shoulders as the man "was sinking under his burden." The prospect of making a humiliating and painful fall, coupled with the awkwardness and even the discomforting psychosexual dynamics of having an Indian man's head set between his legs so distressed the priest that he "got down in spite" of his overloaded companion's wishes and "walked up the hill" unattended. Only after being "compelled" to remount did he allow himself to be carried into town.[63] Nicolas Perrot invoked European metallurgical skills when demurring a ride offered by his Macouten companions. Since he and his colleagues were able to "shape" iron," he assured the Indians that "they had the strength to walk" unaided.[64] For Perrot, carrying carried with it a perceived negative critique of European abilities in general, and he was not prepared to be demeaned by Native habits. La Salle and his party also protested when their Caddoan hosts insisted on carrying them, despite the fact that one of them, Joutel, by his own admission "was of a pretty large size" and loaded down with "clothes, a firelock, a case of pistols, powder and ball, a kettle, and other implements." This must have been quite a sight, since Joutel was reportedly taller than his carrier and it took the aid of two others to hold up the Frenchman's feet, which otherwise "would have hung upon the ground."[65]

A loss of personal control through physical discomfort, an embarrassing loss of dignity, a perceived challenge to one's strength and manhood, and perhaps even some sexual anxiety, all lurked behind some Europeans' dislike of being carried by an Indian, however well-meaning the carriers were. Also, not every carrying technique neatly fit the horse-and-rider metaphor so neatly. As discomfited as Joutel, Perrot, and St. Cosme must have felt at the prospect of mounting an Indian's back, slightly more anxiety attached itself to the thought of being carried in an Indian's arms with, as one initiate described it, his "feet in the air."[66] Jacques Cartier offered a fleeting glimpse into the issues that may have been lurking in the minds of European travelers on an Indian's back or in his arms. Cartier described how, in 1536, the men of Hochelaga picked him up in their arms "as easily as if he had been a six-year-old."[67] Herein lay the central problem for some Europeans. If riding an Indian was at best reassuringly like riding a horse, then being cradled in Indian arms was uncomfortably infantilizing. This was a bigger problem than one might expect, since being a child or a boy was essentially the opposite of being a man, meaning that what was intended as an act of kindness or respect was in part received as a diminution of manhood.[68] It is telling that when the Venetian geographer, cartographer, and travel-narrative editor Giovanni Batistta Ramusio produced his 1550s print of Cartier's Hochelaga map and incidents from the visit, he chose to replace Cartier's recorded infantilizing (and therefore unmanly) ride with the image of two Frenchmen riding in style on the backs of two Hochelagans—a pose not recorded by Cartier at all.[69] Presumably, the European print-buying public preferred to see Indians as beasts of burden and not nursemaids to the exploration heroes such prints celebrated.

Gendered anxieties like these surfaced most prominently in the ways that European men dealt with and wrote about the Native women they met on the trail. Native men generally loomed larger in European travelers' experiences and writing than did women. But as Samuel Hearne's failed Coppermine River trip showed, women were often vital for American travel, even if many Europeans were unwilling or unable to see as much. Like Hearne, many Europeans marginalized women travelers, first by ignoring or working around their abilities, and then by writing them out of their stories.[70]

This was part of the way Europeans constructed the trail and travel as manly and also touched on tensions about being their own ideal travelers. Reliance on women implied a deficient manliness on the part of the traveler and damaged the idea of the trail as somehow male (a problem which itself further jeopardized European travelers' manliness). For many colonial writers, descriptions of Native women as the village's principal agriculturalists, or "squaw drudges" hauling loads like mules, were coded ways in which Europeans suggested that all was not right in Native America. This was a place of inversions, and as such was ripe and ready for colonial improvement by those who better understood things as they were supposed to be—namely, Europeans.[71] But on the trail, these issues became more personal, and what emerged was a gendered anxiety centered on European manliness in travel. Native women played many roles as travelers, depending on how labor was distributed in their society, and women were every bit as skilled in fulfilling their travel roles as their male counterparts in fulfilling theirs were. But when it came to common travel, European travelers limited as much as they could the roles women would play in their own exploits.

All over North America Native women traveled just as did their menfolk. Indeed, many European chroniclers noted the presence of Indian women on the trail and remarked on their skill in the trail's arts. Europeans met Indian women paddling canoes up and down rivers. They noted the presence of women in large travel parties carrying water and baggage or preparing food and shelter. A smaller number of chroniclers went further, and noted the skill and steadfastness of women Indian travelers. English fur trader John Long, for example, noted that the women he met, all experienced in the hunting and travel associated with fur-trade life, knew the land and could draw maps with "great precision."[72] Native women could also get by on horseback pretty well, as one late-eighteenth-century Georgia traveler learned when he met a pair of women "driving ten very fat cattle" to market.[73] When one Frenchman found himself lost in the Canadian woods, it was a pair of female Huron travelers who tried to help him get back on track. Naturalist Lawson remarked that eastern Carolina Native women were "very handy with canoes, and will manage with great dexterity, and skill."[74] In his recording his travels, though, he avoided implying that he had been directly aided by any of these dexterous female paddlers.

In remarking on the fortitude of Native women, European travelers suggested that Indian femininity was somehow less feminine than an elite European ideal. The fact that Indian women could carry heavy burdens, walk long distances, and endure considerable pain and hardship with little more than a grimace all served to bestialize Native women and suggested another way in which Native social order was out of order, and therefore justifiably displaced. But travelers' accounts of female strength also implicitly (and uncomfortably) contrasted Indian female abilities with those of European male travelers. The comparison was not always favorable. One French Jesuit found "really astonishing" the endurance shown by one Algonquian woman "more than seventy years old." This woman had been captured by some Iroquois, who "tore out her toe-nails and finger-nails, and applied burning torches to several parts of her body." Yet despite these injuries this "poor old woman" managed to slip her bonds and escape her captors, making it back to her people. The recording priest was deeply impressed by her fortitude and did not miss the chance to turn her toward Christ. But while his description of her ordeal praised her endurance, it also betrayed an underlying anxiety over the fact that he and his colleagues generally did not fare as well in the face of their sufferings as this aged woman did. The priest's litany of trail woes—the "many thickets," the "armies of mosquitoes with which these countries are infested," and the difficulties of travel in a "wretched Hiroquois canoe"—reflected what the Jesuits themselves found most trying about American travel. When confronted with an elderly woman able to make a similar trip even though hungry, maimed, and burned, the most face-saving tactic was to emphasize her exceptional hardiness.[75]

Samuel Hearne's gender-rich narrative provides another example of this sort of uncomfortable implicit comparison. In the winter of 1772, Hearne was traveling with a large number of Chipewyan Indians led by Matonabbee. Along the trail, some of the party's young men found an odd, small hut which sheltered a young Dogrib woman who had made an escape from Athabascan captors. On her way home she found herself lost and forced to winter on the Barren Ground. Hearne reported that she had been "near seven months without seeing a human face," surviving on partridges, rabbits, and squirrels caught with numerous animal sinew snares she set in the area. She wore the skins of snared rabbits, which she had fashioned into a "suit of neat and warm clothing for the winter," and for all of her trials, Hearne thought she "did not seem to have been in want."[76] In fact, he described her as being "one of the finest women, of an Indian," that he had ever seen in all of his travels.[77]

The Chipewyan men responded to this hardy young woman by listening to her story and looking over her clothes, tools, and ample cache of rabbit meat. They then began to compete for her affections and wrestle each other to see "who should have her for a wife."[78] Hearne's response was to carefully detail the ways this woman caught her food, fashioned her clothes, and made fires, and to wonder at her grit, writing, "it is scarcely possible to conceive that a person in her forlorn situation" could have survived as well as she did.[79] Hearne was indeed impressed, and lavished his praise. But at the same time, his retelling contrasted this woman's fortitude with his own vulnerability and his earlier failures in a very similar situation. When confronted with the Barren Ground winter, Hearne was twice close to giving up the ghost and had to turn back or be rescued. While the Chipewyan men were certainly interested in this woman (and while at least one woman was somewhat resentful), there was no indication that they saw her as being uniquely remarkable for her endurance; after all, winter survival was very much part of Chipewyan life. By portraying this woman's abilities as exceptional, though, Hearne in effect buffered himself against the obvious implications about his own deficiencies.

Native women were not at all rare on the trail, and were often every bit the travelers their male counterparts were. Yet few European travelers were willing to retell their travel stories in ways which showed them as overly dependent on these women. This is in part a facet of selective story telling—leaving out the bits they did not want to report and making their stories fit their models. But the stories, in their selectivity, did reflect a trail reality. Colonial-era European male travelers generally overlooked women's authority and knowledge, and preferred to turn to men when in need. This prejudiced selectivity ensured that men would see other men first and foremost as being the best sources of travel assistance. This pattern relegated Native women to the margins of European travel and the resulting stories while also denying the possibilities of female aid, thus perpetuating their certainty of female inability and sustaining the vision of the trail and travel as being essentially male.

Once again, Samuel Hearne provides one of the clearest examples of how an Englishman's gendered order could be a bone of contention within a travel relationship while also dramatically shaping the outcome of an exploration. The year before he met the hardy Dogrib woman, Hearne was in the midst of another failed attempt to reach the Coppermine River. During the trip's planning, Hearne and the Hudson's Bay Company operatives at Fort Prince of Wales insisted on excluding any women from the trip so as to "avoid all incumberances as much as possible," and so that the party's Native hunters "might have fewer to provide for."[80] Toward that end, Hearne also took steps to ensure that no other Europeans would be on the trip, implicitly suggesting that both women (in the English vision) and European men were nothing but burdens on the trail. The decision not to include women on the second Coppermine trip was a curious one.

Hearne was then a newcomer to the world of tundra travel, and despite having made one earlier failed trip on the barren lands, he largely applied his imported conceptions of femininity to Native women. But the man behind the trip, Governor Moses Norton, was not only familiar with the important role women played in Native travel, but was himself alleged to be the son of a Cree woman and the post's former governor, Richard Norton.[81] Hearne even noted in a later textual aside that Norton knew full well that the party "could not do well without [female] assistance," since women were vital for hauling baggage as well as "dressing skins for clothing," pitching tents, gathering kindling, and other seemingly menial tasks.[82] Why then did the two plan the trip without women? The answer may have to do with the very nature of the trip. Unlike most hunting or hauling parties, this one was to be specifically a scientific exploration. For Hearne and Norton, women may have been fine on routine trips rooted in commerce, or for all-Native parties, but the implicitly manly nature of exploration made this trip exceptional. The expedition's key pieces of scientific apparatus (like its quadrant) marked the trip as at core a male activity. This represented a significant play for control over the behavior and values of the expedition's mostly Indian members. It also doomed the trip by crippling the travelers' ability to fend for themselves before they even set foot outside Fort Prince of Wales.

Food soon became a major concern, and the small party devoted as much time to killing fish and geese as it did to traveling. After nearly two lean months alone, the men spied an encampment of a large group of Indians, whom they soon discovered were mostly the wives and families of Chipewyan hunters who had gone down to Fort Prince of Wales to hunt geese. After joining these people in a deer hunt and passing some time with them, Hearne's principal guide began to act strangely. He began pitching his tent "backward and forward, from place to place" as he decided what his course of action should be. When Hearne questioned him, he learned that the man believed "that the year was far too advanced" to allow for safe travel to the Coppermine River that year. The guide seemed to be deciding whether to pitch his tent with the Chipewyans or stay with Hearne as he had agreed to. But he managed to persuade the Englishman that the best course of action was to "pass the winter with some of the Indians then in company" and try again in the spring. Hearne "could not pretend to contradict him," and agreed to this sensible plan.[83]

The planned lack of women denied the expedition the chance of making the Coppermine River by undermining its ability to feed itself. Yet when things looked bleakest, the guides did score a victory—they found the needed women and persuaded Hearne to take up with them. The good news was that they could at least travel in a familiar and efficient manner. The bad news was that, lacking goods to trade for necessities such as food and functional clothing, they were at the mercy of their hosts, who were not eager to take care of a group of men foolish enough to have created their own disastrous plight and led by a "poor servant, noways like the Governor at the factory."[84] Hearne and his increasingly distant guides spent the next several days "reduced to the necessity of depending on" their "inconsiderate" hosts "for support."[85] Nevertheless, Hearne was determined to continue on his scientific pursuit by gaining what geographic knowledge he could of the lands he traversed—a retention of his manly scientific goal in the midst of his demeaning and emasculating dependency on Native handouts.

The centerpiece of his travel kit was his quadrant. It was the quadrant that turned the trip into a scientific venture, and given the male-female opposition established at Fort Prince of Wales, the quadrant was a talisman symbolizing a singularly European form of manhood, while also being a symbol of controlling both geography and travel. But the quadrant was also a heavy piece of equipment made more burdensome by the addition of a tripod and other surveying and distance-measuring tools.[86] Though at the center of Hearne's vision of the trip, the quadrant was more peripheral to his Indian companions. One of the company made his view of the whole endeavor as clear as he could by simply walking off with a recently met group of Indians, and taking the quadrant and the party's small cache of powder with him. By the time Hearne realized what had happened, it was too late in the day to chase down this "deserter." But the next day, after some searching, they found the "quadrant and the bag of powder lying on the top of a high stone." The bag was missing some of its vital contents, but the quadrant was unharmed. But not for long. The whole enterprise finally collapsed a few days later when a "sudden gust of wind" blew it to the ground and dashed to bits both the quadrant and Hearne's final hope of turning the poorly planned trip to some benefit.

From Hearne's perspective, his trip ended when the quadrant's fragile parts smashed on the Barren Ground's rocks. But he had long since lost the support of his Native companions, who preferred travel with the Chipewyans to following Hearne's scientific quest. The guides took control of their time, as did many other Indians: they left when the situation grew too grim. Hearne was also quick to blame the "misconduct" of his increasingly truculent guides for the trip's utter failure. But when he was busy planning his next attempt, this time heavily aided by the Chipewyan fur captain Matonabbee, the headman voiced a Native version of why the trip had failed. "Women," Matonabbee told Hearne, "were made for labour," and there was "no such thing as travelling any considerable distance, or any length of time, in this country, without their assistance."[87]

Matonabbee agreed that having uncooperative guides had indeed undermined Hearne's plans, but in the final analysis, in Native eyes, it was the lack of women "that occasioned all [the party's] wants."[88] There was a significant gap between Hearne's English view and Matonabbee's Chipewyan view. For Matonabbee, the trip failed due to poor planning and a foolish unwillingness to bring needed women on a long trip. But in Hearne's view, gender dominated. It was the loss of the manly scientific apparatus, and the unmanly behavior of his unfaithful guides, that finished off the trip, not the planned absence of female "incumberances." Hearne's next trip, planned in conjunction with Matonabbee, included women, and for this reason (among others) it succeeded in reaching its goal.

If Hearne and others like him were ready to see Native women as little more than "incumbering" mouths to feed, many European men were willing to see that Native women could sometimes be invaluable travel companions—as sex partners. Native women serving the sexual needs of European travelers not only made travel more pleasant, but did so in a way that reified perceived male dominion, and thus ameliorated common travel's gendered anxieties.[89] It is hard to know just how common sex with Native women was for European men on the trail. But there are hints.

When Harmen Meyndertsz van den Bogaert and his fellow Dutch emissaries traveled across Iroquoia in 1634, the resulting account of their trip was largely a mundane affair full of tales of trade, welcomes, and a few unfriendly encounters. The narrative contained no mention of sex. But the glossary of Iroquoian words the Dutchmen produced offered a sort of counternarrative, suggesting that more was going on than the text reflected. The glossary contained the names of predictable trade terms, like "awl," "knives," and "bead." But it also translated Mohawk words like *canna warori* as "a prostitute," *onera* as "vagina," and *sinekaty* as "to have intercourse."[90] In fact, the Dutch-Mohawk glossary was organized in a random fashion, rather than employing an alphabetical or thematic order. This suggests that its author listed words as they came to him, rather than in any systematic structure like alphabetizing. Viewed in this light, portions of the glossary offer near-salacious vignettes of the Dutchmen's Mohawk adventures. Witness this noticeably narrativizing word and phrase list for example, which reads in Dutch as "slaepen, by slaepen, heel moey, toback" and translates as "sleep, (to have) intercourse, very beautiful, tobacco."[91] The glossary from Virginia governor Alexander Spotswood's jaunt into the Appalachian Mountains also contained seemingly mundane and practical names for animals and plants. But the word list also carried such telling words and phrases as "kiss," "will you kiss me," and "come to bed."[92] Certainly, European travelers would benefit from a wide facility with Native languages, but terms like these leave little doubt about at least one topic of conversation around some campfires.

These lists, with their implied counternarrative of travel, point to an ambiguous mélange of desires and actions which could have been either Native or European, and may or may not have been acted on. But a less ambiguous vocabulary describing Native-European sex soon developed, born of the value both European men and Native women saw in shared sexual relationships. Canadian fur traders practiced marriage "in the custom of the country," whereby traders received the personal and economic benefits of intimate female associations while still suggesting that the habit was Native and not of their own devising. Such "marriages" worked for both partners: they allowed Europeans the comforts and rewards of Native kinship networks during their travels, and granted Native women access to goods, social prestige, economic security, and a host of other benefits, personal and social.[93] In a somewhat gender-bending metaphor, Lawson noted that the typical trader of his experience was "seldom without an Indian female for his bed-fellow," but other travelers took on "Indian wives" while on the trail as well.[94] Some travelers labeled Native women "prostitutes," thus emphasizing what Europeans perceived as an occasional economic basis of Native desire, and turning the many, varied reasons Native women may have sought out European partners (including the formation of valuable family alliances, access to trade goods, and romance) into something base and essentially economical in European eyes.[95] These varied terms and descriptions highlighted the singularity of travel sex. They marked it as outside the regular rules of colonial society and located its onus within Native societies. This allowed European travelers the possibility of sex, while allowing any opprobrium to attach elsewhere.

A few Europeans claimed to have resisted the advances of Indian women. Missionaries, for example, and particularly the celibate ones, not only avoided sexual activity, but were quick to condemn others.' But other Europeans made a point of describing their resistance. Samuel Champlain sent away "with gentle remonstrances" a "shameless girl" whom he claimed "came boldly up to me, offering to keep me company."[96] James Madison and his companions also rejected the offers made by Oneida women, in 1784. Madison injected a class-based comparison into his tale of offered sex by claiming that, while he and his well-born French companions demurred, their servants showed less manly restraint.[97] Even in rejecting sex, men like Champlain and Madison still played out their own masculine travel identities against a backdrop of Native sexuality.

Other travelers were quite willing to literally kiss and tell on the trail—and some were quite direct in their descriptions. Byrd, who was never shy about describing his own exploits, cast the sexual assaults of his 1727 Virginia surveying companions in the most congenial possible terms. The women this party met were subjected to a range of pressures from the surveyors, who seemed to have felt that taking women was as much their charge as was taking measurements. The travelers forced their attentions on the kin and servants of the colonists who offered them hospitality. One "tallow-faced wench" with a sprained wrist was thus "disabled from making any resistance" as one of the party "was ranging over her sweet person."[98] A "dark angel" at another stop "struggled just enough to make her admirer more eager."[99] Indian women were not far from the surveyors' minds, and the surveyors even seem to have discussed whether or not Native women had pubic hair.[100] At Indian villages the surveyors continued their sexual inquiries, perhaps with greater success than at English farms. Byrd noted that at one Nottoway village, the "ladies had put on all their ornaments to charm us," and that members of the party were curious to "try the difference between them [Native women] and other women." Byrd focused on the condition of the men's clothing, that noted delineator in English minds between civility and savagery, as an indicator of sexual activity.[101] One man's advances led to the "disobligation of his ruffles," while, on leaving the Nottoways, Byrd observed his fellows to have their underclothing "discolour'd by the soil of the Indian Ladys."[102]

Byrd provided a rare glimpse into how some European travelers eroticized the trail in a way which also asserted male domination. At least some members of this English party saw travel as providing a chance to give vent to their sexual energies in a setting far removed from possible domestic ramifications. Far from home, families, and familiar hierarchies, these travelers were quick to equate the trail with sexual license. Their readiness to paw the various women they encountered along the way also suggests that, for some, the sampling of female "charms" itself may have been a powerful, though rarely acknowledged, motivation for European male travel.

If would-be travelers were looking for evidence of a sexual paradise awaiting them on the trail, they would have to look no further than Indian trader Nicholas Cresswell's account of his 1775 Ohio Valley adventures. Cresswell described Native women who were models of female acquiescence and sexual availability. Like many traders, Cresswell was a welcome visitor in Native communities, where many people were eager to create lasting personal alliances with a well-connected English friend. Sex and female assistance and companionship filled a need for traders along the trail, and consequently, Cresswell and other traders found no shortage of families ready to offer their womenfolk in hopes of creating a bond. At one stop, three Delaware women quietly took care of his horse, prepared his evening meal, and as Cresswell recorded it, "spread my blankets at the fire and made signs for me to sit down." After some discussion, the youngest of the three began to make advances upon the Englishman. Cresswell claimed to have been slow to see what was taking place—as the girl "placed herself very near me," he noted, "I began to think she had some amorous design upon me." But once in place she began to "creep nearer," and tug suggestively at her target's blanket. Cresswell played right along, remembering, in a sexually charged metaphor centering on his blanket, "I found what she wanted and lifted it up." He went on to praise her appearance, describing her as "young, handsome, and healthy. Fine regular features and fine eyes, had she not painted them with red before she came to bed."[103]

In the morning she obligingly gathered in the horses, saddled them, and got everything together for the day's journey, while the other women prepared breakfast. The new couple continued on together for some while, the girl telling Cresswell an array of things in a language he did not understand. When they finally parted he recalled giving "my Dulcinea a match coat, with which she seemed very well pleased."[104]

As Cresswell kept traveling, he and the other Englishmen who occasionally joined him met other "Dulcineas" along their way. At the home of one Mohawk man, Cresswell slept with his host's "tolerably handsome" sister at the man's request, while his partner bedded with their host's daughter. In the morning, Cresswell's "bedfellow" insisted on going with him. This time the trader decided that if he did not take a woman along he would have to face the same situation at each campfire. This woman, whom he named Nancy, spoke some English and seemed as likely a partner as any, and so the two traveled on for some time. Along the way, Nancy proved to be a valuable companion, fetching horses, cooking meals, and preparing fires, as well as providing access to trading partners, and, of course, offering sex.

Cresswell would certainly have agreed with Lawson's earlier observation that "besides the satisfaction of a she-bed-fellow," traders "find their Indian girls very serviceable to them, on account of dressing their victuals, and instructing 'em in the affairs and customs of the country."[105]

Appraisals like these lauded Indian women's skills and utility on the trail.

But they did so in a way which restricted the roles Native women could play to a few select activities—sex, camp maintenance, and cooking, most notably, with social networking following close behind. It is no accident that these largely conformed to an idealized European division of labor which gendered domestic tasks female. A few European travelers were willing to see women as shaping their courses or directing their travel, but most refused to see Indian women as serving in these capacities. This refusal itself created a travel reality which these narratives reflected, replicated, and amplified.

Just as European men's travel habits and preferences relegated Native women to select roles in their company, some Indians were ready to return the favor by tweaking the genders of some of the same male travelers. When Europeans suggested that Indian men were in some way deficient as men, they did so in ways which focused largely on the Natives' perceived inabilities. Native men could not ride horses well, they were impious, they were superstitious, they did not understand economics, and so on, all absences which cast them as lacking that which marked European travelers as civilized, skilled, and complete. Europeans in general (and men most especially) held to models which defined people as being either male or less than male. These ideas were in flux by the middle of the eighteenth century, but they nevertheless held sway for much of the colonial era. During the colonial era there were many ways to be less than male. The most prevalent was to be a woman, but women were only one category of non-men; there were others too. One could be a child; the fear of this unmanly state surfaced notably in European anxiety over being carried by Indians. One could be an animal, an unthinking brute. One could also be a non-European. Natives and Africans were the most common exemplars of this status in America, and both were subjected to analyses which saw "savages" as combining elements of many non-men: child-like lack of emotional control, beast-like skills and appetites, womanly churlishness, and mendacity.[106] Common travel itself raised uncomfortable questions about these statuses, as it placed European men in the very conditions which, for many, embodied Native savagery.[107] Traveling together risked blurring distinctions which Europeans were most desirous to maintain. Therefore, having a laugh at Natives served to maintain otherwise at-risk distinctions between peoples. When travelers like Byrd or Lawson looked at their Indian companions and laughed, their doing so bolstered their own manliness and marked Native companions as less than men.

The equation was not quite the same for many Natives. Like their European companions, Native men generally saw certain traits as defining male identities and marking them as good travelers. Fortitude, stealth, wisdom, and respectfulness are only a few of the traits which defined a Native man as a manly traveler. Like Europeans, Natives guides sometimes looked at their fellow travelers and found them lacking the right stuff. But these guides often came from Native societies employing gender systems quite different from the ones operative in European and colonial societies. Therefore, Native diminution of European travelers' manhood came in different forms. Many Native guides were quick to suggest that Europeans were foolish, slothful, and graceless on the trail. But Indians concluding that their companions were less than manly had a wide range of explanatory possibilities, including a third gender, neither man nor woman. The story of Peter Fidler, a late-eighteenth-century Canadian fur trader, provides clues as to how perceived European deficiencies and manliness could play themselves out on the trail, and how gender could function as a language for cultural difference.

In September 1791, Peter Fidler set off for the Northwest Territories' Slave River in the company of a group of Chipewyan Indians. Fidler's mission was to study the area and strengthen trade connections between the Natives and his employer, the Hudson's Bay Company.[108] Laden with trade goods and surveying equipment, he lumbered off, diligently recording the distances and directions of his daily marches. Like Hearne before him in quite similar conditions, Fidler put great stock in his use of surveying equipment to view, chart, and thereby possess the lands he traversed. But what he did not seem to know was that while his hosts were willing, even eager, to build new trade ties, they did not think much of the travel abilities or manliness of the company's representative. Fidler was unable to hunt, the principal task of the Chipewyan men at whose pleasure he traveled. He therefore could not participate in a central defining act of his fellows' masculinity. This inability seems to have raised questions for the Indians about the exact nature of their companion's gendered identity. Fidler's notebooks record how, step by step, his Chipewyan companions re-gendered him, seemingly without Fidler understanding what was going on. Early on, the men began to leave Fidler behind with the women as they set off to hunt game. He became a member of one of the party leader's coterie, making Fidler analogous to a wife when it came to issues of food and protection. In fact this situation closely paralleled the ways that Samuel Hearne earlier had become a sort symbolic wife to Matonabbee through the former's reliance on the great man's skill and protection.[109]

On September 16, Fidler recorded that "all the men went on hunting and the women and myself took the canoes thro the swamp."[110] On its surface this was no big deal; after all, Englishmen were not the hunters the Chipewyans were and Fidler with his notebooks and quadrant would only get underfoot. But it was only the beginning.

The pattern set on September 16 continued for the rest of the fall: the men went out to kill beavers and buffalo while Fidler and the women followed them, bringing in the carcasses of the fresh kills, cutting up the meat, preparing the camps, and repairing canoes and clothing. During all this, Fidler was content to record the directions of his travels and take his measurements. He sometimes participated in the women's work. Other times he passed his time taking measurements, tending his kit, and on occasion shooting at beavers. He explained away his marginal participation on the party's activities, writing that "the more an European does of work with them [the Indians] the worse he is respected by them."[111] Fidler cast his low-level activity not as stemming from a lack of skills, but rather as a sign of his privileged status as "an European." But it may have been more complex for his Native companions. For the Chipewyans, labor defined gender—men had their tasks, women had theirs. Work was a constant; what varied was which tasks an individual performed. But Fidler (and other Europeans, by his reckoning) did no work, meaning that their status eluded the gender-defining world of labor. This created an important ambiguity in Chipewyan eyes: Fidler seems to have been not quite a man and not quite a woman because he defied the usual definitions. Such people were not entirely unfamiliar in many Native societies. European observers struggling for the words to explain these people cribbed Native terms like "berdaches," or fell back on their own references for sexual ambiguity, sometimes (wrongly) calling them "hermaphrodites." But berdaches, while not ten a penny, were nevertheless frequent and familiar figures in many Native societies, often playing a variety of respected roles, ranging from the medical and the spiritual to the diplomatic.[112] Indians had a variety of well-developed social-role vocabularies for explaining gradations of sexual variation. Chipewyan responses to Fidler's inabilities suggest that these travelers saw their guest as falling into a space between male and female—perhaps not quite a berdache as term has come to be used, or in the way many other Native societies understood these people, but at the same time neither properly male nor female.[113] Here Natives saw Englishness not in terms of cultural differences or a concept of race, but instead as a matter of defining gender roles. For Fidler's Chipewyan companions, Englishness, at least as Fidler enacted it on the trail, seemed to be a gender in and of itself.

As the Canadian winter gradually crept up on the party, it had become routine for Fidler to be left behind with the women on an almost daily basis. As the weather turned colder, the Indians gradually began to mark their companion as not being male in the same way as were the party's real men. Seeming oblivious to the implications of his acquisition, Fidler wrote that he "got a cap made of a beaver skin after the *manner of the womens* which is very well adapted for keeping snow from ones neck going thro the woods" (emphasis added).[114] The hat may well have been an effective covering, but it was also a visible symbol of the ambiguity of his status within the party. When, a few weeks later, Fidler tore his "old cotton trousers all to pieces," he had no recourse left to keep warm but to "wrap a blanket about me *like a womans petticoat* to protect me from the cold" (again, emphasis added).[115] At this point the skirted man in the woman's hat trudging around with the group's women and children must have cut quite a figure, embodying the betwixt and between nature of his gender.[116]

Fidler's comical clumsiness only made matters worse. On one occasion he leaned too close to a large cooking fire when a sudden "flame of wind" blew the hotter flames right into his face. The result was what Fidler called "the most expeditious shave I ever had tho' somewhat disagreeable" when the flames took off his beard "as clean as if it had just been shaved."[117] Once, while trying to take "the altitude of Venus" with his sextant, Fidler just narrowly "escaped being knocked down by the falling of a tent pole."[118] Another time he reentered a tent after taking some star readings. Hoping to get a good look at his quadrant in the firelight and "read off the observation," he instead found himself pinned "prostrate" to the ground and covered with drying meat when the drying racks collapsed on his head.[119]

It is significant that this particular blunder centered on the suddenly aptly named Fidler's use of his surveying equipment. Tools like these were central to the colonial mission of Fidler's and others' travels—taking measurements, creating charts, and returning to share the information were part and parcel of the expansion of European ambitions. But these tools were thus also defining elements of a territorial explorer's masculinity—they were the vehicles with which they played out their manly roles as conquerors. What is more, when traveling in the company of Indians in places far from home, taking measurements and using equipment helped these explorers to see themselves as independent, purposeful Europeans, as opposed to vulnerable dependents. Hearne, for example, lost his quadrant to the Barren Grounds' rocks, and thus suffered a sort of colonial castration as he suddenly found himself largely alone, unable to conduct his mission, and under the direction of Indians unimpressed with his skills and uninterested in his fate. Confronted with this grim situation, Hearne turned to recriminations and derision of his insufficiently manly companions.

In some cases, surveying equipment could elicit Native curiosity, or Indian ire, like that of the Native headman in 1770s Georgia who angrily asserted that he knew his lands better than that "little wicked instrument" upon which English surveyors relied.[120] But in Fidler's occasionally unsteady hands, something else was at work. Already occupying an ambiguous gender role, Fidler's fumbling with his instruments made these less a means of manly colonial domination and more the playthings of someone whose gendered status was in question. Fidler and many of his fellows understood their actions as the needed front edge of empire, the courageous endeavors of men willing to brave the unfamiliar in aid of colonial enterprises. But Fidler's story suggests that, at the same time, the objects and facilitators of these colonial endeavors—the Native people—could see these people, things, and actions as being very different than Europeans may have imagined.

When William Byrd suggested that travelers and husbands shared crucial traits, he described his ideal traveler in gendered terms. For Byrd, a traveler was to be composed, skillful, and of course, dominant. He and his fellows played out these traits though a regime of mutual observation and restraint in which ridicule and some corporal punishments served to enforce manhood. They also played out their aggressive manliness by helping themselves to the women they met in travel, in some cases regardless of their preys' willingness. By bringing together definitions of husbands and travelers, they combined the sexual rights of the husband with the territorial range of the traveler, and suggested that the ideal traveler governed his trail as the ideal man governed his home and family. Women had a role to play for these and other European travelers, but the roles they most preferred women to occupy were those which best reinforced their own visions of their own manliness and their ability to be the best manly ideal traveler.

When Fidler's male Chipewyan companions left the explorer behind with the women and children, and gradually re-dressed him in an ambiguous fashion, they also used gender, in this case to make sense of their companion and his mixed abilities on the trail. These Chipewyans, like their kinsman Matonabbee, and many other male Native travelers, knew full well that women were often essential for successful travel. Yet they also were, in their way, concerned about questions of gender on the trail, both regarding themselves and their companions.

When Native and European travel companions raced, wrestled, or tried to outsing each other, they used competition to judge each other against their own standards and abilities. When they looked at their travel companions and derided their abilities, knowledge, and even their manliness, their discussion of what they saw most lacking in their fellows also revealed what they prized most in themselves.

6

Going Out

In the late eighteenth century, the fur traders of Hudson's Bay used to tell a story about two men and a boat. One man was an unnamed Cree Indian, a member of a tribe with a long and proud history of northern fur trading. By the time of this story, the Crees had long been essential partners in all European fur trade activities, both in their home territories and far afield. The other man was a Scots Hudson's Bay Company employee with the remarkably singular name of Magnus Twatt. Twatt was one of the countless traders whose livelihood depended on their North American travel skills, and so was an adept traveler familiar with the trail's rigors.

The story goes this way: Sometime around the 1784, the two men were on one leg of a fur-trading expedition. The rather routine commerce venture saw them paddling a small canoe together in which there were a mere "four pieces of goods." Their shared travels brought them to what was called Cross Lake, "a sheet of water about twenty miles from north to south but only three miles wide," located in what is now Canadian Saskatchewan.[1] A river intersected this linear lake right in its middle, giving it its name, although the name also tellingly recalls the century-old Jesuit's lament that the American trail could be "full of crosses."[2] It was on this river that the two men traveled, and it was Cross Lake which the two had to cross—offering perhaps an alternative genesis of the lake's name.

A three-mile pull should not have been a particularly challenging task to experienced fur-trade paddlers, but a place like Cross Lake could be tricky. Its long length made it susceptible to strong winds funneled along its flat surface. Winds combined with the river's current to make this crossing point potentially quite perilous. Twatt and his partner fell prey to this climatological phenomenon. According to David Thompson, the two made it into the middle of the lake when they found themselves suddenly caught up in a "small gale" formed by north winds whipping southward and wreaking havoc with the river's current. The resulting "awkward waves" knocked the canoe about and threatened the lives of its paddlers.

The danger was obvious, but Thompson related that it was the Indian who took the first action. The boat was the most dangerous place to be in this storm—should it flip over it could easily pin a paddler under water long enough to drown him. It was also better policy choose the moment of one's dunking rather than to wait until it came by surprise. With that in mind, the Cree "threw off his belt and loose coat and got ready to swim." He called out to Twatt, urging him to do the same; "strip strip man not be long in canoe now man or you will be drowned drowned man." But stripping down was less simple for Twatt. He was "fast buttoned up in a tight jacket and had on trowsers," making undressing a slow, awkward affair. What is more, the man could not swim in the first place. Therefore, Twatt's only option was to stick by his paddle and hope to make it to the shore's shelter before the worst could happen. Yelling above the wind, struggling to remove clothing, and all the while pulling hard on their paddles, the two somehow made it to the relative safety of a "large patch of tall rushes," where they were able to cower "until the wind moderated." The paddlers, canoe, and goods all survived Cross Lake to continue their travel.[3]

Thompson's story was a parable of risk and the differences between travelers on the trail. Both Twatt and the Cree were skilled and experienced travelers sharing the labors and the many intimacies of travel in a small boat. Yet despite their proximity, shared conditions, and potentially shared fates, there were nevertheless marked differences in how they approached the trail. The Cree trader saw his survival in his readiness to abandon the canoe and swim to safety. For Twatt, the boat itself was the vehicle of both peril and survival. By staying in the boat he increased the danger, but like a dangerous gamble, if he pulled his paddle hard enough he might survive. As it happens, his plan was the one that worked, but it could just as easily have gone otherwise.

Thompson's retelling also focused on clothing as the locus of differences between an Indian and a European, not a new rhetorical tack at all for European observers, who often used nudity as an indication that non-Europeans were insufficiently civilized. On the trail, fellow travelers had long borrowed elements of each other's clothing—such items were easy to transfer and were often quite practical. European adoption of Native snowshoes, soft moccasins, and protective leggings were matched by Native uses of woolens, billowy shirts, and hats. This cultural cross-dressing certainly made for some hybridized or even heterogeneously attired mixed-travel parties. But the clothes did not fully make the men, and even when outward appearances converged, ideals of how best to travel still could diverge wildly. It was not so much what they wore, but how they wore it. Both Twatt and the Cree wore what made the most sense for how they planned to deal with what travel might throw their way. For the Cree, a plan to jump ship would have been facilitated by loose clothing ready to be jettisoned in a crisis. Twatt, on the other hand, dressed in a European mode which fully covered the body, protecting it against cold, sun, and insects. His belt was also a crucial part of the ensemble, and useful for carting items like knives and purses. Both sets of clothing reflected travel experience and a material dialogue between the trail, travelers, and the homefront sources of clothing production and fashion. Both men dressed for success in their shared travels, even though definitions of success may have varied somewhat.[4]

But most importantly, both men were ready, willing, and able to cope with the hard work and numerous risks of Canadian travel. It may be too much to claim the two as having been equals based solely on Thompson's brief retelling, but neither were they leader and led.

By the time Thompson recorded this story, men like the Cree had long been familiar figures in travel stories and on the trail itself. But European travelers like Twatt, men equal in their way to Indian companions, were gaining prominence in both North American travel and its documentation. The colonial woodsman was not a completely new figure. Far from it; from colonization's earliest days there had been no shortage of colonists adept at North American travel. The skin and fur trades had long been the principal engines creating these skilled travelers; and in time, explorers, diplomatists, and even missionaries of many European nations also earned their laurels on the American trail. But as the numbers of these men grew, their presence on the trail had a significant impact on Indian-European travel relationships. Most significantly, the availability of skilled and experienced European paddlers, translators, and trail guides made it increasingly possible for less-skilled European travelers to turn to their countrymen for assistance rather than to Native aids. Employing Europeans (and American colonials) in these roles sidestepped the many issues of Native-European conflict which defined intercultural travel. European woodsman travel partners were solidly enmeshed in colonial economies and were generally part of colonial societies. This meant that both leaders and crew would often be returning to the same world; hence, authority and discipline could successfully draw on off-trail ramifications. It also meant that travelers brought to the trail the domestic conflicts over class, manhood, and other issues which marked the divides within colonial and European societies.

The availability of large numbers of fully naturalized, well-connected, highly skilled and experienced fur trappers, traders, hunters, paddlers, and other woodsmen ready and willing to participate in a variety of travels and fluent in Native languages also spelled changes in the roles of Indians within European travel parties. It meant that, in some travels, Indians played more marginal roles than they would have played on similar trips a century earlier.

The two best-documented transcontinental treks, Alexander Mackenzie's 1793 crossing of the Canadian Rockies, and Lewis and Clark's 1803 to 1806 extended voyage, were both examples of something that was changing in Indian-European travel relationships. Both trips were largely river trips, making it possible for them to rely particularly heavily on the travel skills of non-Indians, mostly men associated with the northern fur trade and the new United States military. These men performed as paddlers and hunters, roles which often had been performed by Indian allies and employees. Indians were still involved, at times even central, in these to late expeditions, fulfilling many of the same roles they had always played—providing food, local geographic information, and acting as translators. But at the same time, these cross-continental expeditions were far less dependent on Natives than were earlier trips. In that way they represent a shift away from the patterns of relationships which had typified similar travel since the sixteenth century's great entradas yielded to the more cooperative models of the seventeenth and eighteenth centuries.

Sir Alexander Mackenzie was like many other adventure-minded fur traders. Like Samuel Hearne before him, he set out northward to track a useful water passage to the Arctic, this time to the benefit of the North West Company. In 1788, Mackenzie set out from Alberta's Fort Chepeweyan in the company of Matonabbee's successor Nestabeck, to follow the route of the river which to this day, fairly or unfairly, bears the Scotsman's name. Building on that experience, four years later, he directed his boats westward from the same fort to cross the Rockies, and located a river trade route through to the Pacific. During his 1793 trek across the Canadian Rockies, Mackenzie again relied on Indians in a variety of ways. Throughout the trip Mackenzie talked with Indians, accepted their gifts of food, queried them about the road ahead, and brought along a few as short-term guides. Indeed, before his Artic trip, Mackenzie recognized what all traders and most interior travelers knew, that "without Indians" he had "very little hopes of succeeding."[5]

But despite this admission, Mackenzie's Pacific trip was quite different from his own and others' earlier travels. Mackenzie's Pacific trip, in both planning and actuation, marginalized Indians and limited their participation more than many similar previous ventures. For one thing, this was the first major venture of its type to not be led, or at least heavily aided, by a well-traveled Native fur captain. Instead, Mackenzie and his right-hand man, Alexander MacKay, would themselves lead the party, picking up geographical knowledge as they went—a plan reminiscent more of Soto than of Mackenzie's immediate precursors. Also, few Indians were integral to the party's structure. Instead, Mackenzie's Canadian paddlers bore the bulk of the work. These men had considerable experience taking on the rapids and portages they would face in crossing the Rockies. Two of the crew had accompanied Mackenzie to the Arctic, and the rest seemed equal to the task. His crew list showed the French Canadian background of his company—Landry and Ducette, both of whom had previous experience with Mackenzie, joined Beaulieux, Bisson, Courtois, and Beauchamp to make a party more comfortable in French than in Scots-inflected English. These men were products of the fur trade, and many may even have been the scions of the Native-European marriages so common in and around trade forts. The party also included two Indians as hunters and translators, one of whom the crew derisively called "Cancre," or Dunce.[6] Mackenzie considered these Canadian paddlers "the most expert canoe-men in the world," an assumption only abandoned on seeing the remarkable skill and dexterity of the Indian paddlers living along British Columbia's Bella Coola River.[7]

Nevertheless, the Canadians were the core of the party, and Mackenzie worked hard to maintain his control over them and their travels. This struggle created a distinct platform for the party's intercultural travel relationships. Despite the presence of a few select Indians, all along the way, Mackenzie directed and limited contact between his party and the Native people they encountered. Mackenzie sometimes had his party camp separately from Indians, at times he limited personal contact between members of his party and people along the way, and he even encouraged competition between his men and Natives, all with an eye toward maintaining distinctions and bolstering his own ability to control the behavior of his French Canadians. The Scotsman's mistrust of Indians and his fear that unrestricted contact with them jeopardized his travels came out in small ways, and on many occasions Mackenzie was "not without some apprehension respecting" the Indians they met.[8] For example, when the Canadians "drove" one of their canoes onto "a stony bank," thus necessitating its repair, Mackenzie blamed not only the paddlers, but also the group of Beaver Indians who ran "along the bank conversing with my people," distracting them from their work.[9] Despite his desire for Native geographic information, Mackenzie was quick to distrust his would-be informants, and his account is rife with the fur trader's suspicions of Indians. Rather than being grateful for Native aid, Mackenzie felt a desire to "chastise" one guide for having been less than forthcoming in answering his questions.[10] He saw the Natives, in general, as being weak willed and "inclined to magnify evils of any and every kind."[11] And, most tellingly, when Native testimony about the way over the mountains painted a bleak picture, thus threatening to "disconcert the project on which [his] heart was set, and in which [his] whole mind occupied," Mackenzie simply concluded that "from fear, or other motives," these Indians had to be lying.[12]

Of course, like many other traveler writers, Mackenzie's doubts and bluster allowed the writer to emerge from his text as the travel-savvy man in control. But his text and the actions it reflects also reveal confidence that his goals could be achieved with minimal Native service at the core of the party. To some extent he was right, and his willingness to buck the advice of Native informants sometimes paid off. But Mackenzie's confidence was itself facilitated by the ready availability of experienced European paddlers to stock his team.

The conflicts that emerged from Mackenzie's separate and not quite equal travel policy were revealing. At one point in the trip, the Canadians and their Athabascan fellows found themselves in dire straits on a particularly difficult stretch of British Columbia's Parsnip River. This hazardous stretch of the river became a vehicle for conflict between Natives and Europeans, quite in keeping with the pattern of travel conflict. But this incident also revealed the shape of tensions within Mackenzie's relatively homogeneous party of Canadians, and particularly how a language of manliness served the explorer's need for order.

On seeing the raging river, Mackenzie's Athabascan guides had "manifested evident symptoms of discontent" at the prospect of paddling through this leg of the river, which was choked with "fallen trees, and large stones," in addition to having a fearsome snowmelt-swollen current.[13] The head guide pointed out a not-too-distant mountain and assured the traders that it was "on the other side of a river, into which this empties."[14] In other words, the local Sekani guide suggested that it made more sense to bypass the present rapids and lakes by hoofing it to the gentler waters on the other side of the mountain.

But Mackenzie and his men, driven by the explorer's relentless need for speed in travel and a manly travel ethic that "urged the honour of conquering disasters," preferred to avoid such a long and uphill trudge loaded down with heavy food supplies, hunting and mapping gear, and trade goods.[15] Instead, they chose to take their chances on the water. On the morning of June 13 all was ready to go. At the last moment, Mackenzie had second thoughts and suggested that it may be wiser for him to accompany the Indian guides. But his companions urged him to join them, with an appeal to fellowship that echoed William Byrd's "laws of travel." They told him that "if they perish," then Mackenzie "should perish with them."[16] Such an appeal to group identity and Mackenzie's personal manliness was too strong to be ignored, so he took his place in the large bark boat. No sooner had they set off than a disaster offered them the chance for honor. The "violence of the current" drove the boat sideways only to "break her on the first bar" and then send the fractured vessel back and forth between rocks, which smashed its bow and stern respectively until not much was left of either. As the crew and contents spilled out, one of the endangered paddlers, hoping to stabilize what was left of the boat, grabbed a low-hanging tree branch, only to be "jerked on shore in an instant, and with a degree of violence that threatened his destruction." The party's ammunition was lost and most of their goods and supplies soaked and damaged. With no option left, Mackenzie and his rattled crew, "almost in a benumbed state," set about retrieving what they could of their belongings.[17]

When confronted with the icy snowmelt raging downriver, the Athabascans saw no need to push through by boat. Other, less-perilous routes were available, and the Natives did not share Mackenzie's notion of limited time. Nor did they share a travel ethic that saw such obstacles as worthy challenges, at least not while other prudent options were available. Upon seeing the rocks and freezing rushing water turn the canoe into kindling, they assumed the worst and "sat down and gave vent to their tears," without, as Mackenzie bitterly noted, "making the least effort to help."[18] As the fur traders laid out their belongings to dry, repaired their shattered boat, and planned their next move, the guide who had expressed the gravest doubts about the river run assumed what Mackenzie called "an air of contentment."[19] The Scotsman believed this was due to smoke visible in the distant sky, meaning that other Indians could soon be counted upon to serve this impetuous and unwise group of white men. Mackenzie may have been right that the guide sought release from a service "which he had found so irksome and full of danger," but the guide's demeanor probably also carried at least a touch of "I told you so."

Mackenzie made sense of the disaster by falling back on his idea of the ideal traveler and his own understanding of manly behavior. When the party's morale was at its lowest ebb, Mackenzie tried to bolster their courage with some rum and a speech in which he told them that "our late experience would enable us to pursue our voyage with greater security." In Mackenzie's view, the boldness of the attempted passage was enough to trump the stigma of bad judgment, and the lessons learned in the failure would make the next attempt better executed and ultimately successful; indeed, through a mixture of carrying some goods and carefully manipulating the much lighter repaired vessel, the fur traders made it past the worst of the obstacles on June 15.[20] Mackenzie also reminded his fellows that he "did not deceive them"; they knew full well of the trip's risks before they had embarked, and of the "great disgrace that would attend them on their return home, without having attained the object of the expedition." Mackenzie's speech was a string of appeals to his fellows' manliness, all suggesting that to not continue would mean that they would be failing not just as travelers, but as men. But not all of them saw the situation, or its reflection on their manliness, in quite the same way.

On June 15, paddler Jacques Beauchamp "peremptorily refused to embark in the canoe." This was the "first example of absolute disobedience which had yet appeared during the course of the expedition," and Mackenzie, always jealous of his authority, was not about to let this behavior at such a risky juncture go unpunished. Physical or fiscal punishments would have been difficult to enact on the trail, so Mackenzie instead used a tactic that seems like one taken directly from Byrd's "laws of travel." He made fun of the man, "representing" him to the crew "as an object of ridicule and contempt for his pusillanimous behavior," and concluded that he was "unworthy of accompanying us," despite the fact that he had always been a "very useful, active, and laborious man."[21] Mackenzie saw this form of punishment by ridicule and rhetorical isolation as being "very severe." In the manly world of travel, ridicule and a removal from the bonds of fellowship (however symbolic) were strong sanctions indeed.

Mackenzie's speeches and behavior were partly designed to send his Indian companions a message about British manly fortitude and perseverance. But first and foremost, the Scotsman used a shared language of manhood to cajole and browbeat his paddlers into good behavior. Derision and promises of glory were the stick and carrot of Mackenzie's style of leadership—a style shared by many in his age. In this case, this tactic worked to restore order and ensure the party's ability to continue ahead, precisely because Mackenzie's travel plans rested on a fairly homogeneous travel party.

Mackenzie and his men paddled canoes, ate food, and perhaps even wore clothing derived from originals of Native design. Along their way they relied on Native information, supplies, and some help as well. In these ways, Mackenzie's travels, like those of so many other European travelers, were not possible without Indians. But while being in debt to Indians and the material fruit of centuries of contact, Mackenzie's Pacific travel style worked to marginalize actual Native individuals, even while depending on an array of Native technologies and knowledge.[22]

If Mackenzie's travels pushed Indians to his company's margins, Meriwether Lewis and William Clark's transcontinental journey of 1803 to 1806 took the model even further. Mackenzie's crossing the Rockies, gaining the Pacific, and returning to write about it was an important inspiration for Thomas Jefferson's sending his personal secretary to venture his own trip.[23] The Lewis and Clark expedition was intended to be a natural-science-focused reconnaissance of the vast lands the new United States purchased from a cash-strapped Napoleonic France. Like Mackenzie before them, Captains Lewis and Clark's westward travels depended heavily on Indian supplies and goodwill along the way, and help in setting up their winter camps. But also, like Mackenzie, the Corps of Discovery relied exclusively on Euro-American leadership, and though still eager to trade and learn from Indians, the party was largely Indian-free for most of its travel. The result was a marginalization of Indians within the travel party, and thus a severe limiting of the possibilities for the types of dynamic, challenging travel relationships which had been the norm since the mid-sixteenth century.

This American exclusivity was built into the expedition from its earliest planning. Both the party's leaders were armed with captain's commissions in the United States Army, making their authority more than mere persuasion. They were able to, and did, use the lash to keep their men (mostly soldiers as well) in line when these got too unruly or slept on duty. The language and use of military authority and discipline imposed eastern hierarchy onto the travelers and marked clear lines between real participants, those to whom the rules applied, and those along for the ride, to whom these rules did not apply. The desire for ranked hierarchy envisioned a trip largely free of Native participation except at its edges, as no one expected that Indians met along the way could be brought successfully in harness of rulebooks, sergeants, and regulations. Lewis himself considered the best people to accompany him on this trip to be the "unmarried" frontier-post "soldiers" from "some of the companies stationed at Massac, Kaskaskias, and Illinois."[24] These men were to do all the jobs which Indians had so often performed with European travelers. They would manage the trip's first boat—not fur-trade canoes as Mackenzie and others used, but instead a specially built, sailable and rowable keelboat, loaded to the waterline with supplies and equipment. Beyond the point where "navigation is practicable" for the keelboat, they would need to paddle canoes—canoes the planners envisioned the men would have to make themselves from "bark or rawhides," or, as it happened, carved out of logs.[25] The captains felt confident that their soldiers could handle this work without needing to turn to Indian paddlers or canoe builders.

Along the way, Lewis and Clark's men hunted their own game rather than relying on hired Native hunters. They made their own clothes, paddled their own boats, and built their own shelters. In all these matters, Lewis and Clark were the beneficiaries of years of travel experience which had taught Euro-Americans the skills of survival on the trail, thus creating a growing pool of non-Indian (and presumably more tractable, or at least differently tractable) travelers, hunters, and intermediaries, ready to be hired. The trip's principal translators were not multilingual Indians, as had so often been the case previously, but instead were French fur traders with long experience of Native peoples. At times, the party took on guides—particularly on the overland stretch across the Rockies. The only long-term Native member of the party was the teenaged wife of one of the French translators.

Lewis and Clark's travels went quite smoothly, with no violent flare-ups on the way out and only one on the return trip. The relative homogeneity of the party and its military ethos went some of the way toward keeping order within the party. But Native reaction along the way also helped keep the party's peace. Right from the beginning, the Indian peoples the Corps of Discovery met understood what was taking place, what the party symbolized, and how best to benefit from the Americans' presence. While the party traveled along the lower Missouri River, many Natives saw the Captains' flat boat as less a threatening incursion and more of an opportunity to build potentially valuable friendships and maybe hitch rides upriver. The captains and their mostly Anglo-American companions benefited from centuries of travelers' comings and goings on the trail.

David Thompson's tale of Twatt and his Cree boatmate, and the story of the exclusivity of party leaders like Mackenzie and Jefferson's captains, offer two different visions of travel relationships at the turn of the nineteenth century. In Thompson's retelling of the crisis on Cross Lake, we see intercultural travel companions sharing the intimacy and interdependence fostered by a frail canoe. Both men were adept travelers, though each was skilled in slightly differing ways and marked his identity in a variety of ways. Their differences were there, most visibly located in the paddlers' attire and its potential consequences. But the intimacy of their travel, the shared peril, and the most of all the commonplace comfortable nature of their intercultural relationship highlight all that was shared between Indians and Europeans on the trail.

On the other hand, the travels of Mackenize and Lewis and Clark show that intimacy was not the only possible result of a long history of shared travel. On these transcontinental treks, party leaders relied first and foremost on European and Euro-American travelers to perform tasks like hunting and paddling—tasks which on similar expeditions a century earlier were usually the domain of the Indian guide, paddler, and hunter. Indians still played a role in these trips. Mackenzie needed Native guides all along the trail, as did Lewis and Clark, and both parties relied on Native food and goodwill to get to where they were headed. But at the core of the party's plans was a confidence that the non-Native travelers themselves could do most of what they needed to do to get by. Was this correct? Sometimes yes and sometimes no, but their confidence in their own and their European companions' abilities to traverse the American trail, and their subsequent marginalization of Native participation, mark these late travel relationships as distinct from what came before.

Yet despite how these travel relationships differed from what had predominated before, the single best known Native travel companion in the history of North American shared travel was the Shoshoni wife of Lewis and Clark's translator and guide Toussaint Charbonneau, Sacagawea. This woman, a former captive living with her husband among the easterly Mandans, proved valuable in a few crucial moments—mostly in aiding the party's acquisition of Shoshoni horses and serving as a link in the chain of translators. But as was so often the case with Native women on the trail, she was rarely given the chance to be central to the trip's shape. Despite her strength and endurance, like most women with European travel parties, she played a small role in the larger trip and had little chance to meaningfully shape her travels with the Corps of Discovery.[26] Yet Sacagawea is the single best-known Native guide in the entire history of common travel. In America's travel lore, Sacagawea is a sort of patron saint of Indian guides, and as such she makes a fitting figure with which to end this book.

At the turn of the millennium, the United States Treasury offered a gold-colored dollar featuring a stylized portrait of the Shoshoni captive peering over her shoulder in a pose more reminiscent of a painting by Jan Vermeer than what one would expect along the Missouri River. The backwards glance allowed the portrait to capture Sacagawea's trail-born infant, Jean-Baptiste, sleeping peacefully swaddled and strapped to his mother's back. The image, therefore, emphasized the Shoshoni's femininity through this maternal connection, but also suggested her strength, both in giving birth on the trail and then carrying and caring for the infant along the way. Nevertheless, the choice of Sacagawea is rich in significance. She was not the first woman on an American coin; feminist and suffragist Susan B. Anthony adorned the last attempted dollar coin, and Lady Liberty has long been a coinage staple. Nor was Sacagawea the first Native American on a coin; that honor goes to the profile obverse of the buffalo nickel. What makes this selection interesting was Sacagawea's role in American history. There are many better-known Indian names and faces that might have been on a coin; Sitting Bull, Red Cloud, and Crazy Horse have all achieved icon status for many Americans of non-Indian ancestry. But they, like many others, are best known for *opposing* the growth of the United States and consequently would make ironic, not to mention potentially memory-insulting, choices for a numismatic portrait. As Anglo-America's favorite Indian guide, Sacagawea played exactly the type of role that Americans can most easily officially celebrate. As the Corps of Discovery's best-remembered guide, she was an aide to expansion, and what is more, she participated in an expedition whose scientific stance and relative lack of violence make it a comfortable celebration choice for Americans still weary of the divisive squabbling that surrounded the quincentenary of Christopher Columbus's 1492 landfall.[27] Sacagawea's most enduring mark is her symbolizing feminized and cooperative Native American assistance on the trail. As a woman, she stands for both the feminine availability of a continent ripe for European colonization, and Native peoples cast as submissive to a new order. Yet the reality of the intercultural travel relationships which took shape on the North American trail during the colonial era was quite at odds with the colonial logic underlying Sacagawea's traditional appeal. Common travel was underscored by a prolonged competition which pitted travelers' conceptions of the trail and how best to travel against those of their fellows. This competition took many forms, from the physical to the spiritual, and encompassed questions of economics, sexuality, and of course the basic skills of travel. What began with overt coercion yielded to softer but more-enduring and subtle pressures of economics and alliances. The heavy hand borne of distance, fear, and self-defeating travel strategies which typified the earliest travel relationships became unworkable as Natives exploited the weaknesses of European plans. The spread of European settlements turned visitors into neighbors, and for Indians made the occasional European traveler a commonplace. More Europeans took to the trail for reasons ranging from missionizing to trade, and from exploration to natural science. This increase in travel and travelers opened up a host of new possibilities for travel relationships. Only a decreasing reliance on Native aid and the proliferation of competent, experienced colonial travelers during the eighteenth century began to limit the possibilities for Native-European travel relationships.

The trail was central to all of this. It was both the setting for these competitive intercultural relationships, and a cause of the contest between Natives and Europeans. The shape and nature of these personalized contests could only have taken place on the trail, and through them travel companions defined each other, themselves, and the trail itself. Fellow travelers brought to the trail a host of conceptions, perceptions, and travel habits. This individual baggage comprised each traveler's social background, their beliefs, their previous travel experiences, their specific travel habits, and many other elements, idiosyncratically personal and historically contingent. The trail focused all of this difference, and provided a place and set of experiences through which Natives and Europeans could build understandings of one another, and of themselves in relation to each other and the trail itself. And in turn, these experiences on the trail worked their way into larger understandings of Indian and European identity through travelers' stories. The personalized competition between intercultural travel partners, I have argued, typified relationships on the trail, and was also the most enduring element of colonial shared travel. The locus of the contests shifted somewhat over the centuries, but much of common travel remained a contest between Natives and newcomers over the most basic travelers' skills and attributes. Because what it took to travel changed so little over the colonial era, these fundamental travel skills continued to be bones of contention for some considerable time. What changed most was how intercultural travel partners came together and how the increasing availability of skilled European travelers limited the possibilities for travel relationships.

Fellow travelers tested themselves and one another against the rigors of the colonial-era trail as part of prolonged colonial encounter. Whenever Indians and Europeans met, they observed and formed opinions which informed their interactions. When Indians and Europeans traveled together, they each brought own their own methods and ideas to the trail. The trail in turn provided them with the chance to see each other at work and to make assessments about one another and the relative worth of their values, ideas, and habits. In this way, travel and exploration were far more than getting from point A to point B; they were also a vibrant part of entire Indian-European colonial encounter. On the early American trail, the trip itself was far more than half the journey.

Notes

Preface

1. This preface is my A.T. travels' second published reference. The first was from one of our fellow travelers on the trail, Ian Marshall, a.k.a. Evergreen. Ian collected his A.T. travel experiences and melded them with his study of American literature in his book *Story Line: Exploring the Literature of the Appalachian Trail*. In so far as Evergreen and I both draw on similar literature and similar experiences, these books are themselves fellow travelers.

2. For critiques of the phenomenon of non-Indian appropriation of Indian images and styles, see Deloria, *Playing Indian*; Churchill, "Indians Are Us?" 207–72.

3. See Anderson, *Benton MacKaye*; Sutton, *Appalachian Trail*; Perrino, *Appalachian Trail*; Hare, *Hiking the Appalachian Trail*.

4. See Nash, *Wilderness and the American Mind*. For a challenge to the reigning perception of Indians as the quintessential ecologists, see Krech, *Ecological Indian*. For critiques of the very idea of nature in this context, see Cronon, *Uncommon Ground*; White, *Organic Machine*.

Introduction. Setting Off on the Trail

1. In this way the trail represents an extension of the Atlantic world. For overview thematic essays, see Bailyn, *Atlantic History*; Klooster, "Rise and Transformation of the Atlantic World," 1–42. See also Armitage, "Concept of the Atlantic World," 11–30.

2. The culture of shared North American travel has not received extensive study. James Merrell wrote that "few scholars have examined the culture of travel." Merrell, *Into the American Woods*, 364. Merrell's study emphasizes the dichotomy of the woods and villages. My book offers the trail as a third option. For more on Native travel and travelers, see Axtell, *Invasion Within*, 72–74, and Rountree, "The Powhatans and Other Woodland Indians as Travelers," 21–52. James P. Ronda's 1989 call for cultural studies of exploration is also an inspiration for my book. See Ronda, "Dreams and Discoveries," 145–62.

3. Despite the term's Cold War resonances, the phrase "fellow travelers" appears in a few colonial travel narratives. I use it as it refers to sharing travel while alluding to an underlying masculinity which I see as shaping many travel relationships.

4. See Morgan, "Encounters, 1500–1800," 62–68, for a discussion of the concept of "arenas" in colonization. Merrell, "Indian History during the English Colonial Era," 132. Merrell notes that thematic concerns focused on "trade, diplomacy, warfare, missions," a focus which reflects the concerns of those "keeping the records."

5. For the most recent version of this, see Ambrose, *Undaunted Courage*; Duncan and Burns, *Lewis and Clark*.

6. See Fabian, *Out of Our Minds*, 1–22. Fabian emphasizes the disjunction inherent in nineteenth-century African colonization and its literature. This study of trail life attempts to align with his stated mission of moving beyond resistance studies to look at the chaotic and disunited nature of the colonial process itself. On the other side of the equation is the recent apotheosis of Lewis and Clark as heroes of beneficent scientific exploration. See Ambrose, *Undaunted Courage*; Duncan and Burns, *Lewis and Clark*. See also Goetzmann, *Exploration and Empire*.

7. This concept parallels the way Orlando Patterson described slavery in *Slavery and Social Death*, 35–76. This idea also closely parallels Cary Carson's vision of the motivations for the rise of consumerism in the American colonies in the 1700s. See Carson, "Consumer Revolution in Colonial America," 483–697.

8. There is a temptation to see the trail as being a "liminal space." In "Betwixt and Between," Victor Turner built on Arnold Van Gennep's *Rites of Passage* and described "liminality" as being a conceptual point between states of being. For example, during initiation rights (a primary focus of many liminality studies), there is a moment when initiates hover between their old state of being and the new one. One example Turner used was that of a "novice in a male puberty rite," who, for a brief moment, was "not-boy-not-man." Turner, "Betwixt and Between," 6. Turner also sees the liminal space as "a realm of pure possibility whence novel configurations of ideas and relations may arise." Turner, *Forest of Symbols*, 93. This idea of the *limen* as a conceptual place between states of existence and even between rules for behavior has proven quite useful, particularly for those studying the meeting of peoples from vastly different backgrounds. For example, Greg Dening used the metaphor of "islands—cultural worlds" and "beaches—cultural boundaries" to describe how Marqueses Islanders tried to assert their vision of life across the "beach" which, by its nature, was a liminal space. Dening, *Island and Beaches*, 20. Dening and David A. Chappell have both pushed liminality even further by suggesting that even the decks of ships can be *limens*. See Chappell, "Shipboard Relations between Pacific Island Women and Euroamerican Men," 131–32. These conditions of cultural uncertainty and danger, combined with Turner's postulated realm of possibility, helped to condition travelers' experiences. Certainly, travel by definition physically separated people from their most familiar settings and shares many of the defining traits of liminality. But being betwixt and between implies a specific vantage point against which one can be seen as being "between." In the case of some rituals, like circumcision, for example, this state of being between is usually (mercifully) short-term and easy to define. But in the case of travel, it is somewhat harder to say where the betwixt-ness begins and ends. Does it start when one leaves home or at some later time, say when leaving one's home terrain? Does it play out differently on waterborne travels than on land, and will it be different if one is accompanied by familiar people or strangers? Rather than seeing travel and the trail as universal conveyors of liminality, I see the intimacy, the immediacy, and the crucial interconnectedness of the relationships which the trail fostered—travel's social dimensions—as also being defining elements and principal reasons for contest.

9. Since 1991, Richard White's *The Middle Ground: Indians, Empires, and Republics*

in the Great Lakes Region, 1650–1815, has set the dominant paradigm for understanding the meetings of Natives and Europeans. White's metaphor described both a place—the Great Lakes region—and a process. White built on Anthony Giddens's idea of "structuration," which Giddens saw as a way to transcend the unidirectional action implied by the traditional Marxist Base and Superstructure metaphor. Rather than one (base) being the driving force in the shaping of the other (superstructure), Giddens outlined a theory in which the two were mutually formative, one of the other, and vice versa. The idea has great power and can be seen in other work, such as (most germane for this book) Mary Louise Pratt's description of "transculturation." White's model saw discussion and miscommunication (both intentional and accidental) as creating new meanings (often shared) where before two had existed. See Pratt, *Imperial Eyes*, and also Scott, *Domination and the Arts of Resistance*, for one of the defining studies on the working of resistance. There has been a tendency to push White's metaphor somewhat, and use what was both process and place specific as a catchall for *all* Indian-European relations. Nevertheless, the concept is both useful and influential. The ideas and metaphors of "middle" and "between" implied in the Middle Ground concept as used, have brought to the fore a scholarly interest in one strain of Indian-colonial relations study and one particular type of figure within that realm—the culture broker. These people were able to move comfortably in many cultures, and they served as "brokers" able to bring different peoples together and represent interests of one within the other. These figures—inhabitants of the "Middle Ground"—and the very act of brokerage have become a virtual subfield within the large field of Indian-colonial relations. Among the earliest studies to use this model were Wallace, *Conrad Weiser*; Edmonds, *American Indian Leaders*; Sweet and Nash, *Struggle and Survival in Colonial America*; Fausz, "Middlemen in Peace and War"; Richter, "Cultural Brokers and Intercultural Politics"; Kawashima, "Forest Diplomats," 1–14. Richter in particular rooted his vision of culture brokers in sociological theory, specifically Social Node theory. After White's *Middle Ground*, subsequent brokerage studies relied more on the language and the idea of the "middle ground." See Karttunen, *Between Worlds*, xii. See also Hagedorn, "'A Friend to Go between Them'" and "Brokers of Understanding"; Merrell, "Shickellamy," 227–57; Taylor, "Captain Hendrick Aupaumut," 431–57; Merrell, *Into The American Woods*. All of these studies, though, and the very idea of cultural brokerage itself, tend to see cultures as being fairly unified entities—closed circles which one enters or straddles. Instead, my study prefers to avoid abstract definitions of culture and emphasize its locally enacted components. This allows for change and adaptation by individuals without suggesting that they sit somewhere along a cultural continuum from the pure to the debased. Cultures are enacted by individuals who are always both part and not part of their social entities acting on fragmentary knowledge and learned practices which they acquire throughout life. These may come from one culture or another, but are always fit into the logic of one's worldview. In this vision I rely in part on Bourdieu, *Outline of a Theory of Practice* and *The Logic of Practice*.

10. This draws on how Bourdieu described his vision of the "habitus." Bourdieu, *Outline of a Theory of Practice*, 16. Much of my study deals with the location and maintenance of difference between travelers. In recent years the role of Indian relations in the articulation of the concept of race has become a central scholarly concern. Unlike others,

I do not put race at the center of discussions of difference, at least in so far as the trail is concerned. Instead I see many different issues coming into play in ways that do not always fit with the concept of race. Nor do I see a language of race coming to any great or exclusive prominence in the kinds of incidents I examine herein. Nevertheless, the rise of race as a language of differences between colonial-era Indians and Europeans has been an important field of research. See, most recently, Merritt, *At the Crossroads*; Vaughan, "From White Man to Redskin"; Shoemaker, "How Indians Got to Be Red"; and Kupperman, "Constructing Race."

11. The concept and metaphor of the frontier has been falling out of favor in recent years. See Limerick, Milner, and Rankin, *Trails*; Cayton and Teute, Introduction, 1–15. Others have used spatial metaphors to describe Native-European relationships. White's "Middle Ground" is the most prominent, and has helped widen an interest in figures who inhabited that "middle," again layering a spatial metaphor onto social relations. Others have used Pratt's "Contact Zone," and modified versions of the "frontier" as employed by Cayton and Teute. Merritt's "Crossroads" is also a sort of middle-ground metaphor which, noticeably used the image of roads, although her study is less concerned with roads themselves than is this study.

12. Ronda, "Dreams and Discoveries."

13. Michel de Certeau observed that Parisian street signs "make themselves available to the diverse meanings given them by passers-by," thereby enabling each pedestrian to string together a distinctive text of their travels. Certeau, *Practice of Everyday Life*. With slight modification, I see the same thing at play on the trail and within travel relationships. Whereas Certeau's observation highlights the possibilities for multiple meanings, North American intercultural travel brings the conflict of colonization into the observation. For Natives and Europeans, multiple meanings along the trail were sources of long-enduring conflict. See also Soja, *Postmodern Geographies*. Soja offers a call to arms for scholars interested in seeing space and place receive substantive and serious engagement in fields like history. While this study is not one of space or place per se, the relationships this books studies only took place within a particular space. Therefore, space is central to defining this study. See also Tilley, *Phenomenology of Landscape*, 15.

14. Leed, *The Mind of the Traveler*. See also Williams, *Travel Culture*.

15. Helms, *Ulysses' Sail* and *Craft and the Kingly Ideal*; Van Gennep, *Rites of Passage*, 26; Turner and Turner, *Image and Pilgrimage in Christian Culture*.

16. James Merrell uses these rituals in Pennsylvania and New York to demonstrate the danger the woods presented in Native minds. Merrell, *Into the American Woods*, 143–56.

17. The study of travel literature, particularly its cultural and colonial impact, has taken off in the past decades. The literature has become large and diverse. Much of my work here has focused on the literary dimensions and cultural or colonial implications of this type of writing. The central texts in this subfield are Said, *Orientalism*, and Greenblatt, *Marvelous Possessions*. Also crucial is Pratt, *Imperial Eyes*, which brings into focus the contours of colonizer-colonized conflicts within these texts and how these shaped cultures on both sides of the encounter. See also Fabian, *Out of Our Minds*, for a provocative extension of Pratt's ideas into a critique of anthropological discourse and travel

writing. Fabian's work is particularly influential in the present book, in that I share his desire to decenter the European actors and reveal the partial and fragmentary nature of colonial enterprises. These authors focused on European travel writing in Africa and the Middle East. See also Elsner and Rubiés, *Voyages and Visions*; Duncan and Gregory, *Writes of Passage*; Thomas, *Colonialism's Culture*. For similar work on North America, see Liebersohn, *Aristocratic Encounters*; Sayre, *Les Sauvages Américains*. See also Franklin, *Discoverers, Explorers,* Settlers. Most of these studies focus on specific moments and places. Leed and Helms both have tried to build what we may call theories of travel.

18. Helms, *Ulysses' Sail*.

Chapter 1. The Paradox of the Conquistadors' Trail

1. Hoffman, *New Andalucia*, 88. Hoffman notes that Soto's charge was to explore territory and then settle along a choice piece of coastline. As governor he had the authority to grant Indian villages to his followers but also had to construct three forts at his own expense. Hoffman sees the generous terms of Soto's grant as an indication of how undesirable La Florida had become in Spanish eyes by 1539.

2. In *The Spanish Frontier in North America*, David Weber states that Hernando de Soto would have been known to his contemporaries as "Soto," and not "De Soto" as most modern Americans know him. Weber, *Spanish Frontier in North America,* xix. Although Weber prefers to stick with the more common "De Soto," I prefer to follow Patricia Galloway's lead and use the Spanish form "Soto."

3. For more on Soto's life and career, see Hoffman, "The De Soto Expedition, a Cultural Crossroads," 1:1–16, and Lamar, "Hernando de Soto before Florida," 181–206; Hudson, *Knights of Spain, Warriors of the Sun*; Duncan, *Hernando de Soto*. For more on Soto's time in Peru, see Lockhart, *The Men of Cajamarca*.

4. In *De Soto Chronicles*, ed. Clayton, Knight, and Moore (hereinafter *De Soto Chronicles*), 1:263.

5. In *De Soto Chronicles*, 1:262–63.

6. Galloway, "Incestuous Soto Narratives," 11–44. Galloway argues that of the three Soto accounts penned by men who were there, the Rangel account, although retold by Oviedo, comes the closest to being a primary document. The other two, Biedma and Elvas, seem to be as indebted to Oviedo's retelling of the events as they are to the authors' experiences in North America.

7. For brief reviews of precontact Florida, and particularly its village-centered societies, see Milanich, *Florida Indians and the Invasion from Europe*, and Hann, *Apalachee*.

8. *De Soto Chronicles*, 1:262; Weber, *The Spanish Frontier in North America*, 50–53.

9. *De Soto Chronicles*, 1:263–64.

10. Hammond and Rey, *Narratives of the Coronado Expedition* (hereinafter cited as *Coronado*) 194 (Weber says 192). Coronado was acquitted of the charges leveled against him. Weber, "Reflection on Coronado," 10. Coronado's acquittal was not so much a refutation of the charges against him, but more a lack of will and meaningful proof to convict him.

11. McAlister, *Spain and Portugal in the New World*, 98–104. See also Restall, *Seven Myths of the Spanish Conquest*, 1–43.

12. The Black Legend—the vision of the Spanish as singularly cruel by nature—has had mixed fortunes in the literature of American colonization. England and France were quick to exploit the propaganda potential of the colonial condemnations of Spanish observers such as Dominican Bartolomé de Las Casas. See Las Casas, *Devastation of the Indies*. In recent years a form of the Black Legend has resurfaced in scholarship that examines just how destructive the conquest of the Indies was. Most notable among this work is Sale, *Conquest of Paradise*. See also Stannard, *American Holocaust*, and Wilson, *Earth Shall Weep*, for modern work indebted to Black Legend themes and attempts to extend it to all European nations.

13. Stefansson, *Three Voyages of Martin Frobisher*, 50; Prins, "To the Land of the Mistigoches," 175–76. See also Sturtevant and Quinn, "This New Prey," 61–140; Oberg, "Gods and Men," 367–90, and "Indians and Englishmen at the First Roanoke Colony," 75–89.

14. Worth, "Late Spanish Military Expeditions," 104–22.

15. Hoffman, *New Andalucia*, 89. Hoffman points out that Dominican influence over Charles V was at a low ebb between the 1520s and the 1540s. After this time missionaries were more likely than military men to receive Crown grants to take in new lands. Force was still part of the plan, but less central. Early Spanish colonization in general was marked by tensions between churchmen and military conquerors, as both tried to gain royal approval for their vision of how conquest society should be ordered. For more on this conflict, see Hanke, *Spanish Struggle for Justice*.

16. "Laws and Ordinances Newly Made by His Majesty," 13.

17. Hammond and Rey, *Rediscovery of New Mexico*, 6–7.

18. Worth, "Late Spanish Military Expeditions," 111.

19. Juan de Oñate was one notable exception. Between 1598 and 1605, Oñate covered a distance similar to the one covered by Coronado half a century earlier and along many of the same trails, visiting many of the same places. Nevertheless, Oñate's march was tied closely to settlement in the region and did not see the same levels of violence and deception which attended Coronado's failed foray. See Simmons, *Last Conquistador*.

20. Quinn, *New American World*, 2:9; Adorno and Pautz, *Álvar Núñez Cabeza de Vaca*, 1:35.

21. Soto's many pigs were also an attempt to avoid Narváez's errors of poor provisioning.

22. *De Soto Chronicles*, 1:254.

23. Ibid., 1:93.

24. Ibid., 1:70.

25. Ibid., 1:93.

26. Ibid., 1:70.

27. Ibid., 1:267.

28. Ibid., 1:74. Soto's use of porters was on a far larger scale than either Narváez's or Coronado's.

29. Weddle, "Soto's Problems of Orientation," 226. Weddle claims there is no evidence that Soto or his men used navigation aids during their entrada until after Soto's death. Such aids, however, would have been of little use for marchers uncertain of where exactly they wanted to march.

30. Helms, *Ulysses' Sail* and *Craft and the Kingly Ideal*.
31. *De Soto Chronicles*, 1:226.
32. Ibid., 1:254.
33. Helms, *Ulysses' Sail*.
34. Fabian, *Out of Our Minds*.
35. *De Soto Chronicles*, 1:226.
36. Quinn, *New American World*, 2:20.
37. Ibid., 2:22.
38. *De Soto Chronicles* 1:294.
39. Quinn, *New American World*, 2:21.
40. *De Soto Chronicles*, 1:273.
41. Ibid., 1:271.
42. Ibid., 1:266.
43. Ibid., 1:267.
44. Ibid., Elvas, 1:74. Garcilaso de la Vega claimed that the youth was in fact captured at Apalachee, but most scholars tend to favor the details offered by firsthand observers like the Gentleman from Elvas over the later writings of Garcilaso. See Galloway, "The Incestuous Soto Narratives," 11–44; Henige, "The Context, Content, and Credibility," 10–11. Garcilaso claims that Perico was one of over three hundred captives taken at Naputica.
45. *De Soto Chronicles*, Elvas, 1:80.
46. Ibid., Rangel, 1:273; Elvas, 1:80.
47. Ibid., Elvas, 1:80.
48. Ibid.
49. Ibid.
50. Ibid., 1:81.
51. Ibid., 1:84.
52. *Coronado* 219. See also Wedel, "Indian They Called *Turco*," 153–62.
53. The Ottoman siege of Vienna in 1529 ended with a Turkish retreat. But even though stemmed, the fifteenth-century Ottoman expansion left much of southeastern Europe under Turkish control. See Goodwin, *Lords of the Horizons*.
54. Gutiérrez, *When Jesus Came*, 44–45.
55. *Coronado*, 235.
56. Ibid., 301.
57. Ibid., 301, 242.
58. Ibid., 302.
59. Ibid., 242.
60. Ibid., 304.
61. Ibid., 241.
62. Ibid., 242, 304, 336. During later trials the Spaniards could not agree on who killed Turco or by what means. Most of the witnesses claimed him to have been garroted. This was a fairly common form of criminal execution in the sixteenth and seventeenth centuries.
63. Ibid., 23, 305.

64. The Peruvian Garcilaso de la Vega, a nonparticipant and the most embellishment-prone of the four Soto chroniclers, claimed that Perico had been the servant of traders from the interior and that his story was based on his travels with them. In Garcilaso's retelling, a friendly Indian in Spanish service recognized Perico and pointed him out to the soldiers as someone who knew the interior. When asked about his connection to the merchants, Perico replied that "he knew about some of the provinces that he had visited with his masters, the merchants, and he would venture to guide the Spanish twelve or thirteen days' journey." *De Soto Chronicles*, 2:249. The friendly assistance of Garcilaso's Perico is suspect, as are the boy's claims that his merchant masters regularly traded in "yellow" and "white" metals like the silver and gold the Spanish showed him. Garcilaso claimed that the youth was in fact captured at Apalachee. But there is reason to favor the details offered by the three firsthand observers over the later but more rich stories of Garcilaso. See Henige, "Context, Content, and Credibility," 10–11.

65. James Brooks offers an extensive review of the nature and implications of this trade in *Captives and Cousins*. For his discussion of Turco and the Quivira party's makeup, see pp. 46–48.

66. Duncan, *Hernando de Soto*, 262; Axtell, *Indians' New South*, 16–17.

67. Hudson, *Knights of Spain, Warriors of the Sun*, 127.

68. *Coronado*, 302; Wedel, "Indian They Called *Turco*," 159.

69. *Coronado*, 221.

70. Brandon, *Quivira*, 33.

71. *Coronado*, 235. Wedel ("Indian They Called *Turco*,")claims that much of Turco's information came through hand signs.

72. *Coronado*, 221.

73. Ibid.; Wedel, "Indian They Called *Turco*," 155.

74. *De Soto Chronicles*, 1:84.

75. Ibid., 1:226. Although his focus was elsewhere, Weddle rightly points out that due to his lack of navigational aids and an absence of a willing Indian faction, as in Peru, Soto was "often at the mercy of Indian guides, who had their own reasons for giving him false information." Weddle emphasizes deception in Native misguidance. Weddle, "Soto's Problems of Orientation," 217.

76. *De Soto Chronicles*, 1:257.

77. *Coronado*, 204.

78. *De Soto Chronicles*, 1:145.

79. Ibid., 1:146.

80. Ibid., 1:244.

81. While most of the party probably died on their rafts or drowned in the Gulf, it is also quite possible that many washed up on shore and were taken into Indian villages, as was Cabeza de Vaca. Since none were ever contacted again by Europeans, their ultimate fates remain unknown and unknowable to us. See Adorno, *Cabeza de Vaca*, 2:103.

82. The Narváez entrada is overshadowed by the later longer march of its principal chronicler, Cabeza de Vaca, and by the march of Soto. Consequently the discussion of Narváez is shorter than that of his colleagues. Although there is considerable disagreement about the route of the party's march, most scholars concur that poor planning

(particularly poor provisioning) and the weaknesses of Narváez as a leader did in the march. Oviedo's interpretation, formulated in the wake of the events, still holds sway. Samuel Eliot Morison called Narváez "the most incompetent of all who sailed for Spain in this era." Morison, *European Discovery of America*, 518. Similarly Marrinan, Scarry, and Majors argue that Soto's careful provisioning was in part a result of conversations with Cabeza de Vaca and a desire to obviate Narváez's errors. Marrinan, Scarry, and Majors, "Prelude to de Soto," 71–82. Jerald Milanich called the Narváez expedition "star-crossed" and emphasized the lack of provisions and the men's illnesses in his retelling. Milanich, *Florida Indians and the Invasion from Europe*, 116.

83. Adorno, *Cabeza de Vaca*, 1:53.
84. Ibid., 1:53.
85. Ibid., 1:55.
86. Ibid.
87. Ibid.
88. Ibid., 1:59.
89. Ibid., 1:51.
90. Ibid., 1:59.
91. *De Soto Chronicles*, 1:227, 1:72.
92. The route of Narváez's march, like those of almost all other conquistadors, is open to debate. The location of the entrada, as they believed they entered Apalachee, is germane to my interpretation, but not pivotal. Jerald Milanich has argued that Narváez's guides led the Spaniards on a "very circuitous route" through rough country on their way to Apalachee. This would account for the discrepancies between Soto's and Narváez's entradas' vision of the land. Likewise, Milanich believes that the town in which Narváez and his men passed a month was most likely on the edges of the Apalachee heartland, as its description is inconsistent with what we know of the province. Milanich, *Florida Indians and the Invasion from Europe*, 122–23. The guides who led this march were those captured after the entrada's visit at Dulchanchellin's village. Adorno, *Cabeza de Vaca*, 1:51–53. These were probably people from Apalachee, who unlike their enemies from Dulchanchellin, would have had no interest in leading the Spaniards into Apalachee proper.
93. Adorno, *Cabeza de Vaca*, 1:61
94. Ibid., 1:61.
95. Ibid.
96. Ibid.
97. Ibid., 1:63.
98. Hammond and Rey, *Rediscovery of New Mexico*, 94.
99. Ibid., 90.
100. Ibid., 80.

Chapter 2. "Upon Proper Terms"

1. Richter, *Ordeal of the Longhouse*, 88–93. Richter sees the attempt by the five Mohawk guides to ditch the Dutchmen as a sign that many in Mohawk Country were still ambivalent about their trade partners. He also suggests that the villagers' remonstrations

as signs that the Mohawks had better adjusted to the Dutchmen's odd trade habits while the Oneidas still demanded the following of their own customs.

2. Van den Bogaert, *Journey into Mohawk and Oneida Country*, 5.

3. Ibid., 5.

4. Ibid., 6.

5. Ibid.

6. Ibid.

7. Ibid.

8. Ibid., 37.

9. Sqorhea's fate is unclear. Although he seems to have traveled a few days with the Dutchmen, and complained about a few heavy streams, his name soon falls out of the narrative. On December 21 the travelers rested at the "fourth castle" of Osquage, where they met Oquoho, who accompanied them on the trail. The following day the narrative mentions "the old man who was our guide" (8–9) but is not clear about who that man was. Both Sqorhea and Oquoho were staying behind during the winter hunts perhaps because both were aged—indeed the resemblance of Sqorhea's name to the Mohawk word for skeleton suggests a man aged and thinned. Later in the narrative the Dutch again had trouble finding guides suggesting that their travel companions were accompanying them only from one village to the next.

10. Greg Dening described the European mariners who first drifted past the Marquesas Islands as being men of "no settlement," who had "no tomorrows in the places they visited." A similar dynamic was at work in North American travel relationships. Dening, *Islands and Beaches*, 23.

11. Smith, *Complete Works of Captain John Smith* (hereinafter cited as *John Smith*), 2:173.

12. Ibid., 2:178.

13. Ibid.

14. Ibid., 2:167.

15. Ibid.

16. Rountree, *Powhatan Indians of Virginia*, 114–25.

17. Helms, *Ulysses' Sail*, 3–65.

18. *John Smith*, 2:167.

19. Champlain, *Works of Samuel de Champlain* (hereinafter cited as *Champlain Works*), 3:44.

20. Cox, *Journeys of la Salle*, 2:167.

21. Ibid., 2:168.

22. Thwaites, *Jesuit Relations* (hereinafter cited as *JR*), 59:95–97; Burpee, *Journals and Letters*, 302–306; *Champlain Works*, 2:64; Barbour, *Jamestown Voyages under the First Charter*, 88.

23. Helms, *Ulysses' Sail*, 3–65; Helms, "Long Distance Contacts," 157–74; Helms, *Craft and the Kingly Ideal*. One of Helms's most relevant points for this argument is that distance and knowledge of it (through physical and spiritual travel) brings with it power. She defines what she calls "distance specialists" and notes that "political-religious specialists may seek association with geographically foreign phenomena to augment their

status and express qualities of leadership." Helms, "Long Distance Contacts," 161. On one level this serves as an explanation for why leaders were eager to meet new arrivals. But if geographic knowledge is part of obtaining and holding power, then it is logical to conclude that controlling that knowledge once possessed would be a strategy for retaining political power.

24. Salley, *Narratives of Early Carolina*, 94. The Englishman of the story, Robert Sandford, did not claim that the Edisto man was a headman. However, the Indian's name, "Cassique," suggests that he was a leader of some sort.

25. McWilliams, *Iberville's Gulf Journals*, 64.

26. Beauchamp, *Moravian Journals*, 91.

27. La Vérendrye, *Journals and Letters*, 353.

28. Richter, *Ordeal of the Longhouse*.

29. *JR*, 47:97.

30. *JR*, 47:73. For uses and meanings of the Woods' Edge Ceremony, see Merrell, *Into the American Woods*, 19–23; Richter, *Ordeal of the Longhouse*, 91–92, 94–95. For various descriptions of the rituals words and protocols, see Fenton, "Structure, Continuity, and Change," 28–30; Hale, *Iroquois Book of Rites*, 117–21.

31. Richter, *Ordeal of the Longhouse*, 115. See also pp. 112, 114, 117–18, 130–32, 141, 181.

32. Hansen, "Journal of Messrs. Hansen and Van Brugh's Visit to Onondaga," 4:802.

33. Graffenried, *Account of the Founding of New Bern*, 234.

34. See Yerbury, *Subarctic Indians and the Fur Trade*; Fiske, Sleeper-Smith, and Wicken, *New Faces of the Fur Trade*; Francis and Morantz, *Partners in Furs*.

35. Yerbury, *Subarctic Indians and the Fur Trade*, 17–59.

36. Davies, *Letters from Hudson Bay*, xxvii.

37. Van Kirk, *Many Tender Ties*.

38. Hearne, *Journey* (1911), 140.

39. Speck, *Samuel Hearne and the Northwest Passage*, 142–50.

40. See Helm, "Matonabbee's Map," 28–47. Governor Richard Norton commissioned this particular expedition, and the result was a map, Norton's copy of which still exists. On the map, the curvy Canadian coastline is straightened into a single line, but Helm's cartographic analysis of the map confirms the accuracy of its placement of rivers and basins.

41. See Rich, *Fur Trade and the Northwest*, 98–99.

42. The events of these expeditions will be covered in detail in subsequent chapters.

43. Hearne, *Journey* (1911), 100.

44. Speck, *Samuel Hearne and the Northwest Passage*, 145. Speck concludes that Matonabbee was "disillusioned about the impregnability of the fort and the infallibility of his English friends." But he does not deal with the fact that Matonabbee's personal prestige was tied to that of the English Hudson's Bay Company traders at the Churchill River.

45. Speck, *Samuel Hearne and the Northwest Passage*, 145.

46. Nestabeck also appears in English documents under the names "The English Chief" (Mackenzie) and "Aw gee nah" (Fidler).

47. Lamb, *Journals and Letters of Mackenzie*, 163.

48. Fidler, "Journal of a Journey with the Chepawyans," 541. For Nestabeck's associations, see Gough, *First across the Continent*, 55–56.

49. Bliss, "Conducted Tour," 16–24. Bliss argues that Mackenzie's guides conducted him on a tour of the region. Bliss underestimates the degree to which Mackenzie actually shaped the trip's pace and tone. I will pick up this theme more directly in a later chapter. See also Goetzmann and Williams, *Atlas of American Exploration*, 114.

50. For the effects of trade in Chipewyan culture and warfare, see Reedy-Maschner and Maschner, "Marauding Middlemen," 703–43; Sharp, "Caribou-Eater Chipewyan," 35–40.

51. The meaningful differences between gift exchange and pay constitute some of the toughest questions and some of the longest debates in anthropology. The literature is vast, and debate has often focused on the extent to which gifts are free offerings or come with implied quid pro quos of return. Most scholars follow Bronislaw Malinowski and Marcel Mauss and see that gifting is part of a socio-economic tie that used material goods to unite people and peoples. The obligation of return is as much a part of the gift as the gift itself. This raises troubling questions about the differences between Indian and European economic models and if carried too far threatens to blur distinctions that historical actors certainly felt existed. For interpretations of gift exchanges, see Mauss, *Gift*; Sahlins, *Stone Age Economics*.

52. Danckaerts, *Journal*, 172–73.

53. Ibid., 174.

54. The notable exceptions to this are the Spanish marches of the mid and late 1500s, particularly those in the Southwest.

55. Alvord and Bidgood, *First Explorations*, 184.

56. Bossu, *Travels*, 156.

57. Hansen, "Journal of Messrs. Hansen and Van Brugh's Visit to Onondaga," 4:807.

58. Hearne, *Journals of Samuel Hearne and Philip Turnor*, 88.

59. *JR*, 51:185.

60. La Vérendrye, *Journals and Letters*, 78.

61. McWilliams, *Iberville's Gulf Journals*, 55.

62. Leon-Massanet, quoted in Bolton, *Spanish Exploration in the Southwest*, 395.

63. Escalante, "Diary and Itinerary," in Bolton, *Pageant in the Wilderness*, 149.

64. Henday, "York Factory to the Blackfeet Country," 346.

65. Long, *John Long's Voyages*, 77.

66. Johnson, *Saskatchewan Journals and Correspondence*, 52.

67. Danckaerts, *Journal*, 159

68. Mereness, *Travels in the American Colonies*, 316.

69. Marvin, *Five Fur Traders of the Northwest*, 72.

70. Bartram, *Journey from Pennsylvania to Onondaga*, 62.

71. McWilliams, *Iberville's Gulf Journals*, 128.

72. Bolton, *Spanish Exploration in the Southwest*, 395.

73. Ibid., 411.

74. Kalm, *Peter Kalm's Travels*, 355.

75. Post, "Two Journals of Western Tours," 1:189.

76. See Merrell, *Into the American Woods*, 245–46, for more on Essoweyoualand.

77. Lawson, *New Voyage to Carolina*, 29.

78. Danckaerts, *Journal*, 149.

79. Hearne, *Journals of Samuel Hearne and Philip Turnor*, 193. See also Thistle, *Indian-European Trade Relations*, 51–80, for a discussion of Indians and fur trade employees and partners.

80. Lawson, *New Voyage to Carolina*, 31, 62. See also Merrell, *Indians' New World*, 43–44, for a fuller discussion of Enoe Will.

81. Byrd, *Dividing Line*, 159. See also Brown, *Good Wives, Nasty Wenches, and Anxious Patriarchs*, 280, for a treatment of the surveying party that places it in the context of homosocial entertainments and colonial masculinity.

82. Merrell, *Indians' New World*, 58–59; Rights, *The American Indian in North Carolina*, 113–15. Byrd claimed that a George Hix had his plantation three miles from Fort Christianna in 1728. Byrd, *Dividing Line*, 311.

83. Byrd, *Dividing Line*, 305–7.

84. Ibid.

85. Ibid., 107. Byrd recorded that the Meherrins had "lately removed from the mouth of the Meherrin," as they were "frighten'd away from there by the late massacre committed upon 14 of their nation by the Catawbas."

86. I take my number by counting kill references in the text. This method is imprecise at best, but is also the only way to estimate Bearskin's total. Byrd, *Dividing Line*, 163, 165, 169, 189, 189, 193, 195, 209, 211, 213, 217, 223, 231, 237, 249, 261, 267, 273, 279, 281, 295, 287.

87. Byrd, *Dividing Line*, 281; Brown, *Good Wives, Nasty Wenches, and Anxious Patriarchs*, 280. Brown suggests that the Virginia's used the trip and the hunting to appropriate elements of native masculinity to enhance their own "manly vigor." Brown also claims that the English hunters were embarrassingly outdone by Bearskin. This is not quite true. The colonists killed at least eighteen turkeys, six deer, and five bears. This is not a bad showing considering that they devoted most of their time to surveying and were, as Byrd noted, pretty poor hunters. Their totals do not support Brown's claims that the Englishmen returned usually with only the "diminutive carcasses of opossums and raccoons"—animals which were not even mentioned by Byrd. This kind of casual appropriation of Native imagery and symbolism was not rare. See Deloria, *Playing Indian*.

88. Byrd, *Dividing Line*, 168–69.

89. Ibid., 311.

Chapter 3. "Quite Contrary to the Custom"

1. Lawson, *New Voyage to Carolina*, 212.

2. Ibid., 213.

3. Ibid., 214.

4. Rather than passively receiving the "natural world," Indians across the continent worked hard to create and maintain the world so as to have it be of maximum utility. See Krech, *The Ecological Indian*; Cronon, *Changes in the Land*; and White, *Organic Machine*.

5. White, "Indian Peoples and the Natural World," 95–98. White poses the thorny question, how do we get at Native understandings of the land and landscapes? One of the best attempts is Basso's *Wisdom Sits in Places*.

6. Beauchamp, *Moravian Journals*, 41, 46.

7. Woodward, *Woodward's Reminiscences*, 130; Alvord and Bidgood, *First Explorations*, 184.

8. Adams, *Radisson*, 60.

9. *JR*, 12:27, 29:213–15.

10. Beauchamp, *Moravian Journals*, 82.

11. Sagard, *Long Journey*, 253; Bartram, *Journey from Pennsylvania to Onondaga*, 45,

12. Lamb, *Journals and Letters of Mackenzie*, 238.

13. Gates, *Five Fur Traders of the Northwest*, 83.

14. Beauchamp, *Moravian Journals*, 38.

15. *Champlain Works*, 2:268; Cox, *Journeys of la Salle*, 2:208; Long, *John Long's Voyages*, 58; *JR*, 64:43; Lawson, *New Voyage to Carolina*, 63; Henry, *Travels in Canada*, 212–14.

16. *Champlain Works*, 2:268.

17. Long, *John Long's Voyages*, 58.

18. *JR*, 59:139; Cox, *Journeys of la Salle*, 2:208.

19. Beauchamp, *Moravian Journals*, 94.

20. *JR*, 51:181.

21. *Champlain Works*, 1:316.

22. McWilliams, *Iberville's Gulf Journals*, 168.

23. Bland, "Discovery of New Brittaine," 121.

24. Barbé-Marbois, *Our Revolutionary Forefathers*, 188.

25. *JR*, 66:267.

26. Cox, *Journeys of la Salle*, 2:208.

27. Ibid., 1:258.

28. Sagard, *Long Journey*, 41.

29. La Vérendrye, *Journals and Letters*, 427; Celeron, "Celeron's Expedition down the Ohio Rivers," 48; Johnston, *First Explorations of Kentucky*; see also Gist, "Colonel Christopher Gist's Journal," 66.

30. Adams, *Radisson*, 7.

31. Byrd, *William Byrd's Histories of the Dividing Line*, 193.

32. Lamb, *Journals and Letters of Mackenzie*, 179.

33. Bossu, *Travels*, 69.

34. *JR*, 10:89.

35. Ibid., 32:137.

36. Stevens, Kent, and Woods, *Travels in New France*, 104–105.

37. Lamb, *Journals and Letters of Mackenzie*, 267.

38. Lindley, "Expedition to Detroit," 579. Lindley's tale can be read in several ways. On one level it is a story of double stereotyping: the awkward white man meeting his fate through his own incompetence and the lazy Indian snoozing toward his destiny. Lindley

also adds a hint of anti-Indian treachery as an aside by suggesting that it "is supposed that" the canoe left the shore when "some wicked person loosed it."

39. *JR*, 19:127.
40. Ibid., 20:45.
41. Ibid., 55:135.
42. Ibid., 59:97.
43. Linck, *Wenceslaus Linck's Diary*, 49.
44. Hammond and Rey, *Rediscovery of New Mexico*, 297.
45. McWilliams, *Iberville's Gulf Journals*, 147.
46. *Champlain Works*, 2:126.
47. *JR*, 32:71.
48. *Champlain Works*, 2:95. Dennis, *Cultivating a Landscape of Peace*, 71. Dennis sees the questioning of Champlain's dreaming and his subsequent revelation of a propitious dream as meaning that the allied Indians saw the Frenchman as "a qualified actor in the developing play."
49. *Champlain Works*, 2:102.
50. Ibid., 2:102. See also Trigger, *Children of Aataensic*, 254. Trigger points out that many early modern Europeans were not unfamiliar with torture, it being a regular part of the era's many public executions. Trigger suggests that Champlain may have been motivated less by a revulsion at the "cruelty" but rather at a sense that it was wrong to treat a prisoner of war in such a manner.
51. *Champlain Works*, 2:103.
52. See Trigger, *Children of Aataensic*, 71–75.
53. This type of confusion was a central constituent in the making of what Richard White called the Middle Ground.
54. Van den Bogaert, *Journey into Mohawk and Oneida Country*, 20.
55. Lawson, *New Voyage to Carolina*, 31.
56. Bolton, *Pageant in the Wilderness*, 176.
57. Lamb, *Journals and Letters of Mackenzie*, 283.
58. Bartram, *Journey from Pennsylvania to Onondaga*, 82.
59. Henday, "York Factory to the Blackfeet Country," 344.
60. *JR*, 8:79, 9:277, 12:117. See also Axtell, *Invasion Within*, 71–90.
61. *JR*, 9:271, 273, 277; 41:97.
62. *JR*, 24:53.
63. *JR*, 67:217.
64. Lederer, *Discoveries*, 149. For more on Virginia's westward expansion, see Briceland, *Westward from Virginia*.
65. Lederer, *Discoveries*, 149.
66. See also Waselkov, "Indian Maps of the Colonial Southeast," 292–343.
67. Lederer, *Discoveries*, 149–50.
68. Ibid., 150–151.
69. Ibid., 150.
70. Ibid., 151; Briceland, *Westward from Virginia*, 96–98.

71. Cox, *Journeys of la Salle*, 1:141; Hammond and Rey, *Don Juan de Oñate*, 138.
72. *Champlain Works*, 1:415.
73. Cox, *Journeys of la Salle*, 2:182–83.
74. Hansen, "Conference with the Five Nations," 5:375.
75. La Vérendrye, *Journals and Letters*, 334; Lawson, *New Voyage to Carolina*, 23.
76. Hansen, "Journal of Messrs. Hansen and Van Brugh's Visit to Onondaga," 4:804.
77. Linck, *Wenceslaus Linck's Diary*, 63–69.
78. McWilliams, *Iberville's Gulf Journals*, 146.
79. Post, "Two Journals of Western Tours," 1:185–87.
80. See Mancall, *Deadly Medicine*. See particularly chapter 3, "Consumption," 63–84. Scholarship has generally focused on Native drinking rituals and consequences.

Chapter 4. None but the Rattlesnakes!

1. Henry, *Travels in Canada*, 176. For more on the Southern Ojibwas' participation in Pontiac's Rebellion, see White, *Middle Ground*, 269–314; Schmalz, *Ojibwa of Southern Ontario*, 63–77; Dowd, *War under Heaven*.
2. See Vecsey, *Traditional Ojibwa Religion*, 72–77. Vecsey does not discuss the concept of the Manitou Kinibic.
3. Summers, *Malleus Maleficarum*, 63–64.
4. Morris and Morris, *Men and Snakes*, 82–83.
5. Thomas, *Religion and the Decline of Magic*, 513.
6. Jameson, *Narratives of New Netherland*, 169–70.
7. *JR*, 43:155.
8. Ibid.
9. Lindholt, *John Josselyn, Colonial Traveler*, 23, 82.
10. Kellogg, *Early Narratives of the Northwest*, 189–90.
11. Catesby, *Natural History*, 2: plate 41. For an integration of empire building and Catesby's writing and art, see Myers and Pritchard, *Empire's Nature*.
12. Kalm, *Peter Kalm's Travels*, 362.
13. Ettwein, "Ettwein's Notes of Travel," 210.
14. Beauchamp, *Moravian Journals*, 16.
15. Kellogg, *Early Narratives of the Northwest*, 189.
16. Charlevoix, *Journal of a Voyage to North-America*, 2:5.
17. Waller, quoted in Mathews, "Rattlesnake Colonel," 343.
18. Kalm, "Medical and Chirurgical Cases," 287.
19. Byrd, *William Byrd's Histories of the Dividing Line*, 289.
20. Ettwein, "Ettwein's Notes of Travel," 210; Blome, *Present State of His Majesties Isles and Territories*, 86.
21. Lindholt, *John Josselyn, Colonial Traveler*, 20.
22. Buffon, *Natural History*, 5:101. The planter survived his bite, but not without a few days of sweating, extreme pain, and high fever.
23. Cronon, *Changes in the Land*, 132; Thomas, *Man and the Natural World*, 274; Coleman, *Vicious*, 57–58; For more on this phenomenon and Europeans' impact on the American landscape, see Merchant, *Death of Nature*; Silver, *New Face on the Country-*

side. Carolyn Merchant added gender to the picture in Merchant, *Ecological Revolutions*. Londa Schiebinger showed how colonial-era discussions of the natural world worked to reinforce European society's gendered order. See Schiebinger, *Nature's Body*. See also Parish, "Female Opossum and the Nature of the New World," 475–514. Parish shows how fascination with the American opossum's marsupial reproductive system challenged the categories used by colonial naturalists. Rattlesnakes, on the other hand, fit well into the category of fearsome beasts, and thus a very different discussion swirled around them. See also Anderson, *Creatures of Empire*.

24. Smith, *Advertisements for the Unexperienced Planters of New England*, quoted in Irmscher, "Rattlesnakes and the Power of Enchantment," 5.

25. Hennepin, *New Discovery of a Vast Country*, 244.

26. Pilkington, *Journals of Samuel Kirkland*, 141.

27. Long, *John Long's Voyages*, 201.

28. Slaughter, *Natures of John and William Bartram*, 142–47. Slaughter argues that Bartram used his writings to create a self that was less brutal than other travelers. Bartram's letters tell more of his snake killings.

29. Ibid., 150–51; Catesby, *Natural History*, 2:41.

30. Kalm, "Medical and Chirurgical Cases," 284.

31. Klauber, *Rattlesnakes*, 2:1116–244. Klauber has pulled together a wonderful compendium of ethnographic information about Indians and rattlesnakes. Klauber's principal interests were rattlesnakes' habits and varieties. His use of ethnographic and historical sources was principally to debunk what he saw as outdated superstitions or to juxtapose modern herpetological fact with supposed quaint old beliefs. In volume 1 on p. 5, he specifically denies that one can tell a given snake's age by the number of its rattles. Most rattlers grow a new rattle each year, but they are fragile and tend to break off if they get too long.

32. Parker, *Journals of Carver*, 63.

33. Ibid.

34. Sloane, "Account of Some Experiments," 309–15.

35. Van den Bogaert, *Journey into Mohawk and Oneida Country*, 12; *JR*, 68:125.

36. *JR*, 13:193.

37. Bossu, *Travels*, 111.

38. Richter, *Ordeal of the Longhouse*, 39; Dennis, *Cultivating a Landscape of Peace*, 86.

39. Bossu, *Travels*, 95.

40. Strachey, *Historie of Travell into Virginia Britania*, 74.

41. *JR*, 64:187, 33:217, 39:25; Long, *John Long's Voyages*, 201.

42. *JR*, 68:153.

43. Lawson, *New Voyage to Carolina*, 227.

44. Ibid.

45. Gutiérrez, *When Jesus Came*, 27–30. Klauber, *Rattlesnakes* (2:1145–58) offers a detailed account of the Pueblo Snake Dance, with an emphasis on the role and meaning of the snakes. Klauber's account is built primarily from the records of the Bureau of American Ethnology.

46. Bossu, *Travels*, 111.

47. *JR*, 14:167.

48. Masterson, "Colonial Rattlesnake Lore," 214. Masterson also claimed that some Europeans also carried snake images on their bodies. While this suggests, and indeed Masterson asserts, that these people accepted the Indian vision of these as protective marking, it is very hard to know what exactly the images meant to European bearers. Alexander Henry bore a tattoo that he received as part of Ojibwa adoption. For Henry the symbol was mostly one showing his daring and skill as a trader and in no way made him predisposed to see snakes as his adoptive kin did.

49. *JR*, 12:15; Lawson, *New Voyage to Carolina*, 49.

50. *JR*, 43:153; Henry, *Travels in Canada*, 117; Bossu, *Travels*, 200; Long, *John Long's Voyages*, 187; Mooney, *Myths of the Cherokee*, 296.

51. Lindholt, *John Josselyn, Colonial Traveler*, 82; Klauber, *Rattlesnakes*, 2:1196.

52. *JR*, 19:97; 14:103.

53. Ibid., 31:247.

54. Ibid., 10:195.

55. Ibid., 12:27; Oman, *Understanding Lightning*, 85–87.

56. Gutiérrez, *When Jesus Came*, 30.

57. Mooney, *Myths of the Cherokee*, 296.

58. Warner, *History of the Ojibway People*, 67; Vecsey, *Traditional Ojibwa Religion*, 177–79. Vecsey connects the Midewiwin Society origin to the trickster–culture hero Nanabozho.

59. Bragdon, *Native People of Southern New England*, 187–88. Thunderbirds and underwater snakes appear in the stories of many Algonquian tribes.

60. Parker, *Journals of Carver*, 98.

61. Pilkington, *Journals of Samuel Kirkland*, 141.

62. *JR*, 33:211.

63. Mooney, *Myths of the Cherokees*, 297; Adair, *Adair's History*, 92; Timberlake, *Memoirs*, 74–75.

64. Adair, *Adair's History*, 92.

65. Timberlake, *Memoirs*, 74.

66. Catesby, *Natural History*, 2:41; Adams, *Radisson*, 92.

67. Lawson, *New Voyage to Carolina*, 134; Catesby, *Natural History*, 2:41.

68. Kearsley, "Letter," 74.

69. Cresswell, *Journal*, 72.

70. Adair, *Adair's History*, 247; Rountree, *Powhatan Indians of Virginia*, 128.

71. Graffenried, *Account of the Founding of New Bern*, 378.

72. Adair, *Adair's History*, 248.

73. *JR*, 59:101; Cresswell, *Journal*, 72; Masterson, "Colonial Rattlesnake Lore," 214; William Byrd, quoted in Irmscher, "Rattlesnakes and the Power of Enchantment," 5.

74. Adair, *Adair's History*, 251.

75. Parker, *Journals of Carver*, 82.

76. Adair, *Adair's History*, 251.

77. Ibid.

78. Parker, *Journals of Carver*, 82.
79. Ibid., 83.
80. Ibid.
81. Lederer, *Discoveries*, 15. Lederer lists his three Indian companions—Magtakunk, Hoppottoguoh, and Naunnugh—as being from "Shickehamany."
82. Lawson, *New Voyage to Carolina*, 134.
83. Catesby, *Natural History*, 2:41. Kalm, *Peter Kalm's Travels* (293), contains the same story.
84. For more on how various Native American ecologies functioned, see Krech, *Ecological Indian*.
85. Lederer, *Discoveries*, 15.
86. *JR*, 69:167; Slaughter, *Natures of John and William Bartram*, 153. Slaughter claims that while William Bartram restated the belief, he related it as a story told to him by others and avoided confirming or denying it. Barton, *Memoir*, uses Bartram's travels in its attack on the belief in the snakes' hypnotic powers. See Slaughter, *Natures of John and William Bartram*, 150–54; Irmscher, "Rattlesnakes and the Power of Enchantment," 10.
87. For a detailed discussion of this question and the minds of naturalists, see Irmscher, "Rattlesnakes and the Power of Enchantment." Irmscher's primary concern is the role of charming as a literary aspect of naturalists' writings into the nineteenth century. He does not discuss the Indian connection and instead sees the origins of charming stories in Pliny's *Historia Naturalis* (Irmscher,10). Pliny no doubt had some influence, but these stories' Native origins are more immediate. For more on the Bartrams, snakes, and fascination, see Slaughter, *Natures of John and William Bartram*, ch. 6. Slaughter argues that John Bartram stood apart from the mass of snake killers by using his Quakerism as an argument against killing the reptiles.
88. Vecsey, *Traditional Ojibwa Religion*, 178; Ritzenthaler, "Southern Chippewa," 754.
89. Henry, *Travels in Canada*, 178.
90. For more on Nativism, see Dowd, *Spirited Resistance*, 1–89; White, *Middle Ground*, 271–314; Edmunds, *Shawnee Prophet*, 3–93.
91. Henry, *Travels in Canada*, 177.
92. Kalm's observation is noted in Klauber, *Rattlesnakes*, 2:1120. Klauber also cites nineteenth-century observers of the same change in practice. Klauber cites his source for Kalm's observation as "Berattlese om Skaller-ormen . . . Kongel. Vetens. Acad. Stockholm, 1752–53, Vol 13 pp. 308–319; vol 14, pp. 52–67, 185–195." In "An Account of the Rattle-Snake" (p. 288), Kalm claims that "the trading people" passing between Lakes Ontario and Erie "continually destroy" rattlesnakes. It is unclear, however, whether he means Indian or European traders.
93. Picquet, "A 1751 Journal," 375.
94. Alexander Hamilton, 1744, quoted in Mathews, "Rattlesnake Colonel," 344.

Chapter 5. Sex, Difference, and the Ideal Traveler

1. Byrd, *Prose Works*, 395.
2. Ibid., 383.

3. Ibid., 387.

4. For more on William Byrd's connection between sexuality, maleness, and dominance, see Godbeer, "William Byrd's 'Flourish,'" 135–62.

5. Byrd, *Prose Works*, 405.

6. Ibid., 391, 397.

7. Ibid., 391.

8. Ibid.

9. Ibid., 397.

10. Ibid.

11. Neither set of societies had monolithic conceptions, and internal social differences such as class were powerful shapers of concepts of manliness. For discussions of Indian manliness, see Sheidley, "Hunting and the Politics of Masculinity"; Vibert, "Real Men Hunt Buffalo," 4–21. See also Shoemaker's "An Alliance between Men," 239–63. The term "manliness" appears here in preference to the more common term "masculinity," following the lead of Gail Bederman, who argues that "manhood" is a more historically resonant term than "masculinity," which only came to be used after 1890. Also, the point of manly competitions on the trail was the marking and establishing of male identities—the creation of *men*. In this context "manliness," with its connotations of control, restraint, and virtue, make more sense in this discussion than the more overly scientific and historically later term "masculinity." See Bederman, *Manliness and Civilization*. For a review of the growing discussion of colonial-era European and Euro-American conceptions of manliness, see Hitchcock and Cohen, *English Masculinities*; Foster, *Manhood in Early Modern England*; Foster, "Deficient Husbands," 723–44; Rotundo, *American Manhood*, 1–30. John Tosh argues that the eighteenth century saw greater continuity in English gender relations than disjuncture. That observation is supported by evidence from the trail. See Tosh, "Old Adam and the New Man," 217–39. William Byrd II himself is the subject of a singularly large literature for an eighteenth-century man who was neither a governor nor a president. The extensive and personal nature of his diaries make him our best entrée into the minds of early-eighteenth-century Virginia planters. See Lockridge, *Diary and Life of William Byrd II*, and *On the Sources of Patriarchal Rage*; Godbeer, "William Byrd's 'Flourish,'" 135–62; Zuckerman, "Family Life of William Byrd." Byrd was also a key subject in Brown, *Good Wives, Nasty Wenches, and Anxious Patriarchs*.

12. Few scholars have addressed the role of insults and derision in Indian-European relations. See most recently Merrell, *Into the American Woods*, 151–52, for small sample. Most of these comments were made post facto by Europeans recording their experiences with Indians as asides or editorial comments. These comments certainly have much to say about the European creation of the Indian as a savage and child-like other not fit to maintain the American continents. See Pratt, *Imperial Eyes*. In this study, however, only those insults (and compliments where relevant) that pertain specifically to travel or were said to have been uttered while in common company are discussed in aid of creating a picture of how travel companions employed the idea of the ideal traveler to specific travel experiences.

13. Sagard, *Long Journey*, 258.

14. Adair, *Adair's History*, 140.

15. Delanglez, *Journal of Jean Cavelier*, 117.
16. *JR*, 5:149.
17. Ibid., 50:259.
18. Thompson, *Narrative*, 118.
19. *JR*, 7:41–43.
20. Cresswell, *Journal*, 91–93.
21. Ibid., 92.
22. Ibid., 93.
23. Adams, *Radisson*, 84.
24. Ibid., 81.
25. Ibid., 84.
26. Ibid., 62.
27. Byrd, *Dividing Line*, 311.
28. Fontaine, *Journal*, 99.
29. Danckaerts, *Journal*, 84–85.
30. Byrd, *Prose Works*, 405.
31. Markham, *Voyages and Works of John Davis*, 18.
32. *JR*, 9:279.
33. Ibid., 32:137.
34. Adair, *Adair's History*, 341.
35. Alvord and Bidgood, *First Explorations*, 222.
36. Long, *John Long's Voyages*, 49. Long, who is at times a questionable source, did not specify the identity of the Indian in this parable-like tale. The larger context, though, suggests that he was Ojibwa. Long goes on to claim the French name *manquer* also carries the implication "very difficult to kill."
37. Sagard, *Long Journey*, 247.
38. *JR*, 2:37.
39. McWilliams, *Iberville's Gulf Journals*, 150.
40. Ibid.
41. Lamb, *Journals and Letters of Mackenzie*, 217.
42. Parker, *Journals of Carver*, 115.
43. Adams, *Radisson*, 57.
44. *JR*, 57:281, 285.
45. For more on language in the Indian-European encounters, see Axtell, "Babel of Tongues," 46–75.
46. Byrd, *Dividing Line*, 201.
47. Ibid., 203.
48. Thompson, *Narrative*, 79.
49. Ibid., 23.
50. Ibid., 88.
51. Ibid., 87.
52. Adams, *Radisson*, 135.
53. Bossu, *Travels*, 86. This tale made many appearances in many places in American frontier folklore. See also Axtell, "Through Another Glass Darkly," 139, 271.

54. Hearne, *Journey* (1911), 149–50.

55. Ibid., 150.

56. Ibid., 179.

57. It is worth noting that this practice seems to have been largely limited to state societies like the Mississippian chiefdoms seen by Soto and other southeastern conquistadors and their historical descendants in the South and Midwest. The St. Lawrence Iroquois also used the practice, as did some of the eighteenth-century Plains tribes, and the people of the desert Southwest. The more mobile peoples of Canada did not ordinarily carry their leaders, and neither did the northeastern Algonquians, although Powhatan of Virginia was at times borne on a litter.

58. McWilliams, *Iberville's Gulf Journals*, 58; Hammond and Rey, *Don Juan de Oñate*, 131.

59. Quinn, *New American World*, 4:212.

60. Norall, *Bourgomont*, 127; McWilliams, *Iberville's Gulf Journals*, 150–51; Salley, *Narratives of Early Carolina*, 90.

61. Joseph Clark, *Journal*, 375.

62. Cox, *Journeys of la Salle*, 1:69; Lamb, *Journals and Letters of Mackenzie*, 395.

63. Kellog, *Early Narratives of the Northwest*, 358.

64. Ibid., 85. See also Axtell, *Beyond 1492*, 42–43.

65. Cox, *Journeys of la Salle*, 2:174.

66. Quinn, *New American World*, 2:29.

67. Cook, *Voyages of Cartier*, 58. Cartier recorded that Agouhanna, the headman of Hochelaga, was carried by "nine or ten men" on a sort of litter made from a "large deer skin" (63). This means that the form of carrying that Cartier benefited from was not the traditional way of carrying men of at least the highest prestige. Since carrying does not seem to have been widely used in Iroquoian societies, it may have been that the Hochelagans' act was in response to a perceived weakness on Cartier's part.

68. See Rotundo, *American Manhood*, 1–30.

69. Unless Ramusio was simply editing Cartier's experiences, he may have been relying on the somewhat dubious work of André Thevet. Thevet was not in Canada but did produce a highly detailed account of the French experiences there, allegedly based on his conversations with mostly semi-anonymous sources. He told the probably apocryphal morality tale (attributed to "Captain J.C.") of a "young Angevin gentleman" who took to "joy rid[ing]" ("proumener a son plaisir") around on the back of "a certain savage." Over the course of several rides the Angevin increasingly exploited the rider-animal analogy so obvious to European minds. When the "Canadian savage" stumbled while going down a hill, his French rider began to "beat unreasonably with blows of his stick" until the angered Indian unceremoniously dumped his Angevin load "into the depths of the sea." The story ended when another Frenchman stepped in and killed the offending Iroquoian. No one else recorded such a potentially pivotal moment, and surely such an act would have changed the otherwise quiet tone of Cartier's Hochelaga stay. Stabler, *André Thevet's North America*, 101. These experiences better resemble the role that carrying played in colonial-era travel in parts of the Andes where the mountains' steep heights, deeply rutted roads, and trackless thickets made carrying by Natives one of the only ways

European colonial travelers could get around. See Taussig, *Shamanism, Colonialism, and the Wild Man*, 287–335.

70. See Van Kirk, *Many Tender Ties*.

71. Smits, "'Squaw Drudge,'" 281–306. See also Merchant, *Ecological Revolutions*.

72. Long, *John Long's Voyages*.

73. Hawkins "Letters" *Collections of the Georgia Historical Society*, 9:16.

74. Lawson, *New Voyage to Carolina*, 91.

75. *JR*, 16:213.

76. Hearne, *Journey* (1795), 264.

77. Ibid., 264.

78. Ibid., 265.

79. Ibid., 264.

80. Hearne, *Journey* (1911), 70.

81. Hearne is the main source for this rumor, but there is reasonable evidence to cast doubt on this story. See Van Kirk, "Moses Norton," 5:583–85.

82. Hearne, *Journey* (1795), 12. Gordon Speck asserts that Hearne himself argued in favor of bringing women but it was Norton who killed the proposal. Speck would seem to be offering Hearne the most flatteringly possible read of the explorer's argumentative footnote. Speck, *Samuel Hearne and the Northwest Passage*, 126. See also Van Kirk, *Many Tender Ties*, 15–27.

83. Hearne, *Journey* (1911), 90.

84. Ibid., 93.

85. Ibid., 93–94.

86. There is no record of how Hearne's companions viewed this piece of brass apparatus, but there are clues from other travels. When William Bartram was busy surveying Buffalo Lick, Georgia, in 1772, he ran into some trouble from local Indians. An unnamed chief approached the party and told the surveyor that his compass had run the line incorrectly and that the "wicked instrument was a liar." Indians like this defiant chief knew all too well that surveying was a prelude to colonial usurpation of their lands. The "wicked instrument" had put a grid on the land before, and the chief was none too happy about the prospect of further encroachments. The Indians of Canada's Northern Shield would not have the same associations with surveying and measuring tools, living as they did on land too barren for European agricultural settlements. Nevertheless, the quadrant and the misguided planning of its operator could not have been favorites of Hearne's companions. Bartram, *Travels and Other Writing*, 56–57.

87. Hearne, *Journey* (1795), 55.

88. Ibid.

89. See Sayre, "Native American Sexuality," 35–54; Godbeer, "Eroticizing the Middle Ground," 92, and "Dangerous Allure," 154–89. Godbeer's overviews are two of the few of their type. It is worth noting too that "Eroticizing the Middle Ground" relies specifically both the "middle ground" and the "frontier" concepts. The literature on Indian-European sex had generally focused on the role of marriages as an institution either forced on Native peoples or used by them in their experience with colonization or how sexual alliances worked for both sides. Richard White used marriage as a key illustrative example

in building his "middle ground" concept. White, *Middle Ground*, 60–75. Ann Marie Plane emphasized New England native adaptive marriage strategies and the transference and validation of Native systems into and through English law. Plane, *Colonial Intimacies*. Sylvia Van Kirk focused on how Native women used relationships to shape the Canadian fur trade and better their own lives. Van Kirk, *Many Tender Ties*. A few studies also focus on the question of "racial purity," which hung over Indian-English sexual relations and the long seventeenth- and eighteenth-century discussion of the merits or problems with mixed marriages. See Smits on the discussion in Virginia, "'Abominable Mixture,'" 157–92, and in New England, "'We Are Not to Grow Wild,'" 1–31.

90. Van den Bogaert, *Journey into Mohawk and Oneida Country*, 52–63.

91. Ibid., 59.

92. Fontaine, *Journal* 93.

93. Van Kirk, *Many Tender Ties*.

94. Lawson, *New Voyage*, 35.

95. Delanglez, *The Journal of Jean Cavelier* , 91; JR 65:241–43.

96. *Champlain Works*, 3:47.

97. Barbé-Marbois, *Our Revolutionary Forefathers*, 202.

98. Byrd, *Dividing Line*, 59.

99. Ibid., 57.

100. Ibid., 123. The quote "I cou'd discern by some of our gentlemen's linen, discolour'd by the soil of the Indian ladys, that they had been convincing themselves in the point of their having no furr" suggests some previous speculation on the matter.

101. Kupperman, "Presentment of Civility," 193–228.

102. Byrd, *Dividing Line*, 123.

103. Cresswell, *Journal*, 105.

104. Ibid., 106.

105. Lawson, *New Voyage*, 190.

106. This model of sex is from Lacquer's *Making Sex*. See also Kathleen Brown's "'Changed . . . into the Fashion of a Man,'" 39–56, which is one example of these ideas playing themselves out in a colonial setting.

107. Herbert, *Culture and Anomie*.

108. See Rich, *Fur Trade and the Northwest*, 175–81, for the trade context of Fidler's travels.

109. Venema, "Under the Protection of a Principal Man," and "Mapping Culture onto Geography," 9–45. Venema sees Hearne playing the role of wife through a literary lens.

110. Hearne, *Journals of Samuel Hearne and Philip Turnor*, 502.

111. Ibid., 535.

112. Hauser, "Berdach and the Illinois Indian Tribes," 45–70; Williams, *Spirit and the Flesh*. Williams asserts that "Berdaches would often be taken along on a hunting expedition, but usually not as a hunter" (69). See also Roscoe, *Zuni Man-Woman*, for a study of a singularly well-documented berdache. Kathleen Venema explored the gender ambiguity in Samuel Hearne's writings. She suggested that Hearne functioned as a wife of Matonabbee. While this point is compelling and has certainly influenced my analysis of Fidler, Venema's focus was more literary in tone. What she saw was text effect and did

not take into consideration Native American traditions in thinking about gender. See Venema, "'Under the Protection of a Principal Man,'" 162–90.

113. Jean-Guy A. Goulet claimed that the Chipewyans, and other peoples of the Canadian Shield (Dene-Tha), did not have the berdache practice as Williams and Hauser have outlined them. See "'Berdache'/'Two Spirit,'" 683–701, and *Ways of Knowing*, 279.

114. Hearne, *Journals of Hearne and Turnor*, 527.

115. Ibid., 530.

116. In some ways, Fidler's attire parallels the Warroskoyak Virginia court's 1629 decision to manifest the intergendered identity of the hermaphrodite Thomas Hall through her/his clothing. See Brown, "'Changed . . . into the Fashion of a Man,'" 39–56.

117. Hearne, *Journals of Hearne and Turnor*, 544.

118. Ibid., 533.

119. Ibid., 532.

120. Bartram, *Travels and Other Writing*, 57.

Chapter 6. Going Out

1. Thompson, *Narrative*, 39.

2. *JR*, 46:277.

3. Thompson, *Narrative*, 39.

4. For more on the uses of clothing in Indian-European relations, see Shannon, "Dressing for Success on the Mohawk Frontier," 13–42.

5. Gough, *First across the Continent*, 52.

6. Lamb, *Journals and Letters of Mackenzie*, 257.

7. Ibid., 364.

8. Ibid., 259.

9. Ibid.

10. Ibid., 261.

11. Ibid., 282.

12. Ibid., 287.

13. Ibid., 267; Gough, *First across the Continent*, 128–33. Gough identifies Mackenzie's companions at this stretch as being Sekanis. Mackenzie called them the "People of the Rocks." With Mackenzie were nine men, five of whom were French Canadians. Two "young Indians" were also in the canoe, though who they were is obscure. Gough, *First across the Continent*, 123.

14. Lamb, *Journals and Letters of Mackenzie*, 297.

15. Ibid., 299.

16. Ibid., 297.

17. Ibid., 296, 299.

18. Ibid., 267.

19. Ibid., 301.

20. Ibid., 299.

21. Ibid., 301.

22. A small literature argues that Mackenzie was wholly dependent on Natives. Bliss, "Conducted Tour," 16–24. Bliss sees Mackenzie as being more like Samuel Hearne or

Peter Fidler, that is to say following his guides and being more or less a guest. Hardwick, *Helping Hand*. Hardwick and his colleagues attempt to correct an older literature which portrays Mackenzie as unaided. Hardwick was right to make this case, but he went too far.

23. The scholarship of the Lewis and Clark Expedition has been a growth industry in recent years. Popular interest has been stoked by Ambrose's *Undaunted Courage* and Ken Burns's PBS documentary *Lewis and Clark* and its companion book, Duncan and Burns, *Lewis and Clark*. This work is largely uncritical though (particularly Ambrose's) and accepts more chestnuts and canards than it challenges. The most useful correctives come from James Ronda: see Ronda, *Lewis and Clark among the Indians,* and *Voyages of Discovery*. See also Slaughter, *Exploring Lewis and Clark*; and Nelson, *Interpreters with Lewis and Clark*.

24. Jackson, *Letters*, 58.

25. Jackson, *Letters*, 58.

26. There is a large literature on Sacagawea. One of the most forthright, and I believe accurate, assessments of her role on the trip is James Ronda's essay "Note on Sacagawea," 256–59.

27. See Kessler, *Making of Sacagawea*.

Bibliography

Adair, James. *James Adair's History of the American Indians*. Edited by Samuel Cole Williams. New York: Argonaut Press, 1967.
Adams, Arthur, ed. *The Explorations of Pierre Espirit Radisson*. Minneapolis: Ross and Haines, 1961.
Adorno, Rolena, and Patrick Charles Pautz. *Álvar Núñez Cabeza de Vaca: His Account, His Life, and the Expedition of Pánfilo de Narváez*. 3 vols. Lincoln: University of Nebraska Press, 1999.
Alvord, Clarence Walworth, and Lee Bidgood. *The First Explorations of the Trans-Allegheny Region by the Virginians, 1650-1674*. Cleveland: Arthur H. Clark, 1912.
Ambrose, Stephen. *Undaunted Courage: Meriwether Lewis, Thomas Jefferson, and the Opening of the American West*. New York: Simon and Schuster, 1996.
Anderson, Larry. *Benton MacKaye: Conservationist, Planner, and Creator of the Appalachian Trail*. Baltimore: Johns Hopkins University Press, 2002.
Anderson, Virginia DeJohn. *Creatures of Empire: How Domestic Animals Transformed Early America*. New York: Oxford University Press, 2004.
Armitage, David. "The Concept of the Atlantic World." In *The British Atlantic World, 1500-1800*, edited by David Armitage and Michael J. Braddick, 11-30. London: Palgrave-Macmillan, 2002.
Axtell, James L. "Babel of Tongues: Communicating with the Indians." In *Natives and Newcomers: The Cultural Origins of North America*, 46-75. New York: Oxford University Press, 2000.
———. *Beyond 1492: Encounters in Colonial North America*. New York: Oxford University Press, 1992.
———. *The Indians' New South: Cultural Change in the Colonial Southeast*. New York: Oxford University Press, 1997.
———. *Invasion Within: The Contest of Cultures in Colonial America*. New York: Oxford University Press, 1985.
———. "Through Another Glass Darkly: Early Indian Views of Europeans." In *After Columbus: Essays in the Ethnohistory of Colonial North America*. New York: Oxford University Press, 1988.
Bailyn, Bernard. *Atlantic History: Concepts and Contours*. Cambridge, Mass.: Harvard University Press, 2005.
Barbé-Marbois, François, Marquis de. *Our Revolutionary Forefathers: The Letters of François, Marquis de Barbé-Marbois*. Edited and translated by Eugene Parker Chase. New York: Duffield, 1929.
Barbour, Philip L., ed. *The Jamestown Voyages under the First Charter, 1606-1609*. The Hakluyt Society. Cambridge, England: University of Cambridge Press, 1969.

Barton, Benjamin Smith. *A Memoir Concerning the Fascinating Faculty Which Has Been Ascribed to the Rattle-Snake, and Other American Serpents.* Philadelphia: n.p., 1796.

Bartram, John. *A Journey from Pennsylvania to Onondaga in 1743 by John Bartram, Lewis Evans, and Conrad Weiser.* Barre: Imprint Society, 1973.

Bartram, William. *Travels and Other Writings.* New York: Library of America, 1995.

Basso, Keith H. *Wisdom Sits in Places: Landscape and Language among the Western Apache.* Albuquerque: University of New Mexico Press, 1996.

Beauchamp, W. M. *Moravian Journals Relating to Central New York, 1745–66.* New York: Onondaga Historical Association, 1916.

Bederman, Gail. *Manliness and Civilization: A Cultural History of Gender and Race in the United States, 1880–1917.* Chicago: University of Chicago Press, 1995.

Bland, Edward. "Discovery of New Brittaine." In *The First Explorations of the Trans-Allegheny Region by the Virginians, 1650–1674,* edited by Clarence W. Alvord and Lee Bidgood. Baltimore: Clearfield Press, 1996.

Bliss, Michael. "Conducted Tour." *Beaver* 69 (1989): 16–24.

Blome, Richard. *The Present State of His Majesties Isles and Territories in America.* London: H. Clark, 1687.

Bolton, Herbert E. *Pageant in the Wilderness: The Story of the Escalante Expedition to the Interior Basin.* Salt Lake City: Utah State Historical Society, 1950.

———. *Spanish Exploration in the Southwest, 1542–1706.* New York: Charles Scribner's Sons, 1930.

Bossu, Jean Bernard. *Jean Bernard Bossu's Travels in the Interior of North America, 1751–1762.* Edited by Simon Feiler. Norman: University of Oklahoma Press, 1962.

Bourdieu, Pierre. *The Logic of Practice.* Translated by Richard Nice. Stanford, Calif.: Stanford University Press, 1980.

———. *Outline of a Theory of Practice.* Translated by Richard Nice. New York: Cambridge University Press, 1977.

Bragdon, Kathleen. *Native People of Southern New England, 1500–1650.* Norman: University of Oklahoma Press, 1996.

Briceland, Alan Vance. *Westward from Virginia: The Exploration of the Virginia-Carolina Frontier, 1650–1710.* Charlottesville: University Press of Virginia, 1987.

Brooks, James. *Captives and Cousins: Slavery, Kinship, and Community in the Southwest Borderlands.* Chapel Hill: University of North Carolina Press, 2002.

Brown, Kathleen M. "'Changed . . . into the Fashion of a Man': The Politics of Sexual Difference in a Seventeenth-Century Anglo-America Settlement." In *The Devil's Lane: Sex and Race in the Early South,* edited by Catherine Clinton and Michelle Gillespie, 39–56. New York: Oxford University Press, 1997.

———. *Good Wives, Nasty Wenches, and Anxious Patriarchs: Gender, Race, and Power in Colonial Virginia.* Chapel Hill: University of North Carolina Press, 1996.

Buffon, Georges Louis Leclerc Comte de. *Natural History of Birds, Fish, Insects, and Reptiles.* London, H. D. Symonds, 1808.

Byrd, William, II. *Prose Works, Narratives of a Colonial Virginian.* Edited by Louis B. Wright. Cambridge, Mass.: Belknap Press, 1966.

———. *William Byrd's Histories of the Dividing Line Bewixt Virginia and North Carolina.* New York: Dover, 1967.

Carson, Cary. "The Consumer Revolution in Colonial America: Why Demand?" In *Of Consuming Interests: The Style of Life in the Eighteenth Century,* edited by Cary Carson, Ronald Hoffman, and Peter J. Albert. Charlottesville: University of Virginia Press, 1994.

Catesby, Mark. *The Natural History of Carolina, Florida and the Bahama Islands.* Savannah: Beehive Press, 1974.

Cayton, Andrew R. L., and Fredrika J. Teute. "Introduction: On the Connection of Frontiers." In *Contact Points: American Frontiers from the Mohawk Valley to the Mississippi, 1750–1830,* 1–15. Chapel Hill: University of North Carolina Press, 1998.

Celeron, Pierre Joseph de. "Celeron's Expedition down the Ohio Rivers." *Wisconsin State Historical Society Collections* 18 (1908): 36–58.

Certeau, Michel de. *The Practice of Everyday Life.* Berkeley: University of California Press, 1984.

Champlain, Samuel de. *The Works of Samuel de Champlain in Six Volumes.* Toronto: Champlain Society, 1925.

Chappell, David. "Shipboard Relations between Pacific Island Women and Euroamerican Men, 1767–1887." *Journal of Pacific History* 27:2 (December 1992).

Charlevoix, Pierre de. *Journal of a Voyage to North-America.* 2 vols. Ann Arbor: University Microfilms, 1966.

Churchill, Ward. "Indians Are Us?: Reflections on the 'Men's Movement.'" In *Indians Are Us: Culture and Genocide in Native North America,* 207–72. Monroe, Maine: Common Courage Press, 1994.

Clark, Joseph. "Joseph Clark's Account of a Journey to the Indian Country." *Friend's Miscellany* 1 (1831): 367–80.

Clayton, Lawrence A., Vernon James Knight Jr., and Edward C. Moore, eds. *The De Soto Chronicles: The Expedition of Hernando De Soto to North America in 1539–1543.* 2 vols. Tuscaloosa: University of Alabama Press, 1993.

Coleman, Jon. *Vicious: Wolves and Men in America.* New Haven, Conn.: Yale University Press, 2004.

Cook, Ramsey, ed. *The Voyages of Jacques Cartier.* Toronto: University of Toronto Press, 1993.

Cox, Isaac Joslin, ed. *The Journeys of Réné Robert Cavelier Sieur de la Salle.* 2 vols. New York: A. S. Barnes, 1905.

Cresswell, Nicholas. *Journal of Nicholas Cresswell, 1774–1777.* New York: Dial Press, 1924.

Cronon, William. *Changes in the Land: Indians, Colonists, and the Ecology of New England.* New York: Hill and Wang, 1983.

———, ed. *Uncommon Ground: Toward Reinventing Nature.* New York: W. W. Norton, 1995.

Danckaerts, Jasper. *Journal of Jasper Danckaerts, 1679–1680.* Edited by J. Frankin Jameson and Bartlett Burleigh James. New York: Charles Scribner's Sons, 1913.

Davies, K. G., ed. *Letters from Hudson Bay, 1703–40*. London: Hudson's Bay Record Society, 1965.

Delanglez, Jean, ed. *The Journal of Jean Cavelier: The Account of a Survivor of La Salle's Texas Expedition, 1684–88*. Chicago: Institute of Jesuit History, 1938.

Deloria, Philip. *Playing Indian*. New Haven, Conn.: Yale University Press, 1998.

Dening, Greg. *Islands and Beaches: Discourse on a Silent Land, Marquesas, 1774–1880*. Honolulu: University Press of Hawaii, 1980.

———. *Islands and Beaches: Discourse on a Silent Land, Marquesas, 1774–1880*. Chicago: Dorsey Press, 1980.

Dennis, Matthew. *Cultivating a Landscape of Peace: Iroquois-European Encounters in Seventeenth-Century America*. Ithaca, N.Y.: Cornell University Press, 1993.

Dowd, Gregory. *A Spirited Resistance: The North American Indian Struggle for Unity, 1745–1815*. Baltimore: Johns Hopkins University Press, 1992.

———. *War under Heaven: Pontiac, the Indian Nations, and the British Empire*. Baltimore: Johns Hopkins University Press, 2002.

Duncan, David Ewing. *Hernando de Soto: A Savage Quest in the Americas*. New York: Crown, 1995.

Duncan, Dayton, and Ken Burns. *Lewis and Clark: The Journey of the Corps of Discovery*. New York: Alfred Knopf, 1997.

Duncan, James, and Derek Gregory, eds. *Writes of Passage: Reading Travel Writing*. London: Routledge, 1999.

Edmonds, David. *American Indian Leaders: Studies in Diversity*. Lincoln: University of Nebraska Press, 1980.

Edmunds, R. David. *The Shawnee Prophet*. Lincoln: University of Nebraska Press, 1983.

Elsner, Jas, and Joan-Pau Rubiés, eds. *Voyages and Visions: Towards a Cultural History of Travel*. London: Reaktion Books, 1999.

Ettwein, John. "Rev. John Ettwein's Notes of Travel from the North Branch of the Susquehanna to the Beaver River." *Pennsylvania Magazine of History and Biography* 25 (1901): 208–19.

Fabian, Johannes. *Out of Our Minds: Reason and Madness in the Exploration of Central Africa*. Berkeley: University of California Press, 2000.

Fausz, J. Frederick. "Middlemen in Peace and War: Virginia's Earliest Indian Interpreters, 1608–1632." *Virginia Magazine of History and Biography* 95 (January 1987): 41–64.

Fenton, William. "Structure, Continuity, and Change in the Process of Iroquois Treaty Making." In *The History and Culture of Iroquois Diplomacy: An Interdisciplinary Guide to the Treaties of the Six Nations and Their League*, edited by Francis Jennings. Syracuse, N.Y.: Syracuse University Press, 1985.

Fidler, Peter. "Journal of a Journey with the Chepawyans . . . in 1791 and 2." In *Journals of Samuel Hearne and Philip Turnor*, by Samuel Hearne, edited by J. B. Tyrrell. Toronto: Champlain Society, 1934.

Fiske, Jo-Anne, Susan Sleeper-Smith, and William Wicken. *New Faces of the Fur Trade: Selected Papers of the Seventh North American Fur Trade Conference, Halifax, Nova Scotia, 1995*. Lansing: Michigan State University Press, 1998.

Fontaine, John. *The Journal of John Fontaine an Irish Huguenot Son in Spain and Virginia,*

1710–1719. Edited by Edwin Porter Alexander. Williamsburg: Colonial Williamsburg Foundation, 1972.

Foster, Elizabeth. *Manhood in Early Modern England: Honour, Sex, and Marriage*. New York: Longman Press, 1999.

Foster, Thomas. "Deficient Husbands: Manhood, Sexual Incapacity, and Male Martial Sexuality in Seventeenth-Century New England." *William and Mary Quarterly*, 3rd ser., 56 (1999): 723–44.

Francis, Daniel, and Toby Morantz. *Partners in Furs: A History of the Fur Trade in Eastern James Bay, 1600–1870*. Montreal: McGill-Queen's University Press, 1989.

Franklin, Wayne. *Discoverers, Explorers, Settlers: The Diligent Writers of Early America*. Chicago: University of Chicago Press, 1979.

Galloway, Patricia. "The Incestuous Soto Narratives." In *The Hernando de Soto Expedition: History, Historiography, and "Discovery" in the Southeast*, 11–44. Lincoln: University of Nebraska Press, 1997.

Gates, Charles Marvin. *Five Fur Traders of the Northwest: Being the Narrative of Peter Pond and the Diaries of John Macdonell, Archibald N. McLeod, Hugh Faries, and Thomas Connor*. St. Paul: Minnesota Historical Society, 1965.

Gist, Christopher. "Colonel Christopher Gist's Journal . . ." In *First Explorations of Kentucky: Doctor Thomas Walker's Journal . . . also Colonel Christopher Gist's Journal . . .*, by Josiah Stoddard Johnston. Louisville: J. P. Morton, 1898.

Glover, Richard, ed. *David Thompson's Narrative, 1784–1812*. Toronto: Champlain Society, 1962.

Godbeer, Richard. "The Dangerous Allure of 'Copper-Coloured Beauties': Anglo-Indian Sexual Relations." In *Sexual Revolutions in Early America*, 154–89. Baltimore: Johns Hopkins University Press, 2002.

———. "Eroticizing the Middle Ground: Anglo-Indian Sexual Relations along the Eighteenth-Century Frontier." In *Sex, Love, Race: Crossing Boundaries in North American History*, edited by Martha Hodes, 91–111. New York: New York University Press, 1999.

———. "William Byrd's 'Flourish': The Sexual Cosmos of a Southern Planter." In *Sex and Sexuality in Early America*, edited by Merril Smith. New York: New York University Press, 1998.

Goetzmann, William H. *Exploration and Empire: The Explorer and the Scientist in the Winning of the American West*. New York: Alfred Knopf, 1966.

Goetzmann, William H., and Glyndwr Williams. *The Atlas of North American Exploration: From the Norse Voyages to the Race to the Pole*. Norman: University of Oklahoma Press, 1998.

Goodwin, Jason. *Lords of the Horizons: A History of the Ottoman Empire*. New York: Picador, 2003.

Gough, Barry. *First across the Continent: Sir Alexander Mackenzie*. Norman: University of Oklahoma Press, 1997.

Goulet, Jean-Guy A. "The 'Berdache'/'Two Spirit': A Comparison of Anthropological and Native Constructions of Gendered Identities among the Northern Athapaskans. *Journal of the Royal Anthropological Institute* 2:4 (1996): 683–701.

———. *Ways of Knowing: Experience, Knowledge, and Power among the Dene Tha*. Lincoln: University of Nebraska Press, 1998.

Graffenried, Christoph von. *Christoph von Graffenried's Account of the Founding of New Bern*. Edited by Vincent H. Todd. Raleigh: Edwards and Broughton, 1920.

Greenblatt, Stephen. *Marvelous Possessions: The Wonder of the New World*. Chicago: University of Chicago Press, 1991.

Gutiérrez, Ramón A. *When Jesus Came, the Corn Mothers Went Away: Marriage, Sexuality, and Power in New Mexico, 1500–1846*. Stanford, Calif.: Stanford University Press, 1991.

Hagedorn, Nancy L. "Brokers of Understanding: Interpreters as Agents of Cultural Exchange in Colonial New York." *New York History* 75 (1995): 379–408.

———. "'A Friend to Go between Them': The Interpreter as Cultural Broker during Anglo-Iroquois Councils," 1740–1770." *Ethnohistory* 35 (1988): 60–80.

Hale, Horatio. *The Iroquois Book of Rites*. Philadelphia: D. G. Brinton, 1883.

Hammond, George P. *The Rediscovery of New Mexico, 1580–1594*, Coronado Cuarto Centennial Publications, 1540–1940. Albuquerque: University of New Mexico Press, 1966.

Hammond, George P., and Agapito Rey. *Don Juan de Oñate, Colonizer of New Mexico, 1595–1628*. Albuquerque: University of New Mexico Press, 1953.

———. *Narratives of the Coronado Expedition, 1540–1542*. Albuquerque: University of New Mexico Press, 1940.

———. *The Rediscovery of New Mexico, 1580–1594*. Albuquerque: University of New Mexico Press, 1966.

Hanke, Lewis. *The Spanish Struggle for Justice in the Conquest of America*. Philadelphia: University of Pennsylvania Press, 1949.

Hann, John. *Apalachee: The Land between the Rivers*. Gainesville: University Press of Florida, 1988.

Hansen, Hendrick. "Conference with the Five Nations." In *Documents Relative to the Colonial History of the State of New York*, edited by E. B. O'Callaghan, 5:372–76. Albany: Weed, Parsons, 1855.

———. "Journal of Messrs. Hansen and Van Brugh's Visit to Onondaga." In *Documents Relative to the Colonial History of the State of New York*, edited by E. B. O'Callaghan, 4:802. Albany: Weed, Parsons, 1855.

Hardwick, Francis. *The Helping Hand: How Indian Canadians Helped Alexander Mackenzie Reach the Pacific*. Vancouver: Indian Education Resource Center, University of British Columbia, 1972.

Hare, Hames R., ed. *Hiking the Appalachian Trail*. Emmaus, Pa.: Rodale Press, 1975.

Hauser, Raymond. "The Berdach and the Illinois Indian Tribes in the Last Half of the Seventeenth Century." *Ethnohistory* 37:1 (winter 1990): 45–70.

Hawkins, Benjamin. "Letters of Benjamin Hawkins, 1796–1806." Collections of the Georgia Historical Society, volume 9. City: Publisher, 1916.

Hearne, Samuel. *Journals of Samuel Hearne and Philip Turnor*. Edited by J. B. Tyrrell. Toronto: Champlain Society, 1934. Includes the "Journal of a Journey with the Chepawyans . . . in 1791 & 2," by Peter Fidler; also, parts of the journals of Malchom Ross, and several other employees of the Hudson's Bay Company.

———. *A Journey from Prince of Wales's Fort in Hudson's Bay to the Northern Ocean.* London: A. Strahan and T. Caldwell, 1795.

———. *A Journey from Prince of Wales's Fort in Hudson's Bay to the Northern Ocean in the Years 1769, 1770, 1771, and 1772.* Toronto: Champlain Society, 1911.Helm, June. "Matonabbee's Map." *Arctic Anthropology* 26:2 (1989): 28–47.

Helms, Mary. "Long Distance Contacts, Elite Aspirations, and the Age of Discovery in Cosmological Context." In *Resources, Power, and Interregional Interaction*, edited by Edward Shortman and Patricia Urban. New York: Plenum Press, 1993.

Helms, Mary W. *Craft and the Kingly Ideal: Art, Trade, and Power.* Austin: University of Texas Press, 1993.

———. *Ulysses' Sail: An Ethnographic Odyssey of Power, Knowledge, and Geographical Distance.* Princeton, N.J.: Princeton University Press, 1988.

Henday, Anthony. "York Factory to the Blackfeet Country: The Journal of Anthony Henday, 1754–55." *Royal Society of Canada Transactions*, 3rd ser., 1 (1908): 307–64.

Henige, David. "The Context, Content, and Credibility of La Florida del Ynca." *Americas* 43 (1986): 1–23.

Hennepin, Louis. *A New Discovery of a Vast Country in America.* Ann Arbor: University Microfilms International, 1982.

Henry, Alexander. *Travels in Canada and the Indian Territories between the Years 1760 and 1776.* Edited by James Bain. Toronto: George N. Morang, 1901.

Herbert, Christopher. *Culture and Anomie: Ethnographic Imagination in the Nineteenth Century.* Chicago: University of Chicago Press, 1991.

Hitchcock, Tim, and Michele Cohen. *English Masculinities, 1660–1800.* New York: Longman, 1999.

Hoffman, Paul. "The De Soto Expedition, a Cultural Crossroads." In *The De Soto Chronicles: The Expedition of Hernando De Soto to North America in 1539–1543*, edited by Lawrence A. Clayton, Vernon James Knight Jr., and Edward C. Moore, 1:1–16. Tuscaloosa: University of Alabama Press, 1993.

———. *A New Andalucia and a Way to the Orient: The American Southeast During the Sixteenth Century.* Baton Rouge: Louisiana State University, 1990.

Hudson, Charles. *Knights of Spain, Warriors of the Sun: Hernando de Soto and the South's Ancient Chiefdoms.* Athens: University of Georgia Press, 1997.

Irmscher, Christoph. "Rattlesnakes and the Power of Enchantment." *Raritan* 16:4 (spring 1997): 1–29.

Jackson, Donald, ed. *Letters of the Lewis and Clark Expedition with Related Documents, 1783–1854.* Urbana: University of Illinois Press, 1962.

Jameson, J. Franklin. *Narratives of New Netherland, 1609–1664.* Original Narratives of Early American History. New York: Charles Scribner's Sons, 1909.

Johnson, Alice M. *Saskatchewan Journals and Correspondence.* London: Hudson's Bay Record Society, 1967.

Johnston, Josiah Stoddard. *First Explorations of Kentucky: Doctor Thomas Walker's Journal . . . also Colonel Christopher Gist's Journal . . .* Louisville: J. P. Morton, 1898.

Kalm, Peter. "Medical and Chirurgical Cases: An Account of the Rattle-Snake, and the Cure of Its Bite, as Used in North America." In *Early Herpetological Studies and Surveys in the Eastern United States*, edited by Kraig Adler. New York: Arno Press, 1978.

———. *Peter Kalm's Travels in North America*. Edited by Adolph Benson. New York: Dover, 1937.

Karttunen, Frances. *Between Worlds: Interpreters, Guides, and Survivors*. New Brunswick, N.J.: Rutgers University Press, 1994.

Kawashima, Yasuhide. "Forest Diplomats: The Role of Interpreters in Indian-White Relations on the Early American Frontier." *American Indian Quarterly* 13 (1989): 1–14.

Kearsley, Dr. "Letter from Dr. Kearsley to Mr. P. Coullinson; dated Philadelphia, Nov. 18, 1735." *Gentleman's Magazine* 36 (1766): 74.

Kellogg, Louis Phelps. *Early Narratives of the Northwest, 1634–1699*. Original Narratives of Early American History. New York: Charles Scribner's Sons, 1917.

Kessler, Donna. *The Making of Sacagawea: A Euro-American Legend*. Tuscaloosa: University of Alabama Press, 1996.

Klauber, Laurence. *Rattlesnakes: Their Habits, Life Histories, and Influence on Mankind*. 2 vols. Berkeley: University of California Press, 1972.

Klooster, Wim. "The Rise and Transformation of the Atlantic World." In *The Atlantic World: Essays on Slavery, Migration, and Imagination*, edited by Wim Klooster and Alfred Padula, 1–42. Upper Saddle River, N.J.: Pearson-Prentice Hall, 2005.

Krech, Shepard, III. *The Ecological Indian: Myth and Meaning*. New York: W. W. Norton, 1999.

Kupperman, Karen Ordahl, ed. "Constructing Race: Special Issue." *William and Mary Quarterly*, 3rd ser., 54 (January 1997).

———. "Presentment of Civility: English Reading of American Self-Presentation in the Early Years of Colonization." *William and Mary Quarterly*, 3rd ser., 54:1 (January 1997): 193–228.

La Vérendrye, Pierre Gaultier de Varennes, sieur de. *Journals and Letters of Pierre Gaultier de Varennes de La Vérendrye and His Sons*. Edited by Lawrence J. Burpee. Toronto: Champlain Society, 1927.

Lacquer, Thomas. *Making Sex: Body and Gender from the Greeks to Freud*. Cambridge, Mass.: Harvard University Press, 1990.

Lamar, Curt. "Hernando de Soto before Florida: A Narrative." In *The Hernando de Soto Expedition: History, Historiography, and "Discovery" in the Southeast*, edited by Patricia Galloway, 181–206. Lincoln: University of Nebraska Press, 1997.

Lamb, W. Kaye, ed. *The Journals and Letters of Sir Alexander Mackenzie*. Cambridge, England: Cambridge University Press, 1970.

Las Casas, Bartolomé de. *The Devastation of the Indies: A Brief Account*. Translated by Herma Briffault. Baltimore: Johns Hopkins University Press, 1992.

"Laws and Ordinances Newly Made by His Majesty." In *The New Laws of the Indies for the Good Treatment and Preservation of the Indians . . .* , edited by Fred. W. Lucas. New York: AMS Press, 1971.

Lawson, John. *A New Voyage to Carolina*. Edited by Hugh Talmage Lefler. Chapel Hill: University of North Carolina Press, 1967.

Lederer, John. "Discoveries of John Lederer." In *The First Explorations of the Trans-Allegheny Region by the Virginians, 1650–1674*, edited by Clarence Walworth Alvord and Lee Bidgood. Baltimore: Clearfield, 1996.

Leed, Eric. *The Mind of the Traveler: From Gilgamesh to Global Tourism*. New York: Basic Books, 1991.

Liebersohn, Harry. *Aristocratic Encounters: European Travelers and North American Indians*. New York: Cambridge University Press, 1999.

Limerick, Patricia, Clyde A. Milner II, Charles E. Rankin, eds. *Trails: Toward a New Western History*. Lawrence: University of Press of Kansas, 1991.

Lindholt, Paul J. *John Josselyn, Colonial Traveler: A Critical Edition of Two Voyages to New England*. Hanover, N.H.: University Press of New England, 1988.

Lindley, Jacob. "Expedition to Detroit." *Michigan Pioneer Historical Society* 17 (1980): 579.

Linck, Wenceslaus. *Wenceslaus Linck's Diary of His 1766 Expedition to Northern Baja California*. Edited by Ernest Burrus. Los Angeles: Dawson's Book Shop, 1966.

Lockhart, James. *The Men of Cajamarca: A Social and Biographical Study of the First Conquerors of Peru*. Austin: University of Texas Press, 1972.

Lockridge, Kenneth. *On the Sources of Patriarchal Rage: The Commonplace Books of William Byrd and Thomas Jefferson and the Gendering of Power in the Eighteenth Century*. New York: New York University Press, 1992.

———. *The Diary and Life of William Byrd II of Virginia, 1674–1744*. Chapel Hill: University of North Carolina Press, 1987.

Long, John. *John Long's Voyages and Travels in the Years 1768–1788*. Edited by Milo Milton Quaife. Chicago: Lakeside Press, 1922.

Mancall, Peter. *Deadly Medicine: Indians and Alcohol in Early America*. Ithaca, N.Y.: Cornell University Press, 1995.

Markham, Albert Hastings, ed. *The Voyages and Works of John Davis the Navigator*. London: Hakluyt Society, 1880.

Marrinan, Rochelle, John Scarry, and Rhonda Majors. "Prelude to de Soto: The Expedition of Pánfilo de Narváez." In *Columbian Consequences: Archaeological and Historical Perspectives on the Spanish Borderlands East*, edited by David Hurst Thomas. Washington, D.C.: Smithsonian Institution Press, 1990.

Marshall, Ian. *Story Line: Exploring the Literature of the Appalachian Trail*. Charlottesville: University of Virginia Press, 1998.

Masterson, James R. "Colonial Rattlesnake Lore, 1714." *Zoologica* 23:9 (1938): 214.

Mathews, Albert. "Rattlesnake Colonel." *New England Quarterly* 10:2 (June 1937): 341–45.

Mauss, Marcel. *The Gift: The Form and Reason for Exchange in Archaic Societies*. New York: W. W. Norton, 1990.

McAlister, Lyle N. *Spain and Portugal in the New World, 1492–1700*. Minneapolis: University of Minnesota Press, 1984.

McWilliams, Richebourg Gaillard, ed. *Iberville's Gulf Journals*. Tuscaloosa: University of Alabama Press, 1991.

Merchant, Carolyn. *The Death of Nature: Women, Ecology, and the Scientific Revolution.* San Francisco: Harper and Row, 1980.

———. *Ecological Revolutions: Nature, Gender, and Science in New England.* Chapel Hill: University of North Carolina Press, 1989.

Mereness, Newton D. *Travels in the American Colonies, 1690–1783.* New York: Macmillan, 1916.

Merrell, James. "Indian History during the English Colonial Era. In *A Companion to Colonial America*, edited by Daniel Vickers. New York: Blackwell Publishing, 2003.

———. *The Indians' New World: Catawbas and Their Neighbors from European Contact through the Era of Removal.* New York: W. W. Norton, 1989.

———. *Into the American Woods: Negotiators on the Pennsylvania Frontier.* New York: W. W. Norton, 1999.

———. "Shickellamy: 'A Person of Consequence.'" In *Northeastern Indian Lives, 1632–1816*, edited by Robert Grumer, 227–57. Amherst: University of Massachusetts Press, 1996.

Merritt, Jane T. *At the Crossroads: Indians and Empires on a Mid-Atlantic Frontier, 1700–1763.* Chapel Hill: University of North Carolina Press, 2003.

Milanich, Jerald. *Florida Indians and the Invasion from Europe.* Gainesville: University Press of Florida, 1995.

Mooney, James. *Myths of the Cherokee.* New York: Dover Books, 1995.

Moore, Francis. "Voyage to Georgia, Begun in the Year 1735." London, 1744. In *Collections of the Georgia Historical Society*, vol. 1. Savannah: Georgia Historical Society, 1840.

Morgan, Philip. "Encounters, 1500–1800." In *Empire and Others: British Encounters with Indigenous Peoples, 1600–1850*, edited by Martin Daunton and Rick Halpern. Philadelphia: University of Pennsylvania Press, 1999.

Morison, Samuel Eliot. *The European Discovery of America: The Southern Voyages.* New York: Oxford University Press, 1974.

Morris, Ramona, and Desmond Morris. *Men and Snakes.* New York: McGraw Hill, 1965.

Myers, Amy R. W., and Margaret Beck Pritchard. *Empire's Nature: Mark Catesby's New World Vision.* Chapel Hill: University of North Carolina Press, 1998.

Nash, Roderick. *Wilderness and the American Mind.* New Haven, Conn.: Yale University Press, 1967.

Nelson, Dale. *Interpreters with Lewis and Clark: The Story of Sacagawea and Toussaint Charbonneau.* Denton: University of North Texas Press, 2003.

Norall, Frank, ed. *Bourgomont: Explorer of the Missouri, 1698–1725.* Lincoln: University of Nebraska Press, 1988.

O'Callaghan, E. B. *Documents Relative to the State of New York.* 15 vols. Albany: Weed and Parsons, 1849.

Oberg, Michael Leroy. "Gods and Men: The Meaning of Indian and White Worlds on the Carolina Outer Banks, 1584–1586." *North Carolina Historical Review* 74:4 (October 1999): 367–90.

———. "Indians and Englishmen at the First Roanoke Colony: A Note on Pemisapan's

Conspiracy, 1585–86." *American Indian Culture and Research Journal* 18:2 (1994): 75–89.

Oman, Martin A. *Understanding Lightning.* Carnegie, Pa.: Bek Technical Publications, 1971.

Parish, Susan Scott. "The Female Opossum and the Nature of the New World." *William and Mary Quarterly*, 3rd ser., 54.3 (July 1997): 475–514.

Parker, John, ed. *The Journals of Jonathan Carver and Related Documents, 1766–1770.* St. Paul: Minnesota Historical Society, 1976.

Patterson, Orlando. *Slavery and Social Death: A Comparative Study.* Cambridge, Mass.: Harvard University Press, 1982.

Perrino, Celeste. *The Appalachian Trail: Seven Decades of Assessing Nature along This Wilderness Footpath.* S.H. Thesis, University of South Florida, Tampa, Fla., 2002.

Pilkington, Walter, ed. *The Journals of Samuel Kirkland, Eighteenth-Century Missionary to the Iroquois.* Clinton, N.Y.: Hamilton College, 1980.

Picquet, Francois Fr. "A 1751 Journal of Abbé Francois Picquet."*New York Historical Society Quarterly.* 54 (1970): 360–81.

Plane, Ann Marie. *Colonial Intimacies: Indian Marriage in Early New England.* Ithaca, N.Y.: Cornell University Press, 2000.

Post, Christian Frederick. "Two Journals of Western Tours." In vol. 1 of *Early Western Travels, 1748–1846*, edited by Reuben Gold Thwaites. Cleveland: Arthur H. Clark, 1904.

Pratt, Mary Louise. *Imperial Eyes: Travel Writing and Transculturation.* New York: Routledge, 1992.

Prins, Harald E. L. "To the Land of the Mistigoches: American Indians Traveling to Europe in the Age of Exploration." *American Indian Culture and Research Journal* 17:1 (1993): 175–95.

Quinn, David B. *New American World: A Documentary History of North America to 1612.* 5 vols. New York: Argo Press, 1979.

Reedy-Maschner, Katherine, and Herbert D. G. Maschner. "Marauding Middlemen: Western Expansion and Violent Conflict in the Subarctic." *Ethnohistory* 46:4 (fall 1999): 703–43.

Restall, Mathew. *Seven Myths of the Spanish Conquest.* New York: Oxford University Press, 2004.

Rich, E. E. *The Fur Trade and the Northwest to 1857.* Toronto: McClelland and Stewart, 1967.

Richter, Daniel K. "Cultural Brokers and Intercultural Politics: New York-Iroquois Relations, 1664–1701." *Journal of American History* 75 (June 1988): 40–66.

———. *The Ordeal of the Longhouse: The People of the Iroquois League in the Era of European Colonization.* Chapel Hill: University of North Carolina Press, 1992.

Rights, Douglas L. *The American Indian in North Carolina.* Winston-Salem, N.C.: John F. Blair, 1957.

Ritzenhaler, Robert E. "Southern Chippewa." In *The Handbook of North American Indians*, edited by William Sturtevant (general editor), vol. 15, *Northeast*, edited by Bruce Trigger. Washington, D.C.: Smithsonian Institution, 1978.

Ronda, James P. "Dreams and Discoveries: Exploring the American West, 1760–1815." *William and Mary Quarterly*, 3rd ser., 46:1 (January 1989): 145–62.

———. *Lewis and Clark among the Indians*. Lincoln: University of Nebraska Press, 1984.

———. "A Note on Sacagawea." In *Lewis and Clark among the Indians*, 256–59. Lincoln: University of Nebraska Press, 1984.

———. *Voyages of Discovery: Essays on the Lewis and Clark Expedition*. Helena: Montana Historical Society Press, 1998.

Roscoe, Will. *The Zuni Man-Woman*. Albuquerque: University of New Mexico Press, 1991.

Rotundo, E. Anthony. *American Manhood: Transformations in Masculinity from the Revolution to the Modern Era*. New York: Basic Books, 1993.

Rountree, Helen. *The Powhatan Indians of Virginia: Their Traditional Culture*. Norman: University of Oklahoma Press, 1989.

———. "The Powhatans and Other Woodland Indians as Travelers." In *Powhatan Foreign Relations, 1500–1722*. Charlottesville: University of Virginia Press, 1993.

Sagard, Gabriel. *The Long Journey to the Country of the Hurons*. Edited and translated by George M. Wrong. Toronto: Champlain Society, 1939.

Sahlins, Marshall. *Stone Age Economics*. Chicago: Aldine Press, 1972.

Said, Edward. *Orientalism*. London: Penguin Press, 1979.

Sale, Kirkpatrick. *The Conquest of Paradise: Christopher Columbus and the Columbian Legacy*. New York: Alfred A. Knopf, 1990.

Salley, Alexander S. *Narratives of Early Carolina, 1650–1708*. New York: C. Scribner's Sons, 1911.

Sayre, Gordon. "Native American Sexuality in the Eyes of the Beholders, 1535–1710." In *Sex and Sexuality in Early America*, edited by Merril Smith, 35–54. New York: New York University Press, 1998.

———. *Les Sauvages Américains: Representations of Native Americans in French and English Colonial Literature*. Chapel Hill: University of North Carolina Press, 1997.

Schiebinger, Londa. *Nature's Body: Gender in the Making of Modern Science*. Boston: Beacon Press, 1993.

Schmalz, Peter S. *The Ojibwa of Southern Ontario*. Toronto: University of Toronto Press, 1991.

Scott, James. *Domination and the Arts of Resistance: Hidden Transcripts*. New Haven, Conn.: Yale University Press, 1990.

Shannon, Timothy J. "Dressing for Success on the Mohawk Frontier: Hendrick, William Johnson, and the Indian Fashion." *William and Mary Quarterly*, 3rd ser., 53:1 (January 1996): 13–42.

Sharp, Henry. "The Caribou-Eater Chipewyan: Bilaterality, Strategies of Caribou Hunting, and the Fur Trade." *Arctic Anthropology* 14:2 (1977): 35–40.

Sheidley, Nathaniel. "Hunting and the Politics of Masculinity in Cherokee Treaty Making, 1763–75." In *Empire and Others: British Encounters with Indigenous Peoples, 1600–1850*, edited by Martin Daunton and Rick Halpern, 167–185. Philadelphia: University of Pennsylvania Press, 1999.

Shoemaker, Nancy. "An Alliance between Men: Gender Metaphors in Eighteenth-Century American Indian Diplomacy East of the Mississippi." *Ethnohistory* 46:2 (spring 1999): 239–63.

———. "How Indians Got to Be Red." *American Historical Review* 102 (June 1997): 625–44.

Silver, Timothy. *A New Face on the Countryside: Indians, Colonists, and Slaves in South Atlantic Forests, 1500–1800.* New York: Cambridge University Press, 1990.

Simmons, Marc. *The Last Conquistador: Juan de Oñate and the Settling of the Far Southwest.* Norman: Oklahoma University Press, 1991.

Slaughter, Thomas. *Exploring Lewis and Clark: Reflections on Men and Wilderness.* New York: Alfred A. Knopf, 2003.

———. *The Natures of John and William Bartram.* New York: Alfred A. Knopf, 1996.

Sloane, Sir Hans. "An Account of Some Experiments on the Effects of the Poison of the Rattlesnake by Captain Hall." *Philosophical Transactions of the Royal Society of London* 35:399 (1727): 309–15.

Smith, John. *The Complete Works of Captain John Smith, 1580–1631.* 3 vols. Edited by Philip Barbour. Chapel Hill: University of North Carolina Press, 1986.

Smits, David. "'Abominable Mixture': Toward the Repudiation of Anglo-Indian Intermarriage in Seventeenth-Century Virginia." *Virginia Magazine of History and Biography* 95 (1987): 157–92.

———. "'We Are Not to Grow Wild': Seventeenth-Century New England's Repudiation of Anglo-Indian Intermarriage." *American Indian Culture and Research Journal* 11 (1987): 1–31.

Smits, David D. "The 'Squaw Drudge': A Prime Index of Savagism." *Ethnohistory* 29:4 (1982): 281–306.

Soja, Edward. *Postmodern Geographies: The Reassertion of Space in Critical Social Theory.* New York: Verson, 1989.

Speck, Gordon. *Samuel Hearne and the Northwest Passage.* Caldwell, Idaho: Caxton Printers, 1963.

Stabler, Arthur, ed. *André Thevet's North America: A Sixteenth-Century View.* Montreal: McGill and Queen's University Press, 1986.

Stannard, David E. *American Holocaust: The Conquest of the New World.* New York: Oxford University Press, 1992.

Stefansson, Vilhjalmur, ed. *The Three Voyages of Martin Frobisher.* London: Argonaut Press, 1938.

Stevens, Sylvester, Donald Kent, and Emma Edith Woods, eds. *Travels in New France.* Harrisburg: Pennsylvania Historical Commission, 1941.

Strachey, William. *Historie of Travell into Virginia Britania.* Edited by Louis B. Wright. London: Hakluyt Society, 1953.

Sturtevant, William, and David B. Quinn. "This New Prey: Inuits in Europe in 1567, 1576, 1577." In *Indians in Europe: An Interdisciplinary Collection of Essays*, edited by Christian Feest, 61–140. Lincoln: University of Nebraska Press, 1989.

Summers, Montague, ed. *The Malleus Maleficarum of Heinrich Kramer and James Sprenger.* New York: Dover Publications, 1971.

Sutton, Ann. *The Appalachian Trail: Wilderness at the Doorstep*. Philadelphia: Lippincott, 1967.

Sweet, David G., and Gary B. Nash, eds. *Struggle and Survival in Colonial America*. Berkeley: University of California Press, 1981.

Taussig, Michael. *Shamanism, Colonialism, and the Wild Man: A Study in Terror and Healing*. Chicago: University of Chicago Press, 1987.

Taylor, Alan. "Captain Hendrick Aupaumut: The Dilemmas of an Intercultural Broker." *Ethnohistory* 343 (1996): 431–57.

Thistle, Paul. *Indian-European Trade Relations in the Lower Saskatchewan River Region to 1840*. Winnipeg: University of Manitoba Press, 1986.

Thomas, Keith. *Man and the Natural World: Changing Attitudes in England, 1500–1800*. New York: Oxford University Press, 1983.

———. *Religion and the Decline of Magic*. New York: Oxford University Press, 1971.

Thomas, Nicholas. *Colonialism's Culture: Anthropology, Travel, and Government*. Princeton, N.J.: Princeton University Press, 1994.

Thompson, David. *David Thompson's Narrative, 1784–1812*. Edited by Richard Glover. Toronto: Champlain Society, 1962.

Thwaites, Reuben Gold. *The Jesuit Relations and Allied Documents*. 73 vols. Cleveland: Burrows Brothers, 1896–1901.

Tilley, Christopher. *A Phenomenology of Landscape: Places, Paths, and Monuments*. Oxford, England: Berg, 1994.

Timberlake, Henry. *Memoirs, 1756–1765*. Edited by Samuel Cole Williams. Marietta, Ga.: Continental Book, 1948.

Tosh, John. "The Old Adam and the New Man: Emerging Themes in the History of English Masculinities, 1750–1850." In *English Masculinities, 1660–1800*, edited by Tim Hitchcock and Michele Cohen, 217–39. New York: Longman, 1999.

Trigger, Bruce. *Children of Aataensic: A History of the Huron People to 1660*. Montreal: McGill-Queen's University Press, 1987.

Turner, Victor. "Betwixt and Between." In *Betwixt and Between: Patterns of Masculine and Feminine Initiation*, edited by Louise Carus Mahdi. London: Open Court Publishing, 1987.

———. *The Forest of Symbols: Aspects of Ndembu Ritual*. Ithaca, N.Y.: Cornell University Press, 1967.

Turner, Victor, and Edith Turner. *Image and Pilgrimage in Christian Culture*. New York: Columbia University Press, 1978.

Tyrrell, J. B., ed. *Journals of Samuel Hearne and Philip Turnor*. Toronto: Champlain Press, 1934.

van den Bogaert, Harmen Meyndertsz. *A Journey into Mohawk and Oneida Country, 1634–1635: The Journal of Harmen Meyndertsz van den Bogaert*. Edited by Charles T. Gehring and William A. Starna. Syracuse, N.Y.: Syracuse University Press, 1998.

Van Gennep, Arnold. *The Rites of Passage*. Chicago: University of Chicago Press, 1960.

Van Kirk, Sylvia. *Many Tender Ties: Women in Fur-Trade Society, 1670–1870*. Norman: University of Oklahoma Press, 1980.

———. "Moses Norton." *Dictionary of Canadian Biography*. Toronto: University of Toronto Press, 1966.
Vaughn, Alden T. "From White Man to Redskin: Changing Anglo-American Perceptions of the American Indian." In *Roots of American Racism: Essays on the Colonial Experience*, 3–33. New York: Oxford University Press, 1995.
Vecsey, Christopher. *Traditional Ojibwa Religion and Its Historical Changes*. Philadelphia: American Philosophical Society, 1983.
Venema, Kathleen. "Mapping Culture onto Geography: Distance from the Fort in Samuel Hearne's Journey." *Studies in Canadian Literature* 23:1 (1998): 9–45.
———. "Under the Protection of a Principal Man: A White Man, the Hero, and His Wives in Samuel Hearne's Journey." *Essays on Canadian Writing* 70 (spring 2000).
Vibert, Elizabeth. "Real Men Hunt Buffalo: Masculinity, Race, and Class in British Fur Traders' Narratives." *Gender and History* 8:1 (April 1999): 4–21.
Wallace, Paul A. W. *Conrad Weiser, 1696–1760, Friend of Colonist and Mohawk*. Philadelphia: University of Pennsylvania Press, 1945.
Warner, William. *History of the Ojibway People*. St. Paul: Minnesota Historical Society, 1984.
Waselkov, Gregory. "Indian Maps of the Colonial Southeast." In *Powhatan's Mantle: Indians in the Colonial Southeast*, edited by Peter Wood, Gregory Waselkov, and Thomas Hatley, 292–343. Lincoln: University of Nebraska Press, 1989.
Weber, David. "Reflection on Coronado." In *Myth and the History of the Hispanic Southwest*. Albuquerque: University of New Mexico Press, 1987.
———. *The Spanish Frontier in North America*. New Haven, Conn.: Yale University Press, 1992.
Weddle, Robert. "Soto's Problems of Orientation." In *The Hernando de Soto Expedition: History, Historiography, and "Discovery" in the Southeast*, edited by Patricia Galloway, 219–33. Lincoln: University of Nebraska Press, 1997.
Wedel, Mildred Scott. "The Indian They Called *Turco*." In *Pathways to Plains Prehistory: Anthropological Perspectives of Plains Natives and Their Pasts*, edited by Don G. Wycoff and Jack Hoffman, 153–62. Duncan, Okla.: Cross Timbers Press, 1982.
White, Richard. "Indian Peoples and the Natural World: Asking the Right Questions." In *Rethinking American Indian History*, edited by Donald Fixico. Albuquerque: University of New Mexico Press, 1997.
———. *The Middle Ground: Indians, Empires, and Republics in the Great Lakes Region, 1650–1815*. New York: Cambridge University Press, 1991.
———. *The Organic Machine*. New York: Hill and Wang, 1995.
Williams, Carol Traynor, ed. *Travel Culture: Essays on What Makes Us Go*. Westport, Conn.: Praeger Press, 1998.
Williams, Walter. *The Spirit and the Flesh: Sexual Diversity in American Indian Culture*. Boston: Beacon Press, 1986.
Wilson, James. *The Earth Shall Weep: A History of Native America*. New York: Atlantic Monthly Press, 1999.
Woodward, Thomas Simpson. *Woodward's Reminiscences of the Creek, or Muscogee, Indians*. Reprint. Mobile: Southern University Press, 1965.

Worth, John E. "Late Spanish Military Expeditions in the Interior Southeast, 1597–1628." In *The Forgotten Centuries: Indians and Europeans in the American South, 1521–1704*, edited by Charles Hudson and Carmen Chaves Tesser, 104–22. Athens: University of Georgia Press, 1994.

Yerbury, J. C. *The Subarctic Indians and the Fur Trade, 1680–1860*. Vancouver: University of British Columbia Press, 1986.

Zuckerman, Michael. "The Family Life of William Byrd." In *Almost Chosen People: Oblique Biographies in the American Grain*. Berkeley: University of California Press, 1993.

Index

Abenakis, 75, 113
Ackquekenonk village, 52, 53
Adair, James, 92, 96, 99, 101, 102; conflict over snake handling, 96
Agouhanna (headman), 168n69
Aguacaleyquen, 11, 12, 13, 17; raided by Soto, 12–13
Alberta, Canada, 137
Algonquians, 52, 65, 74, 92, 113, 168n57; aged woman, 121; allies of Champlain, 70; chiefdoms, 44; eat-all-feast, 74; as foot racers, 112; as French allies, 102, 109; language, 55; snakebite cures, 94
Alligators, 70
Añasco, Juan de, 24
Anouatea (Huron village), 89
Ansen, Hendrick, 73
Apalachee, 31, 154n64, 155n92; Narváez at, 32; Soto visits, 33
Appalachian Mountains, 17, 126
Appalachian Trail, ix, x, 147n1
Archithinues, 73
Arctic Coast, Mackenzie's trip to, 50
Arctic Ocean, 114
Arkansas, 89, 118
Armor, 12
Assiniboins, 78
Atatarho, 89
Atequi, 28
Athabascans, 20, 140; as Mackenzie's guides, 139
Atlantic world, 147n1
Atticameges, 74
Aute, 33; Narváez at, 34
Axtell, James L., x
Aymay, 24

Baja, 78
Banister River, 60
Barren Grounds, 47, 48, 122, 132; travel pitfalls, 49; woman survives on, 121–22
Bartram, John, 72; conflict with Nanticoke guides, 72–73; hires guides, 56
Bartram, William, 88, 163n28, 165nn86–87, 169n86
Batts and Fallam expedition, 54
Bayogoula, 45
Bearskin, Ned (Saponi), 58, 60, 6, 67; as hunter, 59; hunting totals, 60–61; shares cosmology, 115; travel rewards, 60, 159n87
Beauchamp, Jacques (Canandian paddler), 138; defies Mackenzie, 140–41
Beaulieux (Canadian paddler), 138
Beaver Indians: end war with Crees, 64
Bella Coola River, 138
Berdache, 131, 171n113
Bienville, Jean Baptiste, carried, 118
Bisson (Canadian paddler), 138
Blackfeet, 47, 55–56
Black Legend, 152n12
Black Robe, 46, 84. *See also* Jesuits
Blome, Richard, 86
Bogaert, Harmen Meyndertz van den, 72; 1634 trip, 125; Mohawk language glossary, 125
Bossu, Jean-Bernard, 89
Bourgomont, Etienne, 118
British Columbia, 138, 139
Bronze plaques, 66
Brugh, Cornelis van, 54, 78
Buffalo Lick, Ga., 169n86
Buffalo nickel, 144

Byrd, William, II, 7 60, 86, 110, 115, 129, 139, 141, 159n82, 159n85, 166n11; 1727 surveying party, 67; 1728 trip, 58; describes sexual encounters with Native women, 127; describes travel companions, 105; "Discipline of the Woods," 105; gendered comparisons, 105–6, 111; hurts knee on tree, 105; killed rattlesnakes, 86; "Laws of Travel," 139, 141; sees Tuscarora guides as lazy, 106; and snakeroot, 95; toothache on trail, 105; travel partners as hunters, 159n87; travel rules, 106

Cabeza de Vaca, Alvar Nuñez, 154–55n82
Caddoans, 30, 56, 78, 119
Cahainihoua (Caddoan village), 78
Calvinists, 52
Cammerhoff, John: 1750 travels of, 45; visits Senecas, Cayugas, Onondagas, 46
Canada, 77
Canadian paddlers, 138
Canadians, 139
Canagere (Mohawk village), 38
Canandishore, (Mohawk village), 46
Canawarode (Mohawk village), 39
Cancre ("Dunce," Mackenzie Indian guide), 138
Canoes: accidents, 68; lost, 161n38
Captain Tom (Saponi), 59
Captives, women, 18. *See also under* Guides
Caribou, 67
Carier, carried, 119
Carolinas, 63
Carrion Rapids, 56
Carrying bodily, 118–19
Cartier, Jacques 7, 168n67, 168n69
Carver, Jonathan, 88, 92, 114
Castañeda, Pedro de, 28
Catawbas, 159n85

Catawba-Saponi conflict, 59
Catesby, Mark, 88, 92; learns of rattlesnakes "charming" prey, 98
Cayugas, 46, 59
Celeron, Pierre-Joseph, 99
Chain of translation, 27
Charles V, 152n15
"Charming" prey, by rattlesnakes, 98–99, 165n87; herpetology denial of, 99
Champlain, Samuel 65, 70; 1610 travels, 44; battle with Mohawks, 71; dreams 161n48, and torture, 161n48; interferes with torture, 71–72; raid on Mohawks, 70; rejects offers of sex, 126; tells of his dreams, 70–71
Chamuscado-Rodriguez Expedition, 35
Charles V, 11, 18
Charlevoix, Pierre de, 85
Charnonneau, Toussaint, 144
Chaudière Falls, 65
Chawchinahaw (Cree), 49, 57
Cherokees, 92, 98; marvelous snake, 92; views of snakes and water, 92
Cherokee, N.C., ix
Chiametla, Coronado visits, 30
Chickahominy guides, 165n81
Chickahominys, 98
Chickasaws: insults, 108; snake handling, 96
Chickasaw Trade Road, 97
Chiefs: captured by Soto, 13; as guides, 22; offer aid, 22; prestige, 22. *See also* Headmen
Chipewyans, 49, 51, 108, 114, 121, 122, 124, 130, 133; culture, 158n50; men woo Dogrib woman, 122
Chippewas, 65
Chowan-Powhatan peace memorial trail, 65
Christian Indians, conflict with non-Christian kinsfolk, 74

Christianity and snakes, 102
Churchill River, 48, 157n44
Cibola, 24, 25, 26, 30
Circumcision, as ritual, 148n8
Clothing, 141; borrowed, 135; as maker of cultural difference, 135–36
Cody, Iron Eyes, x
Cofaqui, 22
Cofitachequi, 22, 23, 29
College of William and Mary, x
Colonial Wolf bounties, 87
Colorado, 55
Columbus, Christopher, 1492 American landfall, 144
Compass, 76
Competition: between travelers, 106; swimming as, 110; uses of, 108
Conflict: over direction, 76; over rules of travel outlined, 68
Congarees, 58, 63
Conquest, era of ends, 35
Coosa, 19
Coppermine River, 48, 49, 50, 120, 123. 124; Hearne's trips to, 49
Coronado, Vásquez de, 8, 11, 14, 16, 18, 24, 25, 28, 29, 35, 36, 152n19; visits Chiametla, 30
Corps of Discovery, 141, 144; marginalize native participation, 142; military discipline, 142; Natives' view of, 143; personnel, 142
Cortés, Hernan, 13, 31
Courtois (Canadian paddler), 138
Crazy Horse, 144
Crees, 20, 48, 73, 136, 143; end war with Beaver Indians, 64; kill Eskimo woman, 117; traveler rebukes David Thompson, 115; Twatt's travel partner, 134
Cresswell, Nicholas, 95, 127; relationship with Native women on the trail, 128; 1775 travels, 109
Cross Lake, 134, 135, 143
Cuba, 11, 30

Culture brokers, historiography of, 149n9
Cuzco, 20

Dakotas, 92
Dakota snake figures, 92
Danckaerts, Jasper, 56, 110
Dan River, 60
Davis, John, 112
Davis Straight, 112
De Soto, Hernando. *See* Soto, Hernando de
Deganawidah epic, 89
Delawares, 109
Dene-Tha, 171n113
D'Iberville, Pierre Le Moyne, 78; 1700 travels, 45; encouraged singing, 113–14
Dogribs, 47
Dogrib woman, survival on Barren Grounds, 121–22
Dogs, 24; attack guides, 11; war dogs/mastiffs, 30
Dollar coin: Susan B. Anthony, 144; Sacagawea, 144
Du Quen, Father Jean, snake encounter, 84
Ducette (Mackenzie Paddler), 138
Dulchanchellin, 155n92
Dutch burghers, 52
Dutch-French trade rivalry, 37–38
Dutchmen, 53, 57, 62, 72
Dutch-Mohawk trade, 37
Dutch trade goods, 125
Dutch travelers welcomed by Iroquois, 38
Duyn, Gerrit Evertssen van, 52–53

Earl Gregg Swem Library, x
Eat-all-feast, 74
Edistos, 45
Enoe Will (guide), 58; entradas, 11, 12, 13, 14, 43, 137; end of conquest era, 17; end of Soto's, 14; end of, 17; failures of, 15–16; guide procurement strategy, 21

Escalante, Fray Silvestre, 72
Escalante and Dominguez Expedition, hiring of guides, 55
Eskimos, 48, 112, 117
Eskimo woman killed by Crees, 117
Essouweyoualand (Delaware), 57
Etienne (Atticamege), 74–75
Ettwein, John, 86; snake encounter, 85
Europeans: carried bodily by Indians, 118; claim to have rejected sex offers from Native women, 126–27; fear of snakes, 84, 87; uncomfortable in being carried by Indians, 118–19
Evangelico, Fray Juan de, 24

Fidler, Peter, 50; 1791 travels, 130; clumsiness, 130; regendered by Chipewyans, 130–32
Fistfighting, 114–15
Fontaine, John, 110
Food, 108
Foot racing, 112–13
Fort Chipewyan, 137
Fort Christianna, 59, 61
Fort Niagara, 81
Fort Orange, 37, 40
Fort Prince of Wales, 48, 49, 122–23, 124
Fort Stanwix, 1784, 66
Fort Ticonderoga, 57
Fox River, 97
French allies, 102, 109
Fulgarites, 91
Fur trade captain, status of, 51
Fur trade society, 47, 48

Gabriel, Father, 118
Galinée, René de Bréhant de, describes rattles, 85
Gallegos, Balthasar de, 13
Garakontié, 46, 47, 51, 58, 61; as guide, 46; conversion of, 46
Gender ambiguity, 132; Hearne, 170n112

Gender and travelers, 105–6
Gendered anxieties, 120
Georgia, 120, 132
Gift exchange, 56, 158n51
Godefoy (French traveler), 112
God-Satan dichotomy, 91
Goldenrod, 94
Graffenried, Baron Cristoph von, 47
Great Iroquois Long House, 37, 38
Great Slave River, 50
Greetings, 109, 112
Groseilliers, Jean Baptiste de, 109; tricks Sioux with gunpowder, 116
Guat Utima, 13
Guides: captives, 18; chained, 18, 19; chiefs as, 22; coerced, 16; defanging rattlesnakes, 97; drunkenness, 79; escape from Soto, 19; European need for, 43; "fail," 77–78; headmen as, 62; hired, 42, 54; killed, 30; limited geographical knowledge, 20; lost, 20; misdirection by, 21, 30; motivations for, 41; negotiations over services, 55; payment, 56, 57; possibilities seen in guidance, 41; refuse to go farther, 77; rewards received, 56; tortured, 30
Gunpowder, used to trick Indians, 116
Gunshots, 75; as greetings, 109; on trail, 66. *See also* Shooting

Hall, Thomas, 171n116
Hamilton, Alexander, 103
Hand signs, 12, 25, 28, 32
Hans (Algonquian headman and guide), 52, 54, 55, 57, 58, 62; negotiations, 53, 54; view of Christians, 53
Hansen, Hendrick, 54, 78
Harahey, 23, 24, 26, 29; described, 28
Harquebus, 71
Headmen: accompanying, 45; as guides, 62; offer travel warnings, 45
Hearne, Samuel, 7, 48, 49, 50, 51, 54, 57, 120, 121, 122, 130, 137,

169n82, 171n22; Arctic trip of 1771, 116; failure of second Coppermine River trip, 123–24, 125; first Coppermine River trip, 49; gender ambiguity, 170n112; guides take his quadrant, 124; includes Cree women in travel, 125; plans trip to exclude Cree women, 123; quadrant is broken, 124; ridiculed during fight with Eskimos, 117; second Coppermine River trip, 49; third Coppermine trip, 49
Henday, Anthony, 56, 72
Hennepin, Father Louis, 87, 118
Henry, 164n48
Henry, Alexander, 7, 89, 100, 101, 102, 104; almost kills rattlesnake, 81
Hermaphrodites, 131, 171n116
Herpecide, 86, 104
Hix, George, 159n82
Hochelaga, 119, 168n67
Home Guard Indians, 47, 49
Hoppottoguoh (Chichahominy guide), 165n81
Horn blowing, upon arrival or departure, 66
Horsemanship as competition, 110
Horses, dangers of riding, 69
Hudson Bay, 66, 116
Hudson's Bay Company, 47, 50, 62, 122, 130, 134, 157n44
Hudson Valley, 57
Huguenot, 110
Humans changed into snakes, 89
Hummocks, 12
Hurons, 70, 112; allies of Champlain, 7; and disease, 91; snake figure, 92; women, 120
Huronia, 73
Hyco Creek, 60, 61

Ideal traveler, concept of: explained, 106–8; described, 111
Idotleezay (Chipewyan), 48, 49

Illinois, 65, 70, 142
Insults, 106
Iroquoia, 37, 112; trails described, 37
Iroquois, 59, 64, 78, 89; as racers, 112; St. Lawrence, 168n57; welcoming, 38
Isonnaat (Huron), 89
Isopete, 26; challenges Turco, 25

Jackzetavon (Susquehanock), 77
James River, 77
Jamestown, Va., 84
Jean-Baptiste (Sacagawea's child), 144
Jefferson, Thomas, 141, 143
Jesuits (Society of Jesus, France), 54, 65, 66, 73, 75, 91, 115, 121, 134; affect travel, 74; as canoe travelers, 73–74; baptize travel companions, 75; carrying burdens, 108; damage canoes, 74; use of paddlers, expectation of, 46
Johnson, Sir William, 81
Josselyn, John, 85; killing snakes, 86
Joutel, Father, refuses carrying, 119

Kalm, Peter, 57, 86, 88, 102, 118; learns of rattlesnakes "charming" prey, 99; sees Indian snake killers, 102; snake encounter, 85
Kaskaskias, 142
Kent, England, 84
Kirkland, Samuel, interferes with rattlesnakes, 87
Kithcee Manitou, 65

La Florida, 11, 12, 17, 18
La Salle, René-Robert Cavelier, Sieur de, 56, 78, 85; derides Native "superstitions," 66; in Texas 1687, 44; made sick by rattlesnake, 85; protests carrying, 119
La Vérendrye, Pierre Gaultier de Varennes, Sieur de, 78; visits Mandans, 46

194 / Index

Lady Liberty, 144
Lake Athabaskan, 49
Lake George, 65
Lake Superior, 65, 116
Landry (Canadian paddler), 138
Language barriers, 18
Lawson, John, 57, 58, 62, 64, 67, 72, 120, 129; denies rattlesnakes "charming" prey, 99; learns of rattlesnakes "charming" prey, 98; notes "bedfellows," 126; praises Native travel skills, 63
Lead plates, 66
Leaping in greeting, 112
Lederer, John, 77; learns of rattlesnakes "charming" prey, 98–99
Le Jeune, Father Paul, 91
Lewis and Clark expedition, 9, 137, 141, 148n6, 172n23; hunting game, 142; largely trouble-free travel, 143
Lightning, 91
Liminality, 148n8
Lindley, Jacob, 69
Link, Wenceslaus, 78
Long, John, 120; snake encounter, 87
Long house. *See* Great Iroquois Long House
Loon (*maunk*), 113
Louisiana, 55
Lucayo, 13
Luna, Tristan de, 17

Mabila, 21
Mackay, Alexander, 137
Mackenzie, Alexander, Sir, 9, 50, 51, 67, 72, 78, 79, 118, 137, 142, 143, 171n13, 171n22; 1788 Arctic trip, 138; 1789 trip to Arctic Ocean, 114; asserts control, 141; conflicts with Athabascan guides, 139–40; controls behavior of crew, 138–39; crosses Rockies in 1793, 137; French Canadian paddlers, 138; limits reliance on Indians on 1793 Pacific trip, 137; trip to Arctic coast, 50
Madison, James, 66; rejects Oneida women, 127
Magtakunk (Chichahominy guide), 165n81
Mahicans, 38
Maine, 113
Malleus Maleficarum, 84
Manahoac-Nahyssans alliance, 76
Mandans, 144
Manitoba, 48, 49
Manitou, 89, 115
Manitou Kinibic, 82, 100
Manliness, 107, 111, 118, 129, 133, 141, 166n11; competition, 112; Mackenzie appeals to, 140; surveying tools as symbols of, 132; travel virtues, 107
Mannahocks, 42
Marest, Father Gabriel, 66; describes American travel, 66
Marquette, Father Jacques, 95
Marriage, "in the custom of the country," 126
Marxist Base-Superstructure model, 149n9
Masculinity. *See* Manliness
Massac, 142
Mastiffs. *See* Dogs
Matonabbee (Chipewyan), 47, 48, 49, 51, 58, 62, 121, 130, 133, 137; 1767 trip to Arctic coast, 48; biography of, 48; death of, 50; describes need for women in Cree travel, 124; fur trade captain status, 50; prestige, 157n44; status, 51, 54
Megapolensis, Rev. Johannes, and snake encounter, 84
Meherrin River, 59, 110
Meherrins, 159n85
Menominie guide, and superior snake knowledge, 97–98
Métis, 47

Mexico, 11
Middle Ground, 161n53, 170n89; concept of, 149n9, 150n10
Midewiwin Society, 146n58
Mississippi, 113
Mississippian chiefdoms, 168n57
Mississippi Delta, 78
Mississippi River, 65, 78, 109
Missouri River, 143, 144
Missouris, tricked with gunpowder, 116
Mobilians, 65
Mohawks, 37, 38, 40, 46, 52, 54, 55, 62, 67, 73, 78, 155–56n1; Champlain attacked by, 70; villages, 38–39, 156n9
Mole kill-offs, 87
Monacans, 75, 76
Monack. *See* Monacans
Monaughtacunds, 42
Montagnais, 20; allies of Champlain, 70
Montreal, 46, 50, 70, 100
Moravians, 79, 85, 86
Moscoso, Luis, 30
Moss, as compass, 63
Muskogean, 23, 27

Naansis, 108
Nahuatl, 28
Nahyssans-Manahoac alliance, 76
Nanabozho (Ojibwa culture hero), 146n58
Nancy (Cresswell's companion), 128
Nansemonds, 42, 43
Nanticokes, 72; conflicts with John Bartram, 72–73
Narváez, Pánfilo de, 8, 14, 18, 27, 30, 35, 89, 155n92; ambushed, 34; at Apalachee, 32, 33; at Aute, 34; and Cuba, 31; Entrada ends badly, 34; failure of, 31, 32; march to Apalachee, 32; no guides, 18; taking guides, 21; at Tampa Bay, 31

Natchez, 89
Natchitoches, practice of carrying guests, 118
Native Americans: carrying of visitors, 118; landscape markers, 76; landscapes, 76; marvelous snakes, 92; Porters, 12; snake images, 91; snake killing, 89, 102; snake protection habits, 93; Spiritual revival, 101; terms for metals, 29; trade networks, 23; trail memorials, 64–65; trailside signs, 64; travelers' offerings on trail, 65; travelers pass obstacles, 63; travel habits, affected by Christianity, 75; types of travelers, 7–8; views of nonhuman spiritual power, 91
Native American women: aged woman, 121; as "Bedfellows," 126; challenge Europeans' masculinity, 129; as cooks and camp servants, 128; crucial to Cree travel, 125; Dogrib woman survives on Barren Grounds, 121–22; as "Dulcineas," 128; on horseback, 120; Hurons, 120; labeled "prostitutes," 126; marginalized by European travelers, 120–21, 122; in marriages to Europeans, 126; Nancy (Cresswell's companion), 128; participation minimized by Europeans, 107; sex with European travelers, 127; as "Squaw drudges," 120; on trail, 122
Nativists, 101
Naunnugh (Chichahominy guide), 165n81
Nestabeck, 50, 58, 137, 158n48; career history of, 50; as guide, 51; status, 51, 54
New France, 46, 48, 73
New Jersey, 52, 56
New Laws, 1542, 1573, 17
New York (city), 52, 53; cosmopolitan culture circa 1680, 52
New York (region), 46, 54, 57, 59, 73, 78

Niagara Falls, 69
Niagara Portage Trail, 102
Nippisings, 64; lost child, 64
Nondacoa, 30; Moscso at, 30
North Carolina, 59, 90
North West Company, 50
Northwest Territory, 50, 130
Norton, Moses, 49, 169n82; plans Hearne's travels to exclude Cree women, 123
Norton, Richard, 123, 157n40
Nottoways, 127

Ocaneechee Trade Road, 59
Ocaneechees, 59
Oçita, Soto at, 29
Ocute, 22
Ohio, 79
Ohio River, 109
Ohio Valley, 127
Ojibwa, 104; adoption, 164n48; guide a better shot, 113; Midewiwin Medicine Society, 92
Ojibwas, 81, 82, 89, 100, 102, 167n36; offer dogs in lake, 100; offer tobacco, 100; as possible Nativists, 101; separate themselves from Alexander Henry, 100–101; show respect to rattlesnake, 81
Oñate, Juan de, 17, 152n19
Onckehoncka (Mohawk village), 38
Ondiatachiane (Huron divine figure), 91
Oneida, 37
Oneidas, 45, 155n1
Onniont (Huron snake figure), 92
Onondagas, 46, 73
Opossum, 163n23
Oquoho (Mohawk guide), 156n9
Order of Ma-ooty, 60
Ortiz, Juan, 27, 28
Osage, 89; man with snake tattoo, 103
Osquage (Mohawk Village), 156n9
Oswego, 56

Ottawa River, 56, 65
Ottawas, 44
Ottoman siege of Vienna, 153n53
Otzinachson, on Susquehanna River, 65

Painted Rocks, 65
Pardo, Juan, 17
Parsnip River, 139
Paterson, N.J., 52
Patofa, 24, 29
Pawnees, 24
Peace Point, 64
Peace River, Alberta, 64
Pemmican, 67
Pennsylvania, 59, 65, 79
Perico, 23, 28, 29, 154n64; as translator, 27; baptized, 24, 29; fit, 23–24; parallels with Turco, 26–27; renamed "Pedro," 24
Perrot, Nicholas, and refusal to carry, 119
Peru, 11, 154n75
Philadelphia, 57
Piankashaws, 89
Picquet, François, 102, 103
Pigs, 12
Pinneshon (French traveler), 97
Pizarro brothers, in Peru, 13
Pliny the Elder, 165n87
Pocoon (snakeroot), 94
Pond, Peter, 50
Porters, 17; die, 19; escape, 19; killed, 15; from Patofa, 24
Post, Frederick, 57, 79
Potomac chief, 51
Potomac River, 43
Potomacs, 46
Powhatan, 168n57
Powhatan-Chowan peace memorial trail, 65
Practical jokes, 116
Prisoners chained, 12
Puebla, 24
Pueblo Indians, 91; Snake Dance, 163n45; snake rituals, 91–92

Quadrant, 66, 123, 124, 130
Quebec, 46, 112
Querecho, 25
Quivira, 26; Gold of, 25

Race, concept of, 150n10
Radisson, Pierre Espirit, 7, 67, 94, 109, 110; fistfights with canoe partner, 114–15; tricks Sioux with gunpowder, 116
Râle, Father Sebastian, 75
Ramusio, Giovanni Batistta, and 1550s map of Hochelaga, 119
Rangel, Rodrigo, 13, 24
Rattlesnake: called "grandfather," 81, 100; "charming" prey, 98–99; colonist killed by, 86; killing of, 86, 87; paintings, 88; rattles, 163n31; respect shown by Ojibwas, 81; as Revolutionary symbol of defiance, 103; as symbol of bravery, 103
Rattlesnakes, 9, 70, 163n23; attempted killing, 81–82, 83; charming abilities, 165n87; described, 88; disruption by Europeans, 87–88; European fear of, 84; experiments on, 88; Native and European responses differ, 82–83; Native views of, 89; natural science observation, 88; rattles explained, 84–85; sound described, 85
Red Cloud, 144
Richelieu River, 70
Ridicule, 117, 133, 141
Rio Grande, 2
Roanoke River, 60, 61
Rocky Mountains, 137–38
Royal ciphers, 66

Sabbath, 106
Sacagawea: as best-known Native guide, 144; as symbol of America, 144, 145
Sagard, Father Gabriel, 113
Saguenay, 84

Salford, Robert, carried, 118
Santa Fe, 84
Santee Jack (guide), 58
Santees, 57, 63, 78
Saponis, 54, 60, 61, 67, 115; conflict with the Catawbas, 59; fear of Iroquois, 59; leaders as poor horsemen, 110; move north, 59; Virginia relations with, 5
Saskatchewan, 49, 134
Sault Rapids, 56
Sault Saint Marie, 101
Schatsyerosy (Mohawk village), 39
Scientific apparatus of gendered male, 125
Scipio (guide), 78
Sekanis, 139; guides, 171n13
Senecas, 46; as French allies, 102
Seven Years War, 79; consequences of, 81
Sex: alluded to in Bogaert's Mohawk language glossary, 125–26; alluded to in Spotswood's glossary, 126; between European travelers and Native women, 127; offered by Indian women, 126
Sextant, 132
Shamans, 90
Shamokin Daniel. See Essouweyoualand
Shooting: as contest, 115; as greeting, 109; on trail, 66; turkeys, 108
Shoshonis, 144
Siakaris (Mohawk guide), 38, 40, 41, 43, 52, 55, 62; paid, 39
Singing, as contest, 113
Sioux, tricked with gunpowder, 116
Sitting Bull, 144
Slave River, 130
Smith, John, 7, 46; 1608 expeditions, 42; explains need for guides, 44; visits Potomacs, 43
Smokey Mountains, ix, x
Snakebite, 96; cures, 93–94

Snakeroot, 94, 95; differing European and Native logics over use of, 96
Snakes: attributes, 84; bodies as Native objects, 90; as body adornments, 89; Cherokees' marvelous snake, 92; European views of, 83–84; and European witchcraft, 84; and human health, 90–91; humans changed into, 89; images, 90; and Native cosmologies, 91; as Native pets, 90; offerings to, 95; parts heal diseases, 90
Snowshoes, 108, 135
Soto, Hernando de, 8, 11, 13, 16, 29, 30, 31, 35, 36, 137, 154n64, 154–55n82; at Apalachee, 33; death of, 14; end of entrada, 14; multiple accounts of, 151n6; navigation, 152n29; punched in mouth, 22; taking captives,18; visits Oçita, 29
Soussakis, 115
South Carolina, 88, 118
Space, conceptualized, 150n13
Spangenberg, Bishop August Gottlieb, 85; startled by rattlesnake, 86
Sparrows, 87
Spotswood, Alexander, 59; native glossary, 126
Squirrel kills, 87
Sqorhea (Mohawk guide), 41, 53, 54, 55, 56, 62; described, 40; paid, 39; as traveler, 156n9
St. Cosme, Father, carried, 118
St. Lawrence River, 87
St. Marks, Fla., 30
Susquehanna River, 65, 85
Susquehanna Valley, 72
Swimming, 109; as competition, 110; difference between Tuscaroras and Virginians, 106

Taebsas guides, 78
Tamemes. *See* Porters, 22
Tampa Bay, 11; Narváez at, 31
Tattoos, 89–90, 103, 164n48

Tautongo Omlishco (Dakota "Buffalo Snake" figure), 92
Teedyuscung, 79
Tenochtitlan, 20
Texas, 11
Texas Gulf Coast, 56
Thevet, André, 168n69
Thompson, David, 7, 50, 134, 136, 143; rebuked by Cree companion, 115; ridiculed by Native companions, 115–16; ridicules Native beliefs, 115
Tidewater Virginia, 105
Timucuans, 11, 12, 13, 20, 21, 23, 27
Tobacco nation, 91
Tobacco offerings, 65, 81, 100
Torture, 30, 71
Toteros, 63
Totofa, 22
Towns, burned down, 22
Trail markers, European, 65–66
Transculturation, 149n9
Travel: adopt Natives' ways, 67; canoe accidents, 68; competitions, 110, 112, 113, 115; dangers, 68–70; economic logic, 62; economics, 40–42; Europeans, 66; flaunt Native rituals, 66; habits differ, 108–9; horse riding, 69; uses of competition, 108; winter travel, 69
Travelers: competition, 106; conflict over direction, 76. *See also* Ideal traveler
Trumpet blasts, as greetings, 109
Tulla, 22
Turco, El (The Turk), 28, 29; described, 25; as guide, 25; killed, 26, 153n62; parallels with Perico, 26–27; as Pawnee, 26
Turco-Isopete rivalry, 25, 26, 27
Turner, Frederick Jackson, x
Tuscaroras, 47, 111; as guides, 106; criticize Virginians as wasteful, 106
Tuscarora War 1712, 59

Tutelos, 59
Twatt, Magnus, 134, 143; caught in sudden storm, 135

Uktena (Cherokee marvelous snake), 92, 98
Uktena Stone, 92
United States Army, 142
United States Treasury, 144
University of Arizona Library, x
Utes, 55

Van Brugh, Cornelis. *See* Brugh, Cornelis van
Vega, Garcilaso de la, 153n44, 154n64
Vermeer, Jan, 144
Vienna, Ottoman siege of, 153n53
Virginia, 59, 75, 112; Algonquians, 90; Saponi relations with, 59. *See also* Tidewater Virginia
Virginians, as horsemen, 110
Vrees, 78

Walloons, 52
Wappenessaw (guide), 56
War dogs. *See* Dogs
Warroskoyak, Va., 171n112
Welcoming, by Iroquois, 38, 117–18. *See also* Greetings
Welshmen, 52
Widener Library, Harvard University, x
Willamegicken (Delaware guide), 79–80
Williamsburg, Virginia, x
Women. *See* Native American women
Woodsmen, non-Indian, 136–37, 142

Xabe, 25, 26

Yellowknifes, 47
Yupaha, 23, 26

Ziesberger, David: 1750s travels, 45; visits Senecas, Cayugas, Onondagas, 46

Philip Levy is assistant professor of history at the University of South Florida. He is a contributor to *Indian and European Contact in Context: The Mid-Atlantic Region* (University Press of Florida, 2004) and the author of numerous articles on colonial Indian relations and historical archaeology